Practitioners and students of government have long waited for a comprehensive study on how public policy now takes shape. Jonathan Craft and John Halligan have answered the call with a lucid, timely and well documented book. Advising Government in the Westminster Tradition should be on the reading list of practitioners and all senior students of public policy looking for answers to the challenges now confronting policy makers, from a comparative perspective.

Donald J Savoie, Canada Research Chair in Public
Administration (tier 1), Universite de Moncton

Jonathan Craft and John Halligan have provided a thorough and thoughtful account of policy advice in Westminster-style governments. Their analysis demonstrates the complexity of advice structures in these governments, and the ways in which they have adapted to changing political styles and policy demands. This is essential reading for anyone interested in how policy actually gets made in these countries.

Guy Peters, Maurice Falk Professor of Government,
Department of Political Science, University of Pittsburgh

Any government needs policy advice in order to function. This volume is a richly researched analysis of policy advisory systems in the world of Westminster polities. Craft and Halligan are to be applauded for their detailed incisions into the varieties of advisory systems, the different types of actors involved in purveying advice but most importantly, how these systems evolve and transform over time. This study is thoughtful and authoritative in its coverage of Australia, Canada, New Zealand and the UK. It is a 'must read' for those interested in understanding how government use, and do not use, advice.

Diane Stone, Dean, School of Public Policy,
Central European University

Who advises whom, what, when and how' represents a long-standing concern in the study and practice of executive government. This volume offers a fascinating investigation into the world of Westminster political systems. Craft and Halligan's comparative study of policy advisory systems offers an exciting major contribution for anyone interested in how executive government operates.

Martin Lodge, Professor of Political Science and Public Policy,
London School of Economics and Political Science

T0381667

Advising Governments in the Westminster Tradition

In turbulent environments and unstable political contexts, policy advisory systems have become more volatile. The policy advisory system in anglophone countries is composed of different types of advisers who have input into government decision-making. Government choices about who advises them vary widely as they demand contestability, greater partisan input and more external consultation. The professional advice of the public service may be disregarded. The consequences for public policy are immense depending on whether a plurality of advice works effectively or is derailed by narrow and partisan agendas that lack an evidence base and implementation plans. The book seeks to address these issues within a comparative country analysis of how policy advisory systems are constituted and how they operate in the age of instability in governance and major challenges with how the complexity policy issue can be handled.

JONATHAN CRAFT is Associate Professor with the Department of Political Science and jointly appointed to the Munk School of Global Affairs & Public Policy. He is also the founding director of Policy Ready – a research and learning platform focused on revitalising public sector policy making. Jonathan specialises in comparative public policy and administration, policy analysis and Canadian politics. He is particularly interested in the study of the policy process, political-administrative relations, policy advice and the intersection of technology and policy making. He is the author of *Backrooms and Beyond: Partisan Advisers and the Politics of Policy Work in Canada* (2016) and is a co-editor of *Policy Work in Canada: Professional Practices and Analytical Capacities* (2017) and *Issues in Canadian Governance* (2018).

JOHN HALLIGAN is Emeritus Professor of Public Administration and Governance at the Institute for Governance and Policy Analysis, University of Canberra. John publishes on comparative public management, policy and governance, including public sector reform, performance management and political-bureaucratic relationships. He specialises in the anglophone countries of Australia, Canada, New

Zealand and the United Kingdom. He has authored *Reforming Public Management and Governance: Impact and Lessons from Anglophone Countries* (2020) and co-authored *Performance Management in the Public Sector* (2010, 2015); *Public Sector Governance in Australia* (2012); *Managing Performance: International Comparisons* (2008); *Parliament in the 21st Century: Institutional Reform and Emerging Roles* (2007); *Political Management in the 1990s* (1992); and *Political Leadership in an Age of Constraint: The Australian Experience* (1992).

Cambridge Studies in Comparative Public Policy

The **Cambridge Studies in Comparative Public Policy** series was established to promote and disseminate comparative research in public policy. The objective of the series is to advance the understanding of public policies through the publication of the results of comparative research into the nature, dynamics and contexts of major policy challenges and responses to them. Works in the series will draw critical insights that enhance policy learning and are generalisable beyond specific policy contexts, sectors and time periods. Such works will also compare the development and application of public policy theory across institutional and cultural settings and examine how policy ideas, institutions and practices shape policies and their outcomes. Manuscripts comparing public policies in two or more cases as well as theoretically informed critical case studies which test more general theories are encouraged. Studies comparing policy development over time are also welcomed.

General Editors: M. Ramesh, National University of Singapore; Xun Wu, Hong Kong University of Science and Technology; Michael Howlett, Simon Fraser University and National University of Singapore

Advising Governments in the Westminster Tradition

Policy Advisory Systems in Australia, Britain, Canada and New Zealand

JONATHAN CRAFT
University of Toronto

JOHN HALLIGAN
University of Canberra

CAMBRIDGE
UNIVERSITY PRESS

Shaftesbury Road, Cambridge CB2 8EA, United Kingdom

One Liberty Plaza, 20th Floor, New York, NY 10006, USA

477 Williamstown Road, Port Melbourne, VIC 3207, Australia

314–321, 3rd Floor, Plot 3, Splendor Forum, Jasola District Centre, New Delhi – 110025, India

103 Penang Road, #05–06/07, Visioncrest Commercial, Singapore 238467

Cambridge University Press is part of Cambridge University Press & Assessment, a department of the University of Cambridge.

We share the University's mission to contribute to society through the pursuit of education, learning and research at the highest international levels of excellence.

www.cambridge.org
Information on this title: www.cambridge.org/9781009380263

DOI: 10.1017/9781108377133

First published 2020
First paperback edition 2023

A catalogue record for this publication is available from the British Library

ISBN   978-1-108-42149-2   Hardback
ISBN   978-1-009-38026-3   Paperback

The book is dedicated with thanks to the family members who gave us the time to make this work possible, our wives Zoiey Craft and Penelope St Clair, and the very young children Béatrice and Elliot Craft.

Contents

Figures

Tables

Acknowledgements

We benefited greatly from the invaluable reflections of past and present ministers, public servants, partisan advisers, and those in firms and think tanks outside of government. In all four countries participants were keen to share their views and appreciated our objective of offering a fresh and contemporary appraisal of how advisory systems are operating in these Westminster systems. Scheduling them for interviews was another matter. The book would not be possible without their generous contributions.

There is now a thriving community of scholars who work specifically on advisory systems and particular advisers. This is a welcome development, and the book has drawn from advances in how they think about advisory systems and empirical work on various advisers that work within them. We gained much from exchanges, both formal and informal, with Michael Howlett, Evert Lindquist and Amanda Clarke in Canada; Mark Evans, Maria Maley and Anne Tiernan in Australia; Jonathan Boston, Chris Eichbaum, Derek Gill, Bob Gregory and Richard Shaw in New Zealand; Patrick Dunleavy, Catherine Haddon and Jill Rutter in the United Kingdom; and, more generally, Thurid Hustedt. Comments on working papers and presentations of draft materials sharpened our analysis and challenged us to extend it.

Our thanks also go to the three independent reviewers who provided constructive feedback. The book is much improved as a result of their probing questions and thoughtful suggestions. We would also like to thank our Cambridge University Press editor Joe Ng and the series editors Michael Howlett, M. Ramesh and Xun Wu for their support and patience as we revised the manuscript to address changes in government and emergent issues. We also gratefully acknowledge the financial support of the Humanities and Social Sciences Council of Canada.

Completing this book required considerable time away from family and friends. Our biggest thanks are reserved for our respective partners, Penelope and Zoiey. Thank you for your support, for your encouragement and for reviewing materials as they developed. Penelope's extensive editorial work is particularly appreciated. Any errors or omissions are the authors' alone.

We know more remains to be done and cannot claim this to be an exhaustive account of Westminster PAS. This book aspires to significantly advance our understanding about how these systems operate and change and to enrich our comparative understanding. Where there are shortfalls, we encourage our colleagues internationally to respond in kind and to continue the stimulating debates of recent years.

Glossary and Acronyms

ADM	assistant deputy minister
APS	Australian Public Service
APSC	Australian Public Service Commission
AU	Australia
BIS	Department for Business, Innovation and Skills
CA	Canada
CAG	Comptroller and Auditor General (UK)
CCMD	Canadian Centre for Management Development
central agency	cross-government agencies at the centre
CEO	chief executive officer
CFIB	Federation of Independent Business
civil service	used in the United Kingdom – the preferred term elsewhere is 'public service'
CO	Cabinet Office
CPA	Committee of Public Accounts (UK)
CPF	Contestable Policy Fund
CPU	Cabinet Policy Unit
DoF	Department of Finance (AU)
DCLG	Department for Communities and Local Government
DCMS	Department for Culture, Media and Sport
DECC	Department of Energy and Climate Change
Defra	Department for Environment, Food and Rural Affairs
deputy minister	head of department (CA)
department head	Generic term for chief executive officers (NZ), departmental secretaries (AU), deputy ministers (CA) and permanent secretaries (UK)
DfE	Department for Education
DFID	Department for International Development

DfT	Department for Transport
DoH	Department of Health
DPMC	Department of the Prime Minister and Cabinet (AU, NZ)
DRAP	Deficit Reduction Action Plan
DWP	Department for Work and Pensions
EBP	evidence-based policy (as opposed to PBE, policy-based evidence)
EMOs	extended ministerial offices
EU	exempt staff – Canadian term for staff appointed by a minister
FCO	Foreign and Commonwealth Office
G8	Group of Eight
G20	Group of Twenty
GDP	gross domestic product
GFC	global financial crisis
Gomery Report	inquiry into 'sponsorship scandal', with accountability focus (CA)
HC	House of Commons
HMRC	HM Revenue and Customs
HMT	HM Treasury
HO	Home Office
HRSDC	Human Resources and Skills Development Canada
IDC	interdepartmental committee
IGO	international governmental organisation
ILO	International Labour Organization
IMF	International Monetary Fund
IRPP	Institute for Research on Public Policy
IT	information technology
MAC	Management Advisory Committee (AU)
MBIE	Ministry of Business, Innovation and Employment
Ministry	co-exists with departments in NZ and for some agencies in the UK; the term 'department' covers both
MoD	Ministry of Defence
MoJ	Ministry of Justice
MP	Member of Parliament

NAO	National Audit Office (see CAG)
NHS	National Health Service
NGO	non-government organisation
NPM	new public management
No 10	Downing Street, Prime Minister's Office (UK)
NZ	New Zealand
OAG	Office of the Auditor General (CA)
OBR	Office for Budget Responsibility
OECD	Organisation for Economic Co-operation and Development
PAG	policy advisory group
PAS	policy advisory system
PBE	policy-based evidence (as opposed to EBP, evidence-based policy)
PBO	parliamentary budget office
PCO	Privy Council Office (CA)
PMD	prime minister's department, generic term that covers the Australian and New Zealand Department of the Prime Minister and the Cabinet (DPMC), the Canadian Privy Council Office (PCO) and the UK Cabinet Office (CO)
PPS	principal private secretary
PSI	public sector innovation
PMO	prime minister's office, a term in standard use across the four
PWGSC	Public Works and Government Services Canada
reform era	Early 1980s until the present
SCS	senior civil service (UK)
SDP	single department plan(s) (UK)
Spad	special adviser (UK) (also SpAd)
SSC	State Services Commission, a leading central agency in New Zealand
TBS	Treasury Board of Canada Secretariat
UK	United Kingdom
WTO	World Trade Organization

1 Policy Advisory Systems
An Introduction

High-quality policy advice remains essential for good governance in Westminster systems. However, the types of advice needed, who provides it, how and when have evolved dramatically in Canberra, Ottawa, Wellington and Whitehall. The public service role has been transformed as new advisory units have sprung up in and around government, while other long-standing units have been marginalised. Ministers have come under scrutiny for paying insufficient attention to their officials' best advice while focusing on the short term because of political and media pressures. In a contestable environment, public service advice can matter less and can be replaced by that of consultants, think tanks or political aides in ministers' offices. There are questions about public service capability and whether it is equipped to handle increasingly demanding contexts with fewer resources and ambivalent support. These are not easy questions to probe, and they are made more difficult by the considerable turbulence that has characterised the contemporary policy-making milieu. High-stakes trans-boundary policy challenges such as the global economic downturn, climate change, COVID-19, immigration and Brexit have commanded the attention of decision makers in addition to the enduring challenges of governing.

Policy advice is of course not only a matter of high-stakes policy issues but also an essential ingredient in more day-to-day policy matters at the heart of governing. Programs must be designed, regulations developed, services delivered, policy choices large and small made or postponed. These policy challenges are all unfolding in rather fluid, even chaotic political contexts. Stable two-party majoritarian governments have given way to more frequent coalition and minority governments in all four countries with implications for parliamentary exigencies and policy coalition building (Boston and Bullock, 2010; Hazell and Yong, 2012). The amplification of partisanship and the entrenchment of permanent campaigning have become common factors in the pathology of contemporary Westminster governments that no longer concentrate on governing after winning elections but function in continuous election mode (Aucoin, 2012; Marland et al., 2018; Diamond, 2019).

More broadly, pressures for transparency, disclosure and 'open government' have become mainstays and formal government policies. In some cases, this leads to paradoxical situations where citizens and policy stakeholders are promised greater consultation and opportunities for participatory engagement but experience dated processes that favour established powerful voices or the invocation of cabinet confidence or state secrecy to mask government activity.

There have always been tensions like these in democratic politics and public administration – as well as world wars, economic crises and policy issues du jour, which have tested the resolve and capacity of governments to govern effectively. Many observers suggest the pace of contemporary governance has increased, with responses required immediately, raising questions about how much space is left for measured consideration and who has the capacity to undertake the considering. Some worry that advice is increasingly restricted to the inner circles, perhaps an inner cabinet, or, worse, a coterie of sycophantic advisers serving an autocratic prime minister (Savoie, 1999, 2008). Yet, as the charges of centralisation of power continue to be made, prime ministers and those at the centre complain about the lack of effective levers for responding to issues and too little influence over a fragmented system that requires infinite coordination. Prime ministers and ministers struggle to cope, let alone advance their agendas, given the byzantine nature of modern policymaking and the rough-and-tumble requirements of politics in a Web-enabled era (Tiernan and Weller, 2010; Dahlstrom et al., 2011; Marrando and Craft, 2017).

Studying Policy Advice 'Systems'

Practitioners and researchers have long recognised the complex ecology of advice that circulates around government and adjusts to the context within which governments govern (Dror, 1984; Plowden, 1987; Peters and Barker, 1993). The notion of a system has more meaning than a structure to those working within it. The public policy system is seen as 'a vast repository of knowledge for policy' that 'covers the relationships and flows of policy relevant knowledge and information among people, organisations and institutions that have policymaking roles and responsibilities . . . Public policy is the outcome of a complex set of interactions among actors in the system' (IPAA, 2012, 20). These actors include ministers, government departments and agencies, businesses and business organisations, charities and foundations, universities and research institutes, NGOs, consultants and individual citizens. Policymaking occurs within 'a system, rather than a structure, with policy makers acting more as stewards and less as top-down controllers of sharply defined processes' (IPAA, 2012, vi).

The policy advisory system (PAS) has been conceived of as an interlocking set of actors and organisations that provide recommendations for action to policymakers (Halligan, 1995; Craft and Howlett, 2012). This definition has been extensively used, as it captures the plurality of suppliers along with contextual contingencies that may influence how governments navigate the advisory waters.

There are also some important limitations with this definition, which became clear as interviews were conducted with elites inside and outside of government, and in seeking to make sense of the changes that were readily apparent in the composition and operation of these systems. There is a presumption that there is a 'fit' or congruence – and interlocking – of advisory units and practices between the various bodies that engage in advisory activity. This is not invariably the case, as some advisers and advisory practices are in conflict, producing tensions between actors. A healthy tension contributes to dynamism, but it is also a key source of broader conflicts between political and public service elites and between evidence-based policymaking and decision-making based on the interests and values of communities, stakeholders or partisan calculations.

An alternative conception of PAS is of interlocked actors that vary between contexts: sectors, jurisdictions and over time. The important point is the existence of an identifiable system of policy advising that, to a greater or lesser extent, has some coherence and core, secondary and peripheral actors who provide various types of advisory inputs. This notion of a policy advising system has been extensively used in anglophone and European countries because of its value in analysing change (Hustedt and Veit, 2017; Veit, Hustedt and Bach, 2017; OECD, 2017).

Lastly, the notion of systems conjures up a logical and ordered state, similar to the point already made about the interlocking nature of advisory units. Some have pointed out this is misleading and favour alternative terms such as a 'network of advisory bodies' (OECD, 2017).

This is, however, an overly narrow reading of the original intent, which was to eschew the confines of individual advisers and practices and think *systematically* about advice. PAS is therefore conceived as an assemblage of advisory units and practices that exist at a given time with which governments and other actors engage for policy purposes. This captures a wider set of policy advisory work that allows for going beyond the closed deliberations of bureaucrats or prime minister's courts to reflect the push and pull of the demand and supply mediation of advice through various contexts (Savoie, 1999; Rhodes and Tiernan, 2014b; Veselý, 2017; Prince, 2018).

Thinking about advisory systems also blossomed on the cusp of big debates about how much power and influence the state really has any more and the fact that governance, often by semi-autonomous networks, has supplanted the command and control mode of government. The effect has been the decoupling of advisory systems from the dominance of the public service as a unit of analysis (Craft and Wilder, 2017), and shifts from government to governance suggest that the processes of aggregating and brokering community and interest-group aspirations require a different skill set (Mulgan, 2014). Advisory work is about problem definition and framing for the broader policy world, not only for authorised decision makers. It is also about making policy happen, not just figuring out which options are available. There are greater expectations for advisers to position themselves on policy problems and highlight solutions to motivate behaviour from non-governmental actors – firms, citizens, markets, international agencies – or other parts of government. This is not to undervalue government and the public service in particular, but to underscore the environmental reality that government policymakers are not the only audience for policy advice and that broader information wars are a reality of contemporary 'post-truth' Westminster worlds. Disinformation and spin are not new tactics (Hood, 2010; Perl et al., 2018). Several studies involving the four Westminster systems have touched upon issues flagged here but have not drawn on in-depth analysis of policy advice (e.g. Bakvis, 1997; Savoie, 2008; Rhodes, Wanna and Weller, 2009). This book seeks to extend the comparative analysis within a PAS framework to assess how Westminster policy advisory systems are adapting and how various advisers interact and seek to exert influence in policymaking and governance. The book builds on a range of recent developments in policy scholarship that seek to understand actual patterns of policy analysis and influence and how they differ in jurisdictions with shared administrative traditions. The book is anchored by four key themes that guide the analysis:

1. The place of advisory work in the Westminster administrative tradition;
2. Structural and organisational trends in PAS;
3. Comparative analysis of advisory systems' stability and change over time;
4. Managing PAS and implications for policymaking and governance.

PAS and Westminster Traditions

While the previous section makes clear that government is not the only advisory game in town, there is still an important set of conditions and practices that shape how policy advice works in and around government. A first step in understanding context is to comprehend the governance arrangements that exist in a Westminster system. As detailed in Chapter 2, the Westminster administrative tradition is not a firm set of rules but rather a set of shared principles and practices, some more defined than others, which guide how politicians, public servants and others engage in advisory activity and exchanges. The examination of the four classic Westminster systems means that there are some important differences in how the PAS is organised and operates given broader choices about Westminster traditions and country-specific contexts and institutional designs.

The distinctive quality of the anglophone administrative tradition is that it both facilitates and constrains change, a combination that distinguishes it from other traditions and which has played an important role in the modernisation process. This tradition can both enable extensive reform and constrain change where it departs significantly from accepted understandings. The constraints derive from the Westminster model as well as routines and conventions that emerge from experiential learning, while the pragmatism has its origins in British administrative style. A significant trend during the reform era has been the apparent reification of the potential of instrumentalism and pragmatism as governments rose to new levels of reformism.

Managerialism (or new public management) has been most associated with anglophone countries because of their early experiments and where this reform agenda reached its apogee. At the same time, the role of the political executive was being transformed, leading to a redistribution of roles and responsibilities, particularly for policy advice. Both developments were facilitated by the flexibilities in the anglophone administrative tradition (Halligan, 2015, 2020). The consequences of managerialism and politicisation are central to the provision of advice in the evolving policy advisory systems.

At this point it can be noted that the inner contradictions of the administrative tradition have exposed significant tensions and dilemmas with major implications for advisory systems (Pierre 1995; Marrando and Craft, 2017). On the one hand, the tradition has enabled unparalleled reform and flexibility, often centred on maximising further flexibilities and few constraints; but, on the other hand, core elements of both the tradition, and Westminster more generally, have been modified, and fluidity in understandings has fostered ambiguity. The consequences have been disruptive in both senses of the word: preventing progress and effectiveness; and facilitating innovation (Halligan, 2020).

Structure and Operational Trends in PAS

A major aim of this book is to better describe and analyse the state of play with the public service in the twenty-first century and other types of internal and external advisory categories, as well as to improve how they can be analysed and compared. The main actors and advisers' roles and relationship to government are provided in Table 1.1. The actors are generally identifiable because of their formal position or high profile. It has not been possible to cover all the different sources of advice, particularly those that are less tangible. For example, academics, chief science advisers and lobbyists are not examined in detail given data limitations and comparability issues. The inclusion of the relationship to government is not intended to promote the government as the central unit of analysis but rather to help underscore the significance of change with respect to both government organisation and operation and the broader PAS changes set out in the book.

Table 1.1 underscores the significant flexibilities that are prominent in Westminster traditions given the ambiguities and discretion noted earlier. Both structural aspects and operational considerations have characterised recent Westminster PAS. This book details, for instance,

Table 1.1 *Components of policy advisory systems and relationships and roles as policy advisers*

Component	Role	Relationship to government	Issues and questions
Prime minister	Strategic leadership & policy direction	Epitomises the government	Influence of PM's style
Ministers	Policy leadership	Dependent on PM's style	Results of interventions and policy priorities
Departments	Advice provider and organiser; implementation	Dependent and self-generating	Decline in policy role; processing other advice
Central agencies	Policy coordination	Prime minister's department central role	Variable central roles and relationships with PMO
Prime minister's office	Political control	Supports prime minister	Extent of policy role and influence
Ministerial advisers	Political advice and management	Agent and surrogate of employer (minister or government)	Extent of policy role and influence
Government inquiries	Advice to minister or government	Dependent on government for initiation & existence	Depends on what sort of inquiry and level of independence
Government authorities	Specialised advice	Independence depends on funding & referrals	Impact of newer agencies
Parliamentary committees & bodies	Independent advice; reports of inquiries	Depends on source of referrals	Variations in capacity, autonomy, policy impact
Consultants	External expert, specialist advice	Commissioned advice	Providing knowledge & legitimacy for policy
Think tanks	Ideas, analysis, advocacy	Usually independent if not funded	How to demonstrate impact
International bodies	Advice, binding international agreements; coordination and crisis management	Government membership/ signatories to agreements; dependence in times of crisis	How to register impact and implications of influence on domestic PAS actors and levers

clear structural changes to the size and composition of public services, the institutionalisation and deinstitutionalisation of some actors and advisory bodies, such as the addition of parliamentary budget offices, and the widespread increase in the number and influence of ministers' partisan advisers. Orthodox assumptions regarding the way advice is generated, circulated and consumed by decision makers is now in question, with developments that suggest departures in practice as well. The bilateralism of minister–senior-official relations is no longer exclusive with a range of other advisers on call or seeking or requiring attention. The public's expectations have evolved, and there have been attempts to open up policy processes through freedom of information regimes and more participatory and 'open' forms of policymaking. Pre-internet era advisory practices of pen and paper and briefing binders full of departmental advice are being replaced by tablets and e-briefing systems. Google searches and WhatsApp texting chains have moved into the executive suite, raising further implications for PAS.

Stability and Change to Advisory Systems over Time

The focus on policy advisory systems is helpful for recognising that a number of policy advisory components exist (e.g. types of policy advisers, advice and advisory practices) and that important distinctions can characterise their respective configurations and operation across jurisdictions and domains (Craft and Wilder, 2016; Craft and Halligan, 2017). Systems can be used to differentiate various dimensions for analysis, such as simple or complex, organised or disorganised (Snyder, 1993; Jervis, 1997). Policy advisory systems can be analysed over time and compared according to the degree to which they are closed or open, hierarchical or horizontal, centralised or decentralised, and considering the relative importance of the main units. In addition, advisory systems facilitate a dynamic and interactive frame for understanding how advisory components interact and how such systems may themselves change over time (Aberbach and Rockman, 1989; Craft and Howlett, 2013; van den Berg, 2017).

A primary focus in this book is providing a characterisation of each advisory system and comparison of the PAS of the four Westminster countries. This is undertaken for the main dimensions of PAS addressed as well as contextual features such as the administrative tradition. This study examines the similarities and differences that characterise

Westminster PAS, how they have evolved and the variations within the anglophone tradition. Where are Westminster principles the strongest, and where are they eroding from a policy advisory perspective? These four cases are often subject to anglophone stereotypes characterised by the primary change dynamics of externalisation from public service suppliers to external, namely consultant and think tank advisers, and by politicisation of PAS driven by ministers seeking greater congruence of advice with political and policy objectives, often secured by the increased use of partisan advisers working for ministers (Rhodes, Wanna and Weller, 2009; Craft and Howlett, 2013; Veselý, 2013). Evidence of this is apparent in the book, but it is qualified and nuanced. As detailed in the following chapters, closer inspection points to important variations in how these systems have evolved, when and why.

Managing PAS and Implications for Policymaking and Governance

The first of two questions concerns the extent to which, and in what ways, governments can manage PAS. It is unclear how often governments think strategically – or holistically – about an entity approximating PAS as opposed to significant components of it. Even then, decisions may reflect short-term political needs and choices about a ready means for achieving policy objectives rather than the consequences for the functioning of PAS. The reliance on one source rather than another has consequences, often unintended, which become apparent in the medium or long term (such as the rundown of internal capability or the budget blowout of external contracts). Governments can alter PAS through austerity programs, stymie open government and close down forms of public engagement. They can favour particular sources of advice to the relative exclusion of others, which can include bypassing public service advice. They can expand or contract greatly the use of partisan advisers, strengthen the centre of government for policy purposes or devolve roles to departments or beyond. It is also commonplace to govern on a 'whole-of-government' basis. Much depends on the myriad decisions made by ministers and departments about whether to source advice internally or to buy it.

The burgeoning PAS is a product of governments extending their advisory processes outward, but increasingly it concerns societal interests seeking to be part of the policymaking process. The discretion and change that have been suggested earlier in this chapter raise important questions about how the PAS can be better organised and, in the face of less government control over its moving parts, how it can be managed. This raises implications for policymaking and governance of the different approaches to policy advisory systems. These can be quite profound, including a range of effects, such as problems with the supply of policy advice, the quality of advice and reconciling demand and supply.

Contestability has become pervasive and prevails, not only in terms of how modern Westminster systems are now set up but also between departments with specialised units and hierarchical chains of command, constant stakeholder and media scrutiny, and the centre's management of policy processes and strategic direction. Parliamentary committees, auditors general and the media have all seized on significant expenditures to 'external' advisers – and questioned the close links between governments and some policy think tanks.

These systems also require considerable coordination. The fragmentation of policy advice due to new suppliers and advisory needs means governments are now forced to reconcile a broader range of advice within and outside of government. The ensuing chapters detail different strategies and choices with respect to how coordination is sought and, similarly, how ministers and governments have sought to secure political control. There are also persistent questions about how much control government can actually exert any more, as policy and advisory activity often unfolds in arenas and networks less responsive to command and control approaches that may have once worked well. These developments have fueled official reviews and attempts to gain more perspective on how well these systems are serving the needs of contemporary Westminster governments (e.g. Scott, 2010; OECD, 2017) and what is – and can be – done to address their shortcomings.

Main Arguments

The main arguments advanced are linked to the key lenses of analysis set out in this chapter and engaged with throughout the book. Firstly, the policy advisory system is argued to be more dynamic and complex than is currently depicted in the PAS literature. The predominance of the public service as the unit of analysis in PAS research has led to a dominant focus on externalization and politicisation vis-à-vis the public service, at the expense of broader reflections on these dynamics and the condition of the system itself (Craft and Wilder, 2017). In some cases, these are addressed in studies of PAS components and governance trends (e.g. Boston, 2016, 2017).

Secondly, the book argues that politicisation and externalisation continue to be important dynamics in PAS change but that greater care needs to be taken in explaining their drivers, sustaining factors, manifestations and constraints. There is clear evidence to support several forms of each, with implications for how PAS operates. These dynamics are reflections of the leadership in government, the available alternatives outside of the public service and the context within which they operate. This is particularly the case for PAS in Westminster systems that are themselves based on a significant degree of interpretation and ambiguity. Ministers differ in how they have sought political control, ranging from greater reliance on external consultants to expanding ministerial offices and strengthening central agencies to support the prime ministers, or to the impacts of intra-executive politics on how cabinet operates and the constraints both formal and informal that have limited political control. Similarly, while externalisation is, on a longer time scale, a property of all of these cases, there are differences in the type of externalisation and in some cases the demise of the public service as principal, though not exclusive adviser are overstated. These and unique trajectories for PAS change are broached to broaden the frame of reference against which the change of these systems is understood. Similarly, the types of change are linked to different orders of change, to better reflect that PAS involves both transformational changes associated with system-wide and contextual developments linked to overarching governance arrangements, such as the advent of political advisers or the interpretation of the merit principle of the public service, as well as a range of day-to-day changes that can be important for advice activity and systems.

A third argument is that parallel processes have been operating to both increase flexibility in the advice instruments under political control and expand the range of independent agencies. The first trend is at the behest of governments wanting short- to medium-term reviews. The second is the diverse range of sources of advice and expertise that have emerged inside government but not necessarily as part of a government-inspired design for enhancing PAS.

Rather, they have been created because issues of the day demand more independent capacity for developing policy.

Finally, PAS change, in these four cases, has been primarily gradual and endogenous in nature in two respects: the country context and the anglophone group. In all four countries most change is not abrupt or transformational; although that does occur, *most* PAS change unfolds over long periods of time. Leaving aside acute ruptures, such as Brexit and global financial downturns, PAS can become affected by lesser crises and the impact of successive attempts to reform PAS as part of broader managerial and public sector reforms (Aucoin, 1995; Lodge and Gill, 2011; Halligan, 2020).

Contemporary Westminster Policy Advisory Systems

The discussion has pointed to a more expansive understanding of the policy advisory system that takes into account the complexities of public policy in plural and activist societies. This is one that acknowledges the continuing authority and centrality of government but recognises the multitude of changes that criss-cross society. At the macro level, several dimensions of an evolving policy advisory system are identified (see Table 1.2). These have been derived from analysis of trends and the direction of change evident in the several literatures on political advisers, the policy advisory system, governance and executive politics (e.g. Craft and Howlett, 2012; Lodge and Wegrich, 2014; Craft and Wilder, 2017; Eichbaum and Shaw, 2018; Prince, 2018; Halligan, 2020), although several dimensions have been devised for this framework.

The shift from government towards governance remains debated, but the formulation here envisages the state as central out of necessity, as well as inclination, but having to acknowledge a pluralist PAS that may potentially become more multi-centric. The public service is still regarded as a focal point for multiple actors and networks. The conception of PAS as interlocking is associated with the traditional dominant ministers and public servants where actors generally knew their place and were substantially enclosed at the core of a tightly drawn PAS. Under the emergent system, capability is distributed more between intra- and

Table 1.2 *Policy advisory system: dimensions and directions of change*

Dimension	Traditional	Emergent
Focus	Centred on core public service and ministers	Issue-driven and PM/minister-centric; multiple actors and networks
Politicisation	Limited	Pervasive, a central dynamic of PAS
Externalisation	Limited	Central but contingent dynamic of PAS
Capability	Concentrated	Dispersed
Advisory sources	Formalised and narrow	Flexibility in choice; broad
Contestability of advice	Limited	Standard practice
Accessibility	Closed	Selectively open
Coordination of advice	Routine, narrow confines	Multifarious and highly demanding
Commissioning	Confined	Diverse range: consultants & reviewers
State centricity	High	State focus, responsive to society & international pressures
PAS interlocking	Tight	Loose, interacting and bespoke
Elasticity of PAS	Circumscribed	Expandable
Time frame	short-medium-long term	Short-term emphasis with episodic and ad hoc longer-term focus

extra-government organisations, the latter including several forms of commissioned policy work.

Finally, the emergent policy advisory system is expandable, as the demands of additional and new types of actors compete for attention and expect responses from decision makers.

There are various degrees of 'emergence'. Some are fairly well established while others are 'emerging', and the long-term impact is indeterminate. There are also counter-tendencies in the sense of political leaders who might subvert openness, control access, redact reports and even contract the PAS. The lack of stable government because of fissiparous parties is one of many complicating factors.

Research Design and Plan for the Book

The rationale for the country selection is provided in Chapter 2. The book is based on over sixty interviews with senior public servants, ministers, political staff and select external advisers carried out in 2017 and 2018. The interviews were designed to test and probe existing accounts and to update and confirm characterisations of PAS in the four cases. Almost all were taped and transcribed, typically on a not-for-attribution basis. A full list of interviews is provided in Appendix A. These interviews complemented other interviews the authors have undertaken over the past decade with similar actors (see Craft 2016, 2017; Halligan, 2020).

Additionally, the book represents a rigorous engagement with a sprawling set of secondary literatures that tackle individual aspects of PAS. Staffing figures, budget allocations and basic advisory system compositions have long been scattered in a range of different sources. For instance, descriptions and analysis of ministers and political advisers in discreet countries have become available in the 2010s (Maley, 2011; Hazell and Yong, 2012; Rhodes and Tiernan, 2014a, 2014b; Craft, 2016; Shaw and Eichbaum, 2018a), and their analyses and interpretations are used to support the comparative analysis.

The examination of Westminster PAS begins with the backdrop of the broader administrative tradition of Westminster that has fundamentally shaped, and continues to influence, the broad PAS practices in the four cases, as well as the country-specific developments that are subsequently examined. Chapter 2 situates the cases within their overarching administrative tradition, and this overview and comparative context addresses the shared fundamental features of the Westminster-type system and the constituent features of government pertinent to policy advisory systems. It compares public organisation and structures and unique characteristics, focusing on the organisation of the political executives, machinery of government, ancillary public sector advisory agents (e.g. parliamentary, commissions of inquiry). Attention is also given to unique characteristics of the cases, such as distinct patterns of public sector reform that have implications for policy advice and the role of central agencies vis-à-vis departments.

Chapter 3 addresses the prevailing approaches that have become established perspectives through which to understand how policy advisory systems are organised and operate. Some have focused on distributional and locational issues of where policy advice is produced in proximity to government, while others have focused on the location of policy advisory supplies and government control over them, content dimensions of policy advice and how policy advisory systems have changed. Chapters 4 through 7 focus on the principal PAS units, providing comparative insights about key developments and current conditions.

The changing position of the public service is examined in Chapter 4 within the context of the expansion in ministers' policy roles. As the political executive assumed policy leadership, a stronger emphasis has been placed on contestability of advice and increasing use of other advisory sources. The common pattern of policy capacity erosion and the effects on public service roles and relationships is analysed.

Chapter 5 explores the politically appointed staffs who work in ministers' offices. Attention is paid to both prime ministers' and minsters' office staff with respect to how they are used to secure political control, provide additional policy capacity and engage with other PAS units. While clearly influential in all four cases, comparative analysis showcases the flexibility of PAS and the diversity of interpretations of Westminster traditions. In Chapter 6, alternative internal, but non–public service, sources of policy advice are addressed. These cover parliamentary committees, commissions of inquiry, and other traditional and emergent alternatives to the public service that remain within the broader public sector. The externalisation dynamic widely attributed to these four systems is analysed in Chapter 7. Two major external advisory units have become established actors in the contemporary Westminster PAS, think tanks and private sector consultants, although the propensity to use them varies between contexts.

Chapters 8 and 9 analyse the patterns and types of change as well as the state and condition of the respective systems. Chapter 8 leverages the comparative analysis to provide a richer understanding of the types and nature of change by drawing attention to system-wide and localised change to particular advisory instruments or their settings. It highlights some distinct types of changes and focuses on the shared and distinct trajectories that have impacted the configuration and operation of these systems.

Chapter 9 returns to country-level appraisals, taking stock of idiosyncratic PAS configurations and their implications for policymaking.

It profiles the distinctive features of the Australian, Canadian, New Zealand and United Kingdom advisory systems, presents some areas of reform undertaken by governments and concludes with reflections on the implications for policymaking flowing from the changed PAS. Ultimately, there are major questions to be asked about how much more effective the advisory systems have become and the impact on the quality of public policy when countervailing pressures are present.

The main categories used to depict PAS some twenty years ago remain discernable, but their composition and how actors within them engage in the practices of giving advice have in many ways evolved. There is also the added benefit of new approaches and perspectives that help enrich how we think about advisory activity and the systems that exist to serve decision makers and society more broadly. If decision makers are going to make informed decisions, a proposition that may be more in doubt than in the past, then it is important to think about how these systems work and change within the shared administrative tradition.

2 | *Comparative Contexts*

The anglophone countries constitute a coherent set because of their common tradition and their historical and ongoing close associations and interactions. They form a natural group of industrialised democracies with institutional roots in the British administrative tradition and can be classified as classic Westminster cases. The countries can be seen as reasonably homogeneous for analytical and comparative purposes, even though they are in some respects heterogeneous. The four countries share an administrative tradition that is distinguished from those of Europe by the relationship between the political and bureaucratic realms, the focus on governments rather than the 'state', and an instrumental and pragmatic orientation (Halligan, 2010).

This overview of comparative contexts addresses the shared fundamental features of the Westminster-type system and the constituent elements of the core of government pertinent to policy advisory systems. It compares public structures and unique characteristics, similarities in the organisation of the political executives, machinery of government and ancillary public sector advisory agents (e.g. parliamentary, commissions of inquiry). Attention is also given to unique features of the cases, which have implications for policy advice, such as distinct patterns of public sector reform and the role of central agencies vis-à-vis departments.

The Westminster Model and the Anglophone Administrative Tradition

The Westminster model is integral to the four anglophone systems, although several elements do not directly impact on either administrative tradition or public management. The Westminster model is used even though the term is redolent of a specific context as much as a system (but see Aucoin, 1995; Rhodes, Wanna and Weller, 2009), and debates about definitions reflect this (Grube and Howard, 2016).

The constituent features of Westminster are centred on responsible government as defined by the fusion of the executive and parliament. English writers dwell at great length on the continuing centrality of Westminster, despite contesting its characterisation and implications in respects that are peculiar to the British context (Richards, 2008; Rhodes, 2011; Diamond, 2014). The primary features for this study are strong cabinet government, ministerial responsibility and a permanent bureaucracy that is neutral, non-partisan and professional. Other elements commonly identified but less directly relevant here are parliamentary sovereignty, the dominant position of central government and accountability through elections (Richards and Smith, 2002; Rhodes, 2011).

The significance and meaning of elements of the Westminster understanding have varied over time and between countries. Public service leaders have accorded different emphases (Weller and Haddon, 2016), reflecting contexts and issues of the day. The meanings of conventions and the functioning of institutions depend on how prime ministers choose to operate for political purposes (Weller, 2018). This has meant that the beliefs and practices are quite contingent. Nevertheless, there continue to be shared core beliefs about a public service that is permanent even if the most senior appointments are not, separation from the political executive even if the boundaries are porous and shifting, a reliance on professional and internal appointments even if political influence is substantial.

Permanency has largely disappeared, most explicitly where the top appointments are on contract. Where the practice is retained, turnover belies claims of durability in high office. There is general agreement that the bureaucracy remains neutral, non-partisan and professional. In support of this professional role, public servants have been insulated from, although responsible to, the political executive as envisaged by the constitutional bureaucracy. How this works in practice has been the subject of high tension in the reform era since the 1980s. The mounting pressures on the professional standing of public servants have produced requirements for them to be variously 'frank and fearless' and responsive to ministers.

A derivative element is the role of the ministerial department, for which the minister has constitutionally derived responsibilities and where the concept of ministerial responsibility prevails as an operational principle. The role of the public service is to serve the government of the day by providing its best advice and loyally implementing its policy. Collective responsibility is also a central constitutional tenet and may operate differently from multiparty systems and where there is a minority government.

The Westminster model was questioned by Rhodes (1997) as an inaccurate portrayal of the British system because the elitist, top-down dimensions were argued to have acquired the features of a differentiated polity model. This included an emphasis on governance, not government, a segmented executive, a hollowed-out state and power-dependent relationships. An alternative was the asymmetric model that recognised fragmentation but posited that the state continued to be dominant (Marsh et al., 2001; Richards and Smith, 2002). This position seems to have been maintained by central government specialists when confronting the obvious impact of governance (Bell and Hindmoor, 2009), although the conception of the state as 'a loose network of actors engaged in "governance"' is said to have gained currency (Grube and Howard, 2016, 8).

An administrative tradition focus speaks to the culture of countries' public management systems (Pollitt and Bouckaert, 2011). Administrative traditions reflect values and principles that are influential in shaping structures, behaviours and cultures (Painter and Peters, 2010). The starting point for establishing the basis of the tradition is the Westminster model, which provides the framework for the constitutional and governance attributes of the state. In terms of how questions have been posed and resolved, there has been a focus within the tradition on organisational administration to achieve policy objectives rather than on their legal character (Peters, 2003).

The consequence in practice of the combination of the British tradition and the circumstances that emerged in different New World settings is a set of shared components in this administrative tradition. These can be identified in terms of the relationship between public servants and politicians and two aspects of administrative and political culture and style: instrumentalism and pragmatism. The combination of elements is distinctive and has significant implications for the machinery of government, processes of change and relations with society.

The identification of an instrumental administration with Britain resonates with the experience of other anglophone countries.

Instrumentalism is recognised at one level as part of the government tradition and provides the 'significant *potential* to transform administrative structures and practices' (Knill, 1999, 127). The concern here is with the application of instrumentalism to the development of public policy, although it is applied more broadly to government's roles.[1] The public service's primary role is to execute the will of the government of the day. In return the public service is meant to be protected in certain respects from arbitrary decisions at the individual level. However, organisational change has become regarded as fair game for political executives seeking to implement their policies because they have the right to select from a range of options through reform and other instruments, while being mindful of the boundaries of action in areas such as partisanship in appointments and the use of the public service. The strong preference has been for the policy advisory system to be opened up to extensive pluralistic influences, competition in policy advice and routine use of other sources of advice from both within and outside government. Within this expanded advisory system, governments rely on ministerial advisers, make extensive use of expert reviews and analysis and draw on the service of external consultants.

The related attribute of administrative and political style, pragmatism, features in the country literature as an operational characteristic. In the formative years, Anglo-American systems were identified with the 'pragmatic and incremental nature of governing . . . . In contrast to most continental political and administrative systems, ideology plays a relatively minor role in Anglo-American politics, and perhaps even less in public administration' (Peters, 2003, 21–2). Pragmatism is regarded as having its origins both in traditions inherited from Britain and in the colonial development experience where conditions (e.g. lack of political parties with strong ideologies) reinforced it. For its part the British tradition was seen as atheoretical and reliant on experience and working through problems. Many qualities of the civil service were acquired piecemeal and were not the product of major statutory or constitutional changes. The standard explanation was that this was consistent with a system of government that lacked a written constitution (Baker, 1972; Chapman, 1996), which was also a feature of the New Zealand system.

Australian and Canadian administrative traditions have also been represented as pragmatic. In Australia's case, there has been a tendency to blend various ideologies, as expressed in nation building. The administrators were 'utilitarian and pragmatic – and pragmatism triumphed as a creed and ideological position' (Wanna and Weller, 2003, 67). Canada also had a tradition of pragmatism and moderation that applied to political and public service leaders (Gow, 2004; Lindquist, 2006c).

Pragmatism is not of course exclusive to this tradition (compare for example the Nordic style: Lægreid and Rykkja, 2015), but it has been important for how the conception of the state has evolved. What distinguishes pragmatism in this tradition is that it can be readily employed as part of the change agenda to serve the requirements of the government of the day whether under conditions of reform or traditional incrementalism. A pragmatic approach supports change-oriented governments by allowing major reforms to be readily implemented and in the acceptance of the malleability of governance.

The distinctive quality of the anglophone tradition is that it both facilitates and constrains change, a combination that distinguishes it from other administrative traditions and which has played an important role in the modernisation and the evolution of the policy advisory system. The tradition is enabled to both facilitate change and to constrain change where it departs significantly from accepted understandings. The constraints derive from the Westminster model as well as routines and conventions that emerge from experiential learning, while the pragmatism has its origins in British administrative style.

A significant trend during the reform era has been the apparent reification of the potential of instrumentalism and pragmatism as governments rose to new levels of reformism. The chief expressions of this have been managerialism and politicisation. On the one hand the tradition has enabled unparalleled reform and flexibility often centred on maximising further flexibilities and few constraints. On the other hand, core elements of both the tradition and Westminster more generally have been either discarded or subjected to ad hoc departures, and fluidity in understandings has fostered ambiguity. The consequences have been disruptive for traditional relationships and the effectiveness of the policy advisory system.

Implications of Westminster

The implications of these features are important in two areas. First, under the Westminster model, relations between politicians and bureaucrats traditionally centred on the coexistence of the public service and responsible government (Aucoin, 1995). The embedded tension between the two elements – non-partisan and partisan – were kept in balance by applying well-established principles. The relationship was traditionally based on a neutral public service that served the political executive regardless of party. The political executive in turn respected the integrity of the public service by maintaining its apolitical and professional character. Specific features were the career public servant, a permanent official who survived successive governments; and the ministerial department as the repository of policy knowledge and primary adviser to government.

The second area centres on the external boundaries differentiating the state from the non-state parts of society (in particular, the private sector). These have often been imprecise and blurred, as in New Zealand (Mulgan, 1997), and have varied over time. The historical experience of anglophone countries has differed (e.g. Australia's greater reliance on private, or at least non-state, provision in education and health services). Yet there was acceptance that the public and private realms were distinctive, and this was reflected in explicit boundaries around the public services in terms of careers and identity.

Politicians did not however take up these opportunities beyond piecemeal changes. These countries' administrative histories like most others up until the 1980s were littered with unimplemented reform initiatives. Accumulated discretionary responsibilities and the powers of public officials and agencies historically placed brakes on meaningful change (Di Francesco, 2001; Scott, 2010).

Reinforcing Anglo Distinctiveness

Beyond institutional traditions, several factors have reinforced the anglophone identity. Continuing patterns of historically formed interaction, culturally supported by language and heritage, have been highly important. There has been a long tradition of studying the transfer of British institutions, within the Empire and later the Commonwealth. Endogenous communication patterns influenced members of the group through bilateral relations between countries and various types of network. The formal networks derived from relationships developed between Britain and its colonies and were maintained following decolonisation. The Commonwealth has provided a mechanism for communication among Australia, Britain, Canada and New Zealand based on a common language, cultural legacy and institutions (Patapan et al., 2005).

These networks have included agency-level exchanges of staff, importing senior experts to conduct reviews, annual meetings of networks, and constant informal contacts and associated epistemic communities. The specialised networks have been an important source for circulating ideas and the sharing of experience. Over time, these functional-based and relatively informal systems within the anglophone group have been significant for reform transfer within a sector, which often occurred independently of general reform programs (e.g. inland revenue/tax offices or specialised service delivery agencies). Politicians from the left and right have had their own looser political networks.

The long history of the transfer of ideas and reforms between the four countries dates from the transplanting of British institutions into the colonies. The historical movement of policy ideas and innovation between anglophone countries was again stimulated during the recent period of intensive reform. The four systems exhibited similar patterns of development (Halligan, 2007). The emergence of this distinctive set of reforms was the product of patterns of interaction that accorded legitimacy and relevance to initiatives within an administrative tradition facilitating rapid transmission and acceptance of ideas and practice. The early identification of new public management – a somewhat imprecise (and changing) ensemble of reforms – came from British writers who discerned the trend under Thatcher (Pollitt, 1990). In addition to the major reforms in Britain (e.g. privatisation and executive agencies with implications for policy processes), individual country programs gained international significance as exemplified by New Zealand's 'public management model'. All the countries in the anglophone group borrowed from each other's reforms. The reform movement therefore served to reinforce the notion of the anglophone group's identity both internally and externally as distinctive and contrasting with that of other countries.

However, the reform directions had impacts on policy advice and the nature of the policy advisory system. A consistent pattern was to expand the components of the policy advisory system. As examined in Chapter 4, the relegation of the status of policy advice and work with the ascendancy of managerialism, the expansion of sources of advice and the eventual decline in policy capability and quality became fundamental matters for public governance.

Variations between Pathways

Traditions and Pathways

Canada stands out within the Westminster group in terms of its trajectory and mix of characteristics. Canadian public administration has presented a set of features to the external observer that is familiar, as well as elusive in some respects. Several dimensions of the Canadian variant locate it comparatively within the anglophone family and show how it has evolved a distinct identity and developmental pathway. The influence of the United States was significant because of its proximity, and the lack of political traditions meant that Canadians tended to follow debates in the United States to inform their understanding of public administration. Prior to World War I, administrative ideas in Canada came mainly from Britain, but subsequently they were largely American, with Canada following the USA in its progression in management ideas and practice (Dwivedi and Gow, 1999). The majority of significant innovations introduced by federal and provincial governments between 1960 and 1990 were based on US influence (Gow, 1994, 104).

For some purposes, the patterns of convergence and divergence of the North American and other Westminster countries could be considered separately (Halligan, 2003). The United Kingdom, Australia and New Zealand pursued comprehensive programs of public management reform, whereas Canada fitted the category of a partially reformed system until the 2000s produced more explicit agendas at the centre. Despite Canada's North American context, the anglophone tradition remained salient to the debates about ideas and relationships derived from the fundamentals of Westminster and responsible government. These included constitutional conventions, conflicts between values, the implications of ministerial responsibility, the complexities of accountability and the policy relationship between the political executive and the public service (Aucoin, 1995, 2012; Kernaghan, 1997; Savoie, 2003; Aucoin et al., 2004). In these areas, core Canadian issues resonated directly with other anglophone countries. Canada emerges as operating within an anglophone tradition, although tempered more directly than the others by the influence of the USA. As Hodgetts (1983, x) observed, its administrative culture comprises 'the British heritage of institutions and conventions mingled with American ideas and practices, with adaptations of both to meet indigenous features of a federal state, overlaid by regional and cultural factors'.

There is also something definably Canadian about other character-istics (Heintzman, 1997), such as the accommodations of a plural society reflecting major minority concentrations in specific jurisdic-tions. The state in Westminster systems has become more complex, but was this greater in the most devolved system of government, which was responsive to anglophone and francophone identities as well as Indigenous peoples? Canada has made less of systemic instrumental-ism, which has allowed pragmatism to play a more prominent role. The emphasis is explicit in commentary that the public service culture is 'pragmatic, little driven by theory' and that public sector reform is pragmatic and evolutionary (Aucoin, 2002; Gow, 2004, 9, 21; Lindquist, 2006c, 61).

Elements of the Canadian character were also reflected in the use of specific instruments as sources of policy advice: the royal commission was retained for general policy inquiries after other anglophone sys-tems had relegated it in favour of other instruments for policy devel-opment. Similarly, the attachment to an array of central agencies and officers of the parliament signified an attachment to incrementalism and process and to top-down policy processes. The legendary level of centralisation within the core executive and the heavy reliance on political levers differentiated Canada (Savoie, 1999) and was reflected in the policy advisory system (Craft, 2016).

In contrast to Canadian incrementalism, the United Kingdom is in many respects at the other extreme. Of all the anglophone systems, it has been the most prone to a change dynamic, typified as 'chronic reformism' (Pollitt, 2007). This can be attributed to the 'awfulness of the English' (Castles, 1989, 267) in first embracing neo-liberal ideas in the 1980s, although it does not account for what emerged from a longitudinal perspective on reform. Pollitt argues (2007) that con-textual factors allow for serial interventions by governments that had absorbed the tenets of managerialism. The United Kingdom system also became more complex with internal devolution to subnational jurisdictions and its supranational membership in the European

Union. The notion of the United Kingdom as an outlier has continued to receive support (Pollitt and Bouckaert, 2011; Wilks, 2013; Pollitt, 2016), and its new public management credentials have usually been the strongest.

New Zealand displayed exceptionalism in the heyday of its public management (from the late 1980s on) with an original model that was unlike any other country internationally (Boston, Martin, Pallot and Walsh, 1996). Having once been depicted as the perfect example of the Westminster model (Lijphart, 1984), the country's pathway could now be depicted as an 'Archetypal Transplant to Maverick Outlier' (Wanna, 2005). Following the introduction of the MPP electoral system in 1996, there have tended to be coalitions or minority governments. There is a case for arguing that the modified New Zealand model is more similar but still different from the others on several counts. New Zealand was famous for inaugurating the most radical public management model, but it has since displayed fewer NPM tendencies, being more focused on backing away from its model. New public management has been more sustained in the United Kingdom and Australia (Halligan, 2020).

Comparing Structures and Machinery

From the outside, the commonalities look strong, but within this group variations are apparent in governmental institutions, the most significant being whether their structures are federal (Australia and Canada) or unitary (New Zealand and the United Kingdom). The central governments of unitary systems have a different purview because of sub-national functions, including proximity to citizens, extensive service delivery, responsibility for local government, more areas exercising choices (e.g. with utilities and use of third parties) and high-profile policy fields (e.g. policing). The four have also had different-sized public sectors nationally (expenditure as a proportion of GDP): Australia's has been smaller over several decades (mid-30s), the rest being closer to the middle range (40s) for the OECD.

The core executive for the purposes here covers central agencies, departments and political offices, and associated bodies playing supporting roles. The outer public sector has less direct and regular engagement with the policy advisory process and ranges from non-departmental agencies within portfolios to parliamentary committees to independent think tanks within the broader system of government, plus ad hoc bodies and committees.

The prime minister, cabinet and individual ministers, as well as senior officials and ministerial office staff, are the objects of policy advice, and their orientations provide the main dynamic for the operation of PAS. Much has been written about the relationship between them, best summarised by core executive perspectives that recognise their interdependence (Smith, 1999), and about the identification of a spectrum of possible arrangements (Elgie, 1997). The long debate about the standing of cabinet in the face of prime ministerial or court government (Savoie, 2008; Rhodes et al., 2009; Rhodes and Tiernan, 2014b) has been in abeyance as cabinets have come back into favour.[2] Variations in the roles of political leaders centre on the leadership styles of prime ministers and ministers in relation to the policy advisory system, including where advice is sourced and the relative importance of the centre of government in relation to ministers and departments (see Table 2.1).

Table 2.1 *Structures relevant to policy advice within the government system*[*]

	Inner/core executive	Outer and ancillary
Public sector	Departments of state	Non-departmental agencies
	Central agencies	Statutory authorities
	Strategic policy unit	Statutory public service appointments
Political	Prime minister's office	Parliamentarians
	Cabinet and cabinet committees	Parliamentary committees
	Ministers' offices	
Instruments	Hybrid committees, working groups	Productivity commissions (or similar)
	Expert policy reviews	Parliamentary budget offices
	Policy tsars	Commissions of inquiry

[*] The public service–political divide may not hold with mixed compositions of offices and units.

Departments

Departments provide the core organisational unit in all four countries. As ministerial departments they are the primary form and invariably command influence, except where this is muted by a domineering and centralising prime minister or strong central agencies. The numbers for federal systems are eighteen in Australia and twenty-one in Canada; for the unitary countries, with their wider range of functions, there are thirty in New Zealand and twenty-five in the United Kingdom.[3]

Departments vary in functions, size and complexity. Two main organising features are whether a department's functions are primarily cross-agency or not; and whether it specialises in one role or combines several (policy, program delivery, regulation). In the first case it is either a line department or central agency (see next section), although several combine features of both. Departments normally have a significant policy focus and command policy expertise in a specialised field, but they may not have notable service delivery responsibilities. They may be constituted as policy departments or ministries with implementation being undertaken by specialised agencies, departments or third parties. Policy departments may be complex rather than large, with the majority of the work being about policy with only an element of service delivery. The policy expertise of departments may receive less acknowledgement where there is a central drive through the prime minister's department.

Central Agencies

The centre of government provides coordination, strategic focus and direction across the governance system. Much depends on how the functions are constituted, the engagement with the political executive and relationships with other parts, the central capacity to respond to complex demands on government and finally their overall performance. For this purpose, a set of three or four central agencies, and the prime minister's office, exists with common core functions across the four systems, although how these are configured varies (see Table 2.2).

The basis of specialisation at the centre is well established and durable. Individual central agencies specialise in coordinating policy advice for the prime minister, financial management, economic policy and personnel. There is also the prime minister's office for political,

Table 2.2 *Central agencies of government and functions by country*

Country	Political advice, interface management, political coordination	Policy advice to PM, cabinet support, policy coordination, political–public service interface	Human resources & system oversight	Budget & resource management	Economic policy
Australia	Prime Minister's Office	Dept of Prime Minister and Cabinet	Public Service Commission	Department of Finance	Treasury
Canada	Prime Minister's Office	Privy Council Office	Treasury Board Secretariat	Treasury Board Secretariat	Finance
New Zealand	Prime Minister's Office	Dept of Prime Minister and Cabinet	State Services Commission[1]	Treasury	Treasury
United Kingdom	No 10	Cabinet Office	Cabinet Office	Treasury	Treasury

[1] The functions of the New Zealand State Services Commission extend beyond senior appointments to system development.
Source: Partly adapted from Parker et al. (2010), Figure 7.

strategic policy and priority matters, which differs from the public service agencies at the centre in being a political office engaged in partisan activity (Craft and Wilson, 2018; Weller, 2018). The specialisation may be exclusive: e.g. central personnel questions are concentrated in a specialised agency in Australia and New Zealand. Otherwise exceptions and variations become important: public finance is located within a broader treasury in two systems (NZ and the United Kingdom); the personnel function is variously split (over time) between the United Kingdom's Cabinet Office and Treasury. The provision of human resources and personnel is the most diverse, with less direct comparability, but these central agencies are less relevant, with the exception of the New Zealand State Services Commission, whose Commissioner has responsibility for recommending appointments of departmental chief executives, which is elsewhere handled through the prime minister's department (Boston and Halligan, 2012). The Canadian Treasury Board Secretariat covers two functions (although the organisation for personnel is more complicated than elsewhere) and has consolidated its role in public management (Table 2.2).

Political Organisation

Prime Ministers' Offices

At the center there is also the prime minister's office (PMO), which was pioneered by Canada, and is notable in the UK as the main source of policy advice on whole of government (Savoie, 1999; Halligan, 2011; Truswell and Atkinson, 2011, 21). PMOs have played critical but variable roles. They come in two basic forms of either core support for the prime minister or political machines for driving the prime minister's agenda, with variations in between. The former may have a narrow range of functions; the latter, extensive responsibilities and greater policy and strategic authority and control. Much depends on the level of decentralisation the prime minister permits within the political executive and how the role of the prime minister's office is perceived. The first form is not necessarily a concentration of partisans, while the latter is unequivocally about political commitment to the prime minister's objectives. A powerful PMO has a propensity to come into conflict with central agencies and the domains of ministers and their departments. Its status signifies that other agencies at the centre are adjuncts to the overriding objectives of the prime minister. The prime minister's office has been depicted as calling the shots in Canada and at times in Australia (Aucoin, Jarvis and Turnbull, 2011).

Levels of centralisation and control vary between political leaders, and PMO capacity is also highly variable depending on the quality of the staff, how they are led and managed, and the inclinations of the prime minister. Indicators of a PMO's character have been the standing of the chief of staff in the core executive, the degree of partisanship of staff and the relative significance of the process/substance (policy content) split (Rhodes and Tiernan, 2014b).

Canada has set the pace with the PMO. The 'modern version' of the PMO was attributed to Pierre Trudeau (although his predecessor had a staff of about forty in the office) (Radwanski, 2016). The PMO functioned mainly as a 'switchboard' for the prime minister (rather than the 'nerve centre of policy making') with most roles, apart from nuts and bolts, supporting the prime minister in terms of public image, party politics and increasingly short-term tactics and firefighting (Campbell and Szablowski, 1979, 60, 67). The Canadian PMO subsequently became larger with staff numbers ranging from 80 to 120. It was reorganised along the lines of the Executive Office of the President in the United States, and PMO staff members were described as more like those employed there (Savoie, 1999, 101). This centralisation and concentration of power in the Canadian government was frequently acknowledged (Savoie, 1999, 2019). The staff were described as 'partisan, temporary, and above all loyal to the prime minister', in a highly centralised structure (Savoie, 1999, 101).

The Australian office dates from the 1970s and was modelled on Canada's PMO (Tiernan, 2007, 41). It evolved greater responsibilities and complexity over time as the government's reliance on it increased. The office existed principally not to initiate policy but to focus on process and on extending the prime minister's capacity to control the public service (Walter, 1986; Campbell and Halligan, 1992). Early on the PMO was quasi-partisan, becoming less so as the value of public service expertise was appreciated more (Campbell and Halligan, 1992, 64–5). The transition to a more partisan PMO occurred in the following two decades (Rhodes and Tiernan, 2014b, 39), when central agencies were weakened by decentering, and continued while recentring was under way, with the most impact on the Department of the Prime Minister and Cabinet. The chief of staff role was emerging towards the end of the 1980s, influenced by the 'Chef de Cabinet' in Europe and management ideas (Behm, 2015, 2). The PMO covered policy advice and coordination and increasingly became a concentration of partisans committed to the prime minister's objectives. The majority of PMO staff in 2012 were advisers (75 per cent) (Rhodes and Tiernan, 2014a, 2014b, 69).

The PMOs of the other two countries have had either less sustained or fluctuating influence. In New Zealand's case the PMO is small and more concerned with short-term questions and firefighting, which can be engendered by instability in the operation of minority governments. UK's No 10 has been prone to wide swings in capacity and influence. It can be authoritative in dictating the prime minister's preferences on specific issues but less so across a number of fields; its relatively small size, and uneven policy capability, means that it must rely on the departments of Whitehall. Much depends on how the office is led by the chief of staff, a role developed from 1997 (Haddon, 2019), and the use that is made of the potential power inherent in the position. Disciplined centralisation has been engineered in 2019 by the senior adviser to Boris Johnson, the de facto chief of staff (Balls, 2019).

The Minister's Office

The ministerial adviser was the other significant addition to the executive branch during the early reform era. The political executive used advisers to increase the influence of the ministerial office, to enlarge the partisan element within the executive, to extend the minister's authority at the interface with the public service and to redistribute power between administrative and political systems. They often performed tasks that otherwise would be undertaken by public servants and acted as the main communication link between the minister and other institutions.

The personal offices of ministers have been recognised as a legitimate component in conventional anglophone country advisory systems (Halligan, 1995; Esselment et al., 2014) and described as '[o]ne of the most significant examples of institutional innovation within Westminster political systems' (Maley, 2011, 1469). Recent assessments from the anglo cases indicate that partisan advisers have not only grown in number but also become more active in providing policy advice and become influential through sophisticated policy advisory work involving a range of public service and non-governmental policy actors (OECD, 2007, 2011; Eichbaum and Shaw, 2010a, 2010b; Maley, 2011; Craft, 2015b). There are, however, differences in the numbers and institutional location of ministerial staffs with implications for advisory system activity (Chapter 5).

Ministerial or political advisers have also been known as special advisers (or spads) in the United Kingdom and 'exempt staff' in Canada. It is unclear how comparable the terminology is, for it may apply to several types of ministerial staff, ranging from media to technical and policy experts (see Craft, 2016, 5). Whether they have been members of a political party has varied between governments (Halligan and Power, 1992). Partisan appointments have increased over time in Australia but still vary with governments and ministers. Regardless, staffers operating politically rather than as professionals within core executive departments have markedly increased in significance.

The Canadian minister's office expanded in tandem with the PMO. An explicit rival to departments was most clearly articulated by Canadian prime ministers, first by Pierre Trudeau and then by Brian Mulroney when he introduced the chief of staff position for ministers' offices in 1984 (Bakvis 2000). Over the past four decades, political staff added a significant new element to the Canadian government as agents of the minister to whom they were responsible and accountable (Aucoin, 2010, 64). Under Mulroney the number of political staff rose to 460 in the early 1990s (with 99 in the Prime Minister's Office), and subsequently the combined staff exceeded 500, a level maintained despite fluctuations (Aucoin, 2010, 71, 73). By the 2010s the PMO figure was as high as 112, and the total exempt staff was 570. There was also a move towards role specialisation, using small policy teams able to influence policy processes and content (Craft, 2016, table 2.2).

In Australia, the Whitlam Labor government introduced an advisory system in 1972; although partisan advisers existed before, they now became the norm, and the size of the ministerial office increased (Halligan and Power, 1992, 81). The Hawke Labor government sought to strengthen political direction (Campbell and Halligan, 1992) by proposing a political tier within the senior public service but compromised with a new position, the ministerial consultant. Ministerial staff were increasingly interposed between the bureaucracy and politicians, becoming an institutionalised part of government with numbers as high as 470, reached in 2007 (Halligan and Power, 1992; Maley, 2010). The Member of Parliament (Staff) Act 1984 provided for ministers to employ and be responsible for staff, and interventions by parties supported the professionalisation of staff and careers (Tiernan, 2007, 33). Working in a minister's parliamentary or electoral office has been a pathway to a career in parliament (Behm, 2015, 19–20).

In contrast with other anglophone countries, New Zealand was more reluctant to develop ministerial offices. Ministerial suspicions of senior departmental advice in the 1980s led them to rely less on the public service and more on political appointees in their offices, but the position was not institutionalised. The number of ministerial advisers has increased since the 2000s: there were about thirty political advisers (excluding press secretaries) in 2006 (Eichbaum and Shaw, 2007, 465), but numbers remained small (fifty-six in 2011). In addition, ministers usually agreed to the placement of departmental staff in ministerial offices to provide policy advice and liaison (Eichbaum and Shaw, 2010a; Boston and Halligan, 2012).

The UK numbers have fluctuated (Richards, 2008, 180), jumping under the Blair government and increasing overall, but less so under recent prime ministers. Despite constant reviews of the role, the overall numbers have remained comparatively small. A distinction needs to be drawn between the minister's private office, staffed by public servants (who perform roles such as correspondence, departmental liaison and the ministerial diary, elsewhere undertaken by staff in a partisan office), and special advisers appointed by ministers. The latter were fixed at two per minister, with the notable exceptions of the prime minister and deputy prime minister. In addition, there might be an expert policy adviser employed on temporary contracts (Paun, 2013, 6–7; Yong and Hazell, 2014).

Canadian and Australian advisory systems include a much more pronounced and accepted role for such actors compared to the United Kingdom (Maley, 2011; LSE Group, 2012; Craft, 2016). The latter features a significantly lower complement of such staff both in ministers' and first ministers' offices. While all countries developed systems of ministerial staff in the reform era, there were significant variations between them: the smallest and largest systems have 100 to 150; while the two medium-sized federal systems have

450–550.[4] Getting a comparative fix on the composition of the staff can be problematic as it varies over time (e.g. the extent of their partisanship and the use of public servants), although they cover various types of assistant in addition to advisers (Craft, 2016, 5). Australian ministerial staff covered a range of occupations, from administrative and support staff, political and departmental liaisons and the major growth areas, media and ministerial advisers (Tiernan, 2007, 19–20). Ministerial advisers accounted for 71 per cent of staff in Australia (Maley, 2011, 1469). Numbers alone do not of course indicate the influence of advisers, for many may be young and inexperienced, as in Australia and Canada and elsewhere (Aucoin, 2010; Yong and Hazell, 2014). Looking at numbers alone understates the role of individual advisers, particularly in No 10, where there are cases of extraordinarily influential advisers under Blair, May and Johnson (see Chapter 5).

Ancillary Public Sector Organisations

Beyond the main agencies of the core executive there is a range of other sources of advice (as discussed in detail in Chapter 6). They are differentiated according to whether they are directly controlled by government, operate completely independently of government or are subject to its influence to varying degrees. In the first category are hybrid committees and groups reporting to government and policy tsars appointed by government. In the second category are bodies that are independent and ongoing (e.g. the parliamentary budget office), those that are ad hoc and independent but still responsible directly to the government (e.g. commission of inquiry), a mixed bag of reviews and those where government influence may pertain depending on where the parliamentary committee system is located.

Conclusion

This chapter has provided the government and cultural contexts for policy advisory systems in the four countries. It has reviewed features that bind the countries together and examined the similarities (and some differences) and comparable dimensions of the four countries: the centrality of the Westminster principles and a shared administrative tradition, the contestation over their veracity, and the key agencies, structures and relationships, including ancillary agents. The contours of the state were changing in the final decades of the last century (Richards and Smith, 2002), and this has impacted directly on the policy advisory system. The following chapters analyse the different components of, and patterns and trends in, PAS.

3 | Approaches to Understanding PAS and Change over Time

Central to the development of the advisory system concept was the recognition that decision makers could avail themselves of a growing plurality of policy advice from within and outside of the public sector. Parliamentary budget officers, political aides, think tanks, management consultants, temporary commissions and expert panels, and international bodies among others had become ready providers of advice. This challenged the bilateralism traditionally associated with the workings of the Westminster style based on elite minister–public service advisory relationships (Rhodes, Wanna and Weller, 2009). By virtue of its proximity to ministers, knowledge of policy files, and its mastery of government process, the public service had long been the dominant source of policy advice for decision makers. Each of the Westminster PAS being examined in this book includes well-documented instances of politicians accessing advice from confidants, business, labour, academic and non-governmental sectors, or any number of advisers from informal 'kitchen-cabinets' (Plowden, 1987; Bakvis, 1997).

The distinction here is that the distributed nature of advisory systems extends beyond the practice of ministers going elsewhere on an informal and ad hoc basis. Rather, it involves the proliferation and normalisation of alternative forms of *professional* policy advice in Australia, Canada, New Zealand and the United Kingdom. Policy advisory landscapes are now depicted as more contested, dotted by a constellation of advisory actors and practices that challenge the orthodox notions of advisory production, brokerage and consumption. The consensus is that in most instances decision makers now sit in complex webs of advisory activity which include both 'traditional' professional public service analysts; political advisers inside and outside of government; and an assortment of 'expert', professional and other less formal types of advice (Rhodes et al., 2009; Brans, Geneva-May and Howlett, 2017). In such a circumstance the parsimony of a bilateral mandarin–minister relationship has been replaced by a more populated if not more contested alternative, characterised by much less predictability about where ministers turn for advice, when and why. This recasts the public services' policy advisory roles and clouds determinations of influence, raising questions as to how more numerous advisory inputs will interact and ultimately be reconciled by decision makers.

The use of PAS has helped scholars and practitioners grapple with some of these important questions. It broadens the focus of analysis from over-reliance on questions of public service capacity and advisory performance to a synergistic frame of analysis that attends to the configuration, operation, effectiveness and evolution of the systems themselves (Craft and Wilder, 2017). As this book makes clear, the public service in each of the four countries remains an important PAS unit, but its functions, like those of ministers and other advisory system units, have evolved in important ways. This chapter introduces three approaches that have helped focus PAS research: location, content and change dynamics. Each has animated particular approaches to examining PAS which individually and collectively help highlight major fault lines, key tensions and important facets of advisory work that will be teased out via the comparative analysis of the British, Australian, New Zealand and Canadian cases in the pages that follow.

A dominant theme in PAS research, especially early attempts to make sense of the diversifying landscape, was location. That is, PAS has always had a focus on distributional issues of where advisory supply was located and the ability of a government to exert control over it. Considerable efforts went into charting the ascendency and decline of various advisory units, typically with an emphasis on the public service's changing role, and the impacts for policymaking and governing brought about by new supply and shifting demand (Seymour-Ure, 1987; Halligan, 1995).

Second, there has been increased attention to the *content* of policy advice. This recognised that, while location was important, the composition, operation and influence of units within these systems was at least in part a result of the congruence of the content of advice with demand, regardless of location of supply or the ability of governments to exert control over it. A focus on content also sought to move beyond less helpful and in some cases less accurate distinctions between 'political' and 'technical' forms of policy advice (Weller, 1987; Prasser, 2006). This was spurred by increasing recognition that the nature of advisory work was not as clear-cut as some theorists would have liked and that boundaries between the various forms of advising were in many cases becoming less clear. The state of play was more muddied, as new advisers, advisory practices, and shifting policy and governance contexts swirled around PAS (Boston, 1994; Prince, 2007; Connaughton, 2010; Craft and Howlett, 2012).

Third, there is the matter of the *dynamics* linked to the stability and change of individual components or entire systems over time (Aberbach and Rockman, 1989; Craft and Howlett, 2013). To date, the focus has been on the dynamics of externalisation and politicisation of these systems because of their significance and identifiability.

The three approaches are drawn upon throughout the book to shed light on the arrangements and developments of note, as well as to provide a better grip on Westminster PAS and how it has evolved over time, and within a shared administrative tradition. Another approach is to examine the change according to its magnitude: from overarching frameworks down to micro adjustments. While the book explores these in this chapter and those that follow, there is a pressing need to better understand the types and nature of PAS change more generally.

There are also organisational dynamics, as types of units within government rise and fall in significance or change their character (Chapter 6). Of relevance here is institutionalisation, which has long been used as shorthand for systematic formalisation of practices or units within advisory systems, while deinstitutionalisation consists of the discontinuity of a previously institutionalised advisory organisation or activity (Seymour-Ure, 1987; Pierre, 1998; Fleischer, 2009; Kay and Daugbjerg, 2015).

Approaching PAS: Location, Content and System Change

Initial policy advisory work was often conceived of either broadly, in terms of government knowledge utilisation, or more narrowly, as part of the policymaking process (Peters and Barker, 1993; Baehler and Scott, 2010). For the insider, policy advice may simply be an 'output' (DPMC, 2014), which at its core can be seen as 'covering analysis of problems and the proposing of solutions' (Halligan, 1995, 139). That is, advice was often relegated to the formulation stage of policy development. However, this orthodoxy began to wane in the face of ongoing evidence documenting a wider set of practices and activities spanning the policy process, which involved a range of actors beyond those of the professional public service (Scott and Baehler, 2010; Craft 2015a; Veselý, 2017). Policy advice includes a range of 'hard' and 'soft' competencies and practices including, for instance, rigorous formal professional policy advising based on the standardised practices and formal techniques of policy analysis, such as cost benefit and the like, but also research, proposal development, consultation, managing political processes and evaluating outcomes (Gregory and Lonti, 2008, 838). The 'soft craft' of advisory work involved marshalling tacit and experiential knowledge, consultation, brokerage and negotiation, advocacy, and political acuity among others (Tiernan, 2015c; Bromell, 2017; Prince, 2018). Advising then includes the provision of recommendations, guidance and the articulation of preferences in support of policy work. This definitional expansion is well reflected in the evolving conceptual PAS approaches reviewed in this chapter which have sought to make sense of the various aspects of advisory activity.

In general, most conceptual models of policy advisory systems associated different levels of influence with the location of advisers either inside or outside government (Wilson, 2006). This line of thinking underlay early efforts to classify the various components of advice-giving as a kind of marketplace for policy ideas and information. Most often, this was seen as comprising three separate locational components: a supply of policy advice, its demand on the part of decision makers, and a set of brokers whose role was to match supply and demand in any given conjuncture (Lindquist, 1998; March et al., 2009). In these models the members of advice systems are typically arrayed into two or three general 'sets' or 'communities' (Sundquist, 1978; Dunn, 1980). The first set of actors are those 'proximate decision makers' who act as consumers of policy analysis and advice. These are actors with the authority to make policy decisions, including cabinets and executives; parliaments, legislatures and congresses; and senior administrators and officials delegated decision-making powers by those other bodies. The second set is composed of 'knowledge producers' located in academia, statistical agencies and research institutes for example, which provide the basic scientific, economic and social scientific data upon which analyses are often based and decisions made. The third set common in many studies are 'knowledge brokers' who serve as intermediaries between the knowledge generators and proximate decision makers and who repackage data and information into a usable form (Lindvall, 2009). Brokers may include permanent specialised research staff inside government, temporary equivalents in commissions and task forces, and non-governmental specialists associated with think tanks and interest groups among others. Although sometimes ignored in earlier 'two community' models, brokers have been found to be consequential as intermediaries, given their ability to 'translate' research results into useable forms of knowledge – that is, policy alternatives and the rationales for their selection to be consumed by decision-makers (Lindvall, 2009; Verschuere, 2009; Phipps and Morton, 2013). By this spatial logic, influence was understood in relation to the proximity of policy advice to government decision makers (Craft and Howlett, 2012).

The first comparative assessment of the classic Westminster family of PAS systems by Halligan (1995) depicted a tripartite locational approach: the public service, other internal sources beyond the public service and external advisory supplies (Table 3.1). This usefully

Table 3.1 *Location of advice and degree of government influence*

	Government control	
Location	High	Low
Public service	Senior departmental policy advisers Central agency advisers/ strategic policy unit	Statutory appointments in public service
Internal to government	Political advisory systems Temporary advisory policy units: First ministers' & ministers' offices Parliaments (e.g. House of Commons)	Permanent advisory policy units Statutory authorities Legislatures (e.g. U.S. Congress)
External to government	Private sector/NGOs on contract Community organisations subject to government Federal international organisations	Trade unions, interest groups Community groups Confederal international communities/ organisations

Source: Halligan (1995).

highlights that PAS are not only a matter of how the public service relates to other advisory units outside of government; it recognises that the public sector itself includes a variety of available advisory bodies in varying proximity to decision makers and flags important questions of how the various *internal* PAS components interact and evolve. Conventionally, the thinking at the time was that a good advisory system involved a stable and reliable in-house public service, a specialised political unit (generally the minister's office), and a third option in the form of a specialised or central policy unit, typically located in a central agency and drawing on external sources as needed and as possible (Halligan, 1995, 162).

Halligan's analysis pointed to a shared trend of a growing plurality of new advisory units coming online, the reconstitution of public service functions within advice systems and a professionalising of policy competence outside the public service. Importantly, this work identified that there was a plurality of advisory supplies that, while external to the public service, still fell within the umbrella of the broader public sector. Halligan captured the expanding international and domestic supplies of policy advice, with the overall assessment some twenty-five years ago being that, across the Westminster cases, the trend was that of expansion of the 'internal government category' at the expense of the internal public service (Halligan, 1995, 19).

Halligan's approach also combined locational logic with a 'government control' variable to improve the depiction and analysis of influence within these systems. Halligan (1995), and later others, also identified shifts in advisory practices in Westminster systems, with the result being a general process of 'push and pull', partially moving responsibilities outside both the public service and the government and therefore beyond the latter's capacity to exercise direct and close control. This analysis, prescient of subsequent studies of individual cases (see Rhodes, Wanna and Weller, 2009; Smith, 2011a; Zussman, 2015), noted that the public service was increasingly compelled to play a political role or, as Halligan put it, was forced to 'engage more in the politics of policy advice' (1995, 160). Notions of evolving public service advisory functions and more general debates as to 'control' over versus the autonomy of those that provide policy advice have been a perennial concern in public administration and governance in Westminster systems. This is linked to the normative and operational debates as to the optimality and tensions of 'neutral' versus 'responsive' public service competence (Aberbach and Rockman, 1994; Savoie, 2003). Alternative approaches to PAS are set out in this chapter, drawing attention to movement between the three categories and also transformation within categories. However, the continued relevance of location and control as variables of interest are reflected in ensuing chapters. Similarly, the persistence of attempts by government to exert control in PAS remains a dominant theme. In each of the PAS, various strategies and techniques have been put in place by governments to exert control, often with direct linkages to the dynamics of externalisation and politicisation discussed in detail in this book. Conversely, governments are also clearly grappling with the loss of control in Westminster PAS, which now see these systems include a range of advisory inputs and bodies over which government has little to no control.

On Content Dimensions of PAS

PAS provided a very useful and clear advance on earlier approaches that focused attention only upon individual, isolated sets of advisers or single locations of advice, but they were largely silent on content dimensions. But as Peters and Barker (1993, 1) put it, if policy advice is conceived of as a means by which governments both 'deliberately acquire, and passively receive advice on decisions and policies, which may be broadly called informative, objective or technical' then content becomes at least as important as location in determining the nature of the influence of both policy advice and policy advisers.

Subsequent work has focused on the content of policy advice, the processes and practices of advice, and sensitivity to the governance contexts within which that work occurs, in various jurisdictions and policy domains (Lindquist and Tiernan, 2011; Pollitt, 2013; Craft and Wilder, 2017). These studies have picked up from early distinctions rooted in categorising advice along 'political' or 'public service' or 'technical' or expert variants (Meltsner, 1975; Weller, 1987), the instrumentality of advisory work spanning operational and strategic motivations, and in response to short- and longer-term policymaking imperatives (Boston, 1994).

Prasser, in his studies of Royal Commissions in Australia, and more generally concerning the nature of policy advice (2006), suggested that distinguishing between the 'political' and 'non-political' content of policy advice is less insightful than differentiating the content of the advice provided. Here he distinguished between what he termed 'cold' – typically long-term and proactive – versus 'hot' – short-term and crisis-driven – types of advice. Although he noted some overlaps between these categories and the old 'politics' versus 'administration' divides, the general situation he describes is one in which neither partisan nor public service actors have an exclusive monopoly of one type of advice over the other. Such content dimensions can be usefully applied to various non-governmental sources of advice that may be seeking to influence policymakers on a short or long-term basis. Moreover, they further align considerations of policy advisory activity with specific content considerations rather than role-based classifications that continue to be tied to locational factors and/or traditional dichotomies such as technical versus political distinctions.

Others have noted the importance of the procedural aspects of policy advice and taken stock of shifts in the modes of advice-giving from public-service-dominant 'speaking truth to power' (Wildavsky, 1979) to modes of 'sense making' characterized by advisory 'weaving' and 'sharing truth with multiple actors of influence' (Parsons, 2004; Prince, 2018). Basically, this has involved attending to whether advice is provided through closed or open processes, through lengthy or short public consultations, royal commissions, or via traditional public service 'white' and 'green' papers, reports of management consultants or blue ribbon panels, or by way of consultations with partisan advisers, technical experts or stakeholders (Pierre, 1998; Weaver and Stares, 2001; Saint-Martin, 2004; Eichbaum and Shaw, 2008). Table 3.2 indicates how these types of distinctions based on the content of policy advice can help draw out additional aspects of PAS that are not captured by a focus only on location or control.

Going beyond location to questions of how responsive and autonomous these systems are and attending to questions of the content of the advice that circulates within them helps develop more sophisticated analysis. In the chapters that follow, analysis of these four PAS from content-based perspectives helps draw attention to the trends and tensions in the types of advisory inputs that circulate in these systems. Ongoing debates as to evidence-based and informed policymaking, the advisory role of partisan and external advisers, and balances between central agencies and departments are canvassed. There are also

Table 3.2 *Policy advisory system members organised by policy content*

	Short-term/Reactive	Long-term/Anticipatory
Procedural	*'Pure' Political and Policy Process Advice* Traditional Political parties, parliaments and legislative committees; regulatory agencies Plus internal & external political advisers, interest groups; lobbyists; mid-level public service policy analysts & policy managers; pollsters	*Medium to Long-Term Policy Steering Advice* Traditional Deputy ministers, central agencies/executives; royal commissions; judicial bodies Plus agencies, boards, commissions; crown corporations; international organisations (e.g. OECD; ILO, UN)
Substantive	*Short-Term Crisis & Fire-Fighting Advice* Traditional Political peers (e.g. cabinet); executive office political staffs Plus political staffers; cabinet; external crisis managers/ consultants; political strategists; pollsters; media; community organisations/ NGOs; lobbyists	*Evidence-Based Policy-Making* Traditional Statistical agencies; strategic policy unit; senior departmental policy advisers; royal commissions Plus think tanks; scientific & academic advisers; open data citizen engagement driven policy initiatives/ Web 2.0; blue-ribbon panels

Source: Craft and Howlett (2012).

considerations regarding the tensions of short-termism versus longer-term perspective and capacity in these systems, as well as the balancing of the processes by which advisory activity occurs both within the public service and with others within and around PAS.

Each of the above approaches also tackles a third issue regarding the study of how these units and systems change over time. There has long been an accepted view that advisory systems are pluralist vehicles. To some degree, these systems are intentionally malleable; they adapt to meet the particularities of the players, contexts and governance realities of the day (Seymour-Ure, 1987; Halligan, 1995; Craft and Wilder,

2017; OECD, 2017). In these four countries this is all the more so given the flexibilities that flow from the Westminster administrative traditions within which PAS are embedded. As Chapter 2 makes clear, Westminster is not a set of strict institutions and structures but rather a set of principles, practices and beliefs that evolve and are subject to ongoing qualification and interpretation in all four countries (Rhodes, Wanna and Weller, 2009; Grube and Howard, 2016; Lindquist and Eichbaum, 2016). Some governments work well with the public service, others not. Some governments feature greater reliance on partisan advisers, or externals; look to cabinet to govern collectively; or demonstrate strong centralisation around first ministers and their courts. Advisory systems reflect these differences but also provide continuity and established practices that condition and structure how PAS is set up and works.

Understanding and Analysing PAS Change: Externalisation, Politicisation and Other Dynamics

New governments are expected to adapt the machinery of government to suit their governance preferences and advisory needs: creating or restructuring public sector institutions over which they have control, increasing or repurposing ministers' offices political advisers, elevating particular policy objectives over others, and establishing favoured patterns for how advice is provided and from which sources, from within or outside of government. This is well captured by Halligan's (1995) category of 'government control' as a variable to model how these systems were, to varying degrees, responsive to the government of the day. Making sense of enduring and long-term patterns of PAS change has been dominated by attention to two dynamics: 'externalisation', or the displacement of public service advisers by those outside of government; and 'politicisation', or the extent to which partisan-political aspects of policy advice have supplanted non-partisan public sector sources of policy advice (Craft and Howlett, 2013; Hustedt and Veit, 2017).

Supply and demand rationales have been advanced to explain the externalisation dynamic often featuring the hypothesis that externalisation is a by-product of ministers seeking greater political control and responsiveness from the administration. This involves, among other techniques, the increasing use of exogenous sources of policy advice to weaken a perceived public sector policy advisory monopoly (Rhodes and Weller, 2001; Peters and Pierre, 2004; Dahlstrom, Peters and Pierre, 2011). Other analysts contend that globalisation and the rise of so-called 'wicked' policy problems have reduced the perceived capability of the public sector to respond to contemporary policy challenges, thus prompting a decline in demand for advice from that source and a concomitant increase in demand for advice from non-governmental sources (Peters and Savoie, 2000). From a supply-side perspective, it has also been argued that successive public sector reforms have eroded the public sector's capacity to provide timely policy advice (as detailed in Chapter 4). Or, as some have alleged, there is simply a greater exogenous supply resulting in a more competitive 'marketplace' for policy advice (Boston, 1994; Lindquist and Tiernan, 2011).

While externalisation is most often depicted as a matter of formal policy advisory actors displacing the public service, there are characteristics of contemporary PAS that are also salient. For example, externalisation linked to shifting public expectations (e.g. expectations for consultation, and participatory and open government movements) and stakeholder-heavy policymaking where externalisation becomes an embedded feature of policymaking, as opposed to solicited forms arising from seeking out external advisory supplies on an as-needed basis. For some time, observers have noted shifts in the contexts and imperatives for access and participation to policy-advice-relevant activity (Pierre, 1998; Parsons, 2004; Prince, 2018). Greater external supplies, or perhaps more well-resourced supplies, may compel governments to externalise advisory activity as a matter of responding to pressures related to externals' abilities to frame policy issues or mobilise affected parties (Mulgan, 2014). By another token, international contexts or international governmental organisations may compel the externalisation of policy advice due to binding agreements, membership in these organisations, or coordination imperatives given matters of crises or the need for policy coherence.

Politicisation is the second significant dynamic that has reshaped contemporary advisory systems. It has been linked to attempts at reasserting the primacy of politics involving greater engagement of ministers in policy and operations, as well as the use of political appointees, the political involvement in senior public service staffing, the use of performance management and procedural steering (van den

Berg, 2017; Halligan, 2019). Attempts to provide a satisfactory definition of politicisation have resulted in an important broadening from notions that have traditionally emphasised deleterious impacts to the norms, functions and impacts on public service functions, to accounts that have sought to focus more squarely on matters of policy. Peters and Pierre (2004) point out the lack of specificity often associated with the application of the notion of politicisation. They suggest that, at its most basic, 'the politicization of the civil service involves the substitution of political criteria for merit-based criteria in the selection, retention, promotion, rewards, and disciplining of members of the public service' (Peters and Pierre, 2004, 2). Many others have sought to further refine politicisation by linking it to specific types of policy processes and advisory activity (see Mulgan, 2007). Eichbaum and Shaw advanced a notion of 'administrative politicization' – that is 'an intervention that offends against the principles and conventions associated with a professional and impartial civil service' (Eichbaum and Shaw, 2008, 343). They do so through more systematic explorations of how ministers' partisan advisers can 'procedurally' or 'substantively' politicise the public service. This involves activities that limit the ability of public servants to provide free, frank and fearless policy advice to ministers or, in the latter case, affect the content of their advice. Their analysis of advisers is fitting because it is ministers' office advisers that have attracted the most concern and derision regarding their politicising effects, as explored in Chapter 5. As Tiernan and Weller (2010) note, partisan advisers were barely mentioned in *Can Ministers Cope?* (1981) but figure prominently in the more recent treatments.

In addition to these major waves of change – externalisation and politicisation – there are other aspects of PAS evolution that are important but have not garnered similar attention. As this book details, major variation exists related to the types of public service policy capacity erosions and country-specific responses to it, as well as the prominence and functions of various advisory units: partisan advisers, royal commissions, parliamentary officers, and various 'external' advisers including management consultants, think tanks and the like. Some PAS changes have been incremental (e.g. declining public service policy capacity or the rise of central agencies), while others have been more abrupt and transformational (e.g. institutionalisation of partisan political advisers in Australia or their role in New Zealand given the adoption of a proportional electoral system (Maley, 2018a; Shaw and Eichbaum, 2018a).

Confronting the Types and Nature of PAS Change

To understand Westminster PAS there is a need to strive for greater clarity in conceptualising and analysing how these systems change and how influence is gained and exercised within them. While broadly discussed, it remains, as Hustedt and Veit (2017, 46) phrase it, 'the million-dollar question' in research on policy advisory systems. The predominance of the public service as the unit of analysis in PAS research has led to a dominant focus on externalisation and politicisation at the expense of broader reflections on the condition of the system itself (Craft and Wilder, 2017). This can be offset by embracing recent trends in thinking about PAS as a nested or multi-level phenomena (Craft and Howlett, 2012; Veselý, 2017). At one level, PAS change is in keeping with the governance arrangements that condition how the systems work – the formal and informal ideas and rules that determine how power and resources are allocated and exercised (Howlett and Lindquist, 2004; Craft and Howlett, 2012). At another level, as Chapters 4 through 7 emphasise, PAS feature specific advisory units that ebb and flow in terms of their prominence within these systems. Finally, the settings and practices of specific units can be variously modified and evolve.

Change can therefore involve differences in type or 'orders' (Hall, 1993). Hall's work was not developed specifically for PAS but can be modified usefully to help better understand what about PAS is changing. His well-known framework involved three types of change: first-order change (routine adjustments to existing policies); second-order change (changes in the policy instruments used to achieve shared goals); and third-order change (shifts in the goals themselves). Modified, *first-order* PAS changes can be understood as routine adjustments of existing practices or units within accepted bounds of PAS operation – for example, reorienting central agencies to increased monitoring of progress, or the implementation of written advisory practices for partisan advisers (Lindquist, 2006a; Craft, 2016). *Second-order* PAS change involves alterations to the dominance of units or practices within an existing PAS. This is where most PAS analysis has traditionally focused, in particular on changes to the public services' advisory roles and functions within PAS (Plowden, 1987; Halligan, 1995). *Third-order PAS change* involves fundamental changes to the PAS due to the governance arrangements within which PAS operates. For example, NPM reforms in the 1980s involved attempts to transform the foundational political-administrative relations, institutional design and the role of policy advice within the policy process (Boston, 1994; Aucoin, 1995; Halligan, 2010). In a similar way, later debates about shifts from state-centred command and control government to modes of governance raised important questions about basic assumptions regarding state power, and the dependency and relational nature of governing, all with fundamental implications for how we understand advisory systems (Howlett and Lindquist, 2004; Tiernan, 2006; Craft and Howlett, 2012).

While the orders of change approach points to differences in the magnitude or type of change, it also helps illuminate the broad and more specific principles involving power and governance dynamics and applied settings and calibrations of advice. In particular are there major changes to how ministers and officials or externals engage and are accountable for policy advice – or are we dealing with changes to the distribution of advisers within the systems, or with minor and more granular changes to the practices and processes of advice (e.g. changing how briefings are provided)?

This can be supplemented with considerations regarding the pathways or trajectories of change in these four cases and in PAS more generally. Not all changes are immediate or quick, with the gradual erosion of public service policy capacity in all four cases demonstrating gradual change and in some cases flourishes of significant decline or rebuilding (Howlett and Lindquist, 2004; Craft and Halligan, 2017). There are, as set out in the introductory chapter, select examples of quick and transformational changes that require scrutiny as well. Chapter 8 examines questions about the pathways or trajectories of change in greater detail based on analysis of the cases, but it is clear there are instances where the cases demonstrate different tendencies towards integrating or rejecting PAS or broader administrative and managerial reforms. While there are basic similarities in the points of departure owing to shared administrative traditions, the pathways of change have varied in part based on differences in take-up of various reforms or the exigencies of particular country and policy contexts.

First movers or late adopters can be distinguished for instance in the UK case along with a penchant for greater change at the centre involving the creation and disbanding of various policy and strategy units. This has been emulated by some jurisdictions with Canada and Australia developing their own delivery and results units much later. A host of other examples are catalogued in ensuing chapters, including the adoption or discontinuation of specific alternative advisory instruments and practices, such as budget officers, royal commissions and ministers' office partisan advisers.

Lastly, the general sequence often takes a dialectical form: a radical departure is followed by public debate, eventually producing modified principles and/or behaviour (Halligan, 2019). The appointment of externals and partisans to department head positions (Australia and Canada) and the peremptory dismissal of professional public servants (Australia) most clearly fit this category. This also applies to dramatic changes in the use of partisan advisers in Australia, Canada and the United Kingdom or the use of 'purchase advisers' in New Zealand (Boston, 2012; Boston and Halligan, 2012; Maley, 2018b). There are also temporary or more enduring forms of change. The contrast here is most vividly evidenced by the longer-term patterns of consultancy use in Australia and the Brexit-induced increases noted in the UK case examined in Chapter 7. In other instances, change follows pendulum-like patterns, with the public service often cut and then built up or the use of consultants being prominent and then dissipating based on changes in government or fiscal conditions.

4 | *Public Services and Policy Advice*

This chapter traces the shared origins and trends of public service advisory work as the policy advisory system expanded from its once-narrow focus on officials. It looks at the similar and divergent experiences of the previously dominant public service in the policy advisory system. There is a notable tendency for a decline in public service policy capacity, but there are differences across the PAS due to country-specific patterns of public management reforms. Two interpretations are offered. The first is that the expansion of the policy advisory system can be attributed to the emergence of new interests and sources of knowledge and expertise in an increasingly complex public policy environment, as well as to ministers looking beyond the public service for policy advice because of perceived internal limitations. Secondly, ministers were empowered with levers of influence but were reconciled neither to the essential role of officials' advice nor to the rhetoric and practice that supported a renewed public service. The public service has become more disposed to being internally collaborative and externally engaged through policy processes, but regular injunctions for greater connectivity indicated continuing shortfalls. The chapter concludes by appraising whether this latter conception means a restoration of capacity and what the advisory role is for a public service that has been emphasising generalist and process-based functions as a broker and convenor of advisory inputs.

Trends in Public Management and Governance and Models of Policy Advising

The policy advisory system has been impacted by the broader governance arrangements within which it is embedded. Halligan's (1995) review was penned against the backdrop of successive assaults on the traditions of public administration by managerial public sector reforms. Scholars have for some time associated attempts to broaden and diversify available policy advisory supplies with managerial and public sector reforms falling under the banner of New Public Management (NPM). These are directly linked to the divisions of labour among political-administrative elites (Page and Wright, 2007), public sector organisational (re)design, and policy analysis and management techniques predicated on notions of competition and efficiency (Pollitt and Talbot, 2004; Christensen and Laegreid, 2007; Osborne, 2010).

These have clear links with the notions of control and autonomy noted above. Reforms have taken direct aim at the function and role of the public service, affected its advisory capacity through reorganisation and budgetary austerity, or incentivised governments to look to alternative advisers or qualitatively different policy advice that privileged 'results' and 'efficiency' (Boston, 1994; Halligan, 2003, 2010). The take-up of NPM and subsequent reforms has varied across Westminster systems (Aucoin, 1995; Halligan, 2020), which reinforces the need for a careful comparative examination of PAS in the four countries.

By the twenty-first century, the era of government was widely regarded as being superseded by governance. The government model, as identified with British elitism and the top-down policymaking of the 1950s (Richards and Smith, 2002, 3–5), was challenged by alternative formulations that questioned the closed and unified system and the viability of traditional state-led forms of authority and public administration. Government was being replaced by modes of 'governance' both internally (Edwards et al., 2012) and externally, involving dispersed power and societal resources with governments' roles now emphasising managing and steering rather than direct control. From a state-centric perspective (Bell and Hindmoor, 2009), that position ignored the changing role of the state within a governance context. In addition, the claims of governance network advocates have been challenged (Davies, 2011). Nevertheless, the implications from a PAS perspective have been a weakening of central control, and a strengthening of the need to situate PAS within the broader governance arrangements in which it is embedded (Craft and Howlett, 2012).

Two ideal types provide models of policy advising by officials (Table 4.1). This analysis draws on but is significantly different from Prince (2007, 2018 on Canada; Craft and Howlett, 2012; and HM Government, 2012). The advantage of using the two ideal types is

Table 4.1 Models of officials' policy advising

Policy advising	Internalised	Externalised and collaborative
Policy advisory system		
Nature of power	Narrow	Broad
	Top-down levers and authority in policymaking	Shared, co-design with networks and coalitions
Focus of policymaking within government	Departmental hierarchy in vertical portfolios. IDCs.	Short-term task forces, working groups. Horizontal management
Skills of senior officials	Generalists with policy expertise and focus	Generalist policy managers
	Permanent	Policy specialists on tap
		Ongoing or employment contracts
Minister/department head relationship	Complementary: ministers rely on officials for policy advice	Multiple relationships: conflict-based principal/agent; partnership
	Officials dominate policy roles	Shared policy roles
Nature of officials' policy advice	Authoritative advice	Contributing to contested advice
	Neutral competence	Responsive competence
	Internal	External
Locus of policy processes	Largely self-contained within government internal units. Supplementary advisory bodies	Open and receptive to external groups, think tanks, lobbyists
		Expert reviews, consultancies
Role of officials in policy processes	Multiple roles as policy advisers	Multiple roles in policy processes, including broker, implementer and engaging with policy networks
	Filter advice from outside	

that they respectively combine the elements of traditional and modern conceptions of policy advising and allow comparisons between the four countries and benchmarks for change over time. The representations are deliberately stark and provide approximations against which the countries can be analysed for two phases in time (pre-1980s and 2010s) without pinpointing systems or specific times in what have been evolving arrangements.

The first type assembles the characteristics of a public service that internalises the advisory process and emphasises the pre-eminence of the senior officials' role in policy advising without much regard for the outside world. The second envisages a twenty-first-century public service that has shed rigid boundaries and is externally focused. The elements in combination may not be characteristic of any one system overall, and have an aspirational flavour, but they have existed in some form in each anglophone country.

The second ideal type, externalised, collaborative and open, is in sharp contrast to the first in that the nature of power has changed (HM Government, 2012; Woolcott, 2018). Rigid boundaries both within the public service and between it and external groups and organisations have been removed. Exchanges between state and society are routine. Under this type, a broad conception of PAS is envisaged where power is shared, and co-design with networks and coalitions is commonplace. This does not preclude the authority of the state (Bell and Hindmoor, 2009) but does assume that government and the public service must be more transformative.

There are three parts to the consideration of trends with officials and policy advising: what is happening internally (with ministers, department heads and central agencies – but for political advisers see Chapter 5); what is happening with external engagement; and implications for the policy advisory system. But first, traditional policy advising is reviewed and compared to type 1.

Policy Advising in the Traditional System

Under the Westminster model, the relations between politicians and bureaucrats traditionally centred on the coexistence of the impartial public service and responsible government (Aucoin, 1995). The embedded tension between the two elements was kept in balance by applying well-established principles, but their enactment was dependent upon the distinctive, even overarching, role acquired by permanent secretaries. A traditional relationship is based on well-understood norms: an impartial public service that serves the political executive, regardless of party; and a political executive that in turn respects the integrity of the public service by maintaining its apolitical and professional character. Specific features are the career public servant, a permanent official who survives successive governments; senior appointments drawn from the ranks of professional careerists; and the ministerial department as the repository of policy knowledge and primary adviser to government (Roberts, 1987; Aucoin, 1995; Campbell and Wilson, 1995; Halligan, 2001).

Policy advising under the traditional arrangement prior to the enlargement of PAS reflects the internalised type in many respects (Table 4.1). The focus of policymaking within government was the departmental hierarchy culminating in the permanent secretary. Senior career officials were generalists with policy expertise and focus. The relationship between minister and department head was complementary with ministers relying on officials for policy advice. Officials dominated policy roles and provided authoritative neutral advice. Policy processes were largely self-contained within government, with policy advice from others being filtered by officials.

The traditional PAS had a propensity to exhibit the features in type 1, but there were qualifications based on practice and country contexts. The notion of a stand-alone specialised department was accurate in terms of their centrality, but there were internal horizontal relationships. Interdepartmental committees were active and often quasi-permanent under the internalised system and could be deeply embedded in policy processes (e.g. on the United Kingdom, Lee et al., 1998, 5), and as many as 180 permanent and ad hoc committees operated under the traditional Australian system, which covered policy negotiation as well as administrative matters (Spann, 1979, 425). An exemplar of the United Kingdom's closed-door process was the small group of policy experts from four departments that played a significant role in the Whitehall policy process on Commonwealth immigration (Wakamatsu, 1998). In effect they formed a closed policy community and reflected a feature of the time in being insular regarding views from outside.

Clearly external advice was received, including from formal advisory councils and commissions, but it was carefully filtered by the public service. The UK civil service exemplified distinctive features of type 1, which reflected the character of the people recruited and their self-image as a guardian elite. It was also more decidedly a generalist service than the others. There was a sense of policy being developed in isolation, and this was reflected in characterisations of Whitehall. An Australian 'stereotypical view of policy-making was of mandarins in ivory towers, where power and influence was wielded by large, siloed empires of staff who had monopoly control over policy spheres and advice to government' (Smith, 2018, 8).

As detailed in Chapter 2, the Westminster tradition of public administration has involved a symbiotic relationship where the public service was responsible for providing elected officials with its 'free and frank' policy advice, with loyal implementation based on the decision of democratically empowered ministers (Savoie, 2003; Eichbaum and Shaw, 2010b; Halligan, 2010). By the beginning of the reform era in the early 1980s, this type of relationship could no longer be taken for granted and was under challenge. During the last forty years, a new imbalance has become characteristic as politicians expand their authority over the previously ascendant officials. This occurred as part of comprehensive programs of managerial reform although changes to the relationship originated in the politicians' reaction to an entrenched public service that predated the reform era.

Expanding Ministers' Policy Roles

There has been extensive discussion of what constitutes politicisation (for example, Mulgan, 1997; Pierre and Peters, 2004; van den Berg, 2017). In this study, politicisation means the political executive's increasing influence and control within the executive branch. The usage here has been chosen for its simplicity and its inclusiveness (cf. Kemp, 1986), and because politicisation in anglophone countries is expressed through private as well as public pressures on public servants by ministers and their agents. In contrast politicisation in other countries is based on political appointments to public positions, which are well institutionalised as a formal element of government (Rouban, 2014). Politicisation focuses on the use of a range of ministerial levers for extending political influence and resources and for changing relationships. Ministerial influence derives from the exercise of their authority, the use of partisan agents in their offices, something of a preference for non-public service advice (either 'independent' inquiries or external sources of advice) and dictates about how policy advice is to be communicated to them by senior officials. The expansion and contraction of political roles are normal in governance over time, and ministers are constitutionally empowered to exercise their authority subject to rules about accountability and responsibility and a few constraints residing with public servants.

The modes of demarcating politics and administration range from a model that firmly separates political and public service careers to that in which the careers intermingle and boundaries are weak (Pierre, 1995). The relative independence of the political and bureaucratic spheres meant that the apolitical British model could once be represented as being at one end of an international spectrum that envisaged a heavily 'politicised' system (mainly in the sense of political appointments) at the other end. A set of issues for the reform era was whether, to what extent and in what respects systems were moving along this spectrum, as well as what was the impact on effective relationships and the performance of the public management system.

Ministerial policy roles have expanded during the reform era from the early 1980s. All systems have demanding ministers; the prioritisation of ministerial and government business; and diminished internal policy capability. The general movement was from mode 1, a traditional type of conception, towards mode 3 (Table 4.2). In each, the principal or dominant actor is indicated, unless shared. The demarcation is clear under the first mode, which has public servants taking a lead on policy roles and being responsible for implementation. Under the second, the ministers exercise policy leadership. The third mode envisages ministers having roles across the spectrum, including

Table 4.2 *Modes of policy roles*

	Mode 1	Mode 2	Mode 3
Values	Ministers	Ministers	Ministers
Strategy	Shared	Shared	Ministers
Policy initiation	Public servants	Shared	Shared
Implementation	Public servants	Public servants	Shared

NB: Ministers includes their staff.

implementation (and management). As noted for Canada, 'politics enters the policy process much earlier than in the past' (Savoie, 2003, 116).

Note that the modes may not capture the position at the time of heightened concern by a new government about the public service. When uncompromising principal/agent views prevail, the public service can be limited to implementation (examples occurred under Howard, Cameron, Harper and Morrison).

The contrast between traditional operations and those in the reform era is striking. Taking the UK case as illustrative, a duopoly used to exist with the civil servants running the country while ministers provided political direction. Policy was left to departments, which was coordinated through interdepartmental committees, and was then worked through a hierarchical committee system of officials, ministers and cabinet (Lee et al., 1998, 5; King and Crewe, 2014, 333). However, starting in the 1980s, ministers were taking on a range of new roles and politicising the policy process (Richards and Smith, 2016, 503). UK observers gave early attention to senior civil servants shifting from policy adviser to policy executor (Barberis, 1996; Richards, 1997; Van Dorpe and Horton, 2011).

The transformation from the 1980s of ministers' roles in policy initiation was dramatic with the rise of the activist minister in conjunction with governments that wanted to accomplish change and prime ministers who favoured and rewarded active ministers. Thatcher recast the minister's role as leader and 'dynamo of change' and was prone to intervening early in departmental policy processes. The dissolving of the differences in responsibility for policy roles appeared in official documents (Parsons, 2003). Ministers saw a clear distinction between themselves as policy initiators and civil servants' responsibility for policy execution (Lee et al., 1998, 5–6; King, 2007, 225; King and Crewe, 2014, 334). Policy initiation from the public service was also replaced by greater ministerial direction in Canada, Mulroney arguing that policy formulation belonged to ministers (Zussman, 1986, 58), and announcing policy initiatives without public service involvement (Sutherland, 1993, 94). Ministerial roles in New Zealand changed from 'policy legitimators' (according to a former prime minister) to 'policy initiators', and policymaking changed from being inductive to mainly deductive (McLeay, 1995, 120–5).

Minister's agents were also highly important where there was a profusion of advisers (see Chapter 5) because of their extensive roles in policymaking: working with the departments in generating ideas, policy development, and implementation and through supervising and mobilising (Maley, 2015; Craft, 2016; Wilson 2016b; Eichbaum and Shaw, 2011). Canadian advisers provided policy directly and were transmitting policy advice. PMO staff were engaged early in the policy process and offered written partisan-political advice in parallel to that of the public service (Craft, 2018, 40).

Implementation was once the core function of public officials and largely exclusive. However, this function received direct attention in the reform era: first, by agencification; second, by delivery being outsourced to third parties; third, through the use of monitoring and reporting instruments; and, importantly, by ministerial engagement and interventions as they embraced more active policy roles. Clearly managerialism played a role, particularly at the height of the new public management. The separation of departments from implementation established precedents, which came to mean that this responsibility was no longer exclusive but simply one of the structural options in play. Shifting the functions to external agencies underscored this, even though now twice removed. In addition, boundaries that once existed by convention regarding political and administrative interaction meant that assertive political executives were scrutinising departmental activities more intrusively and were more insistent on results. This occurred most explicitly through the centre (implementation units), executive ministers (who wanted to direct involvement in departmental management and policy implementation) and the activities of ministerial advisers.

The Australian transformation of roles was apparent in the 1980s, although secretaries for the most part were still maintaining the distinction in the early 1990s (Halligan and Power, 1992, 84; Dunn, 1997). This became more difficult when greater political control was exercised and as the number of ministerial advisers multiplied. New Zealand ministers were assigned new responsibilities under the public management model of the late 1980s. The erroneous assumption was made that they would be capable of handling their clarified responsibilities and would make use of purchase agreements with chief executives (Scott, 2001). The executive minister has been prominent in the United Kingdom as manifest through their roles in policy implementation (CAG, 2016b, 4). This executive role has extended to dictating requirements (e.g. the detail and timing of policy implementation), designing policy details and keeping close involvement in project delivery. Greater ministerial engagement in implementation began under Blair when ministers were monitoring the delivery of performance. Recent involvement in 'practicalities' was regarded as assisting with more effective policy design (HC Committee of Public Accounts, 2016b, Q108, Q109).

Advisory Role of Departmental Heads

The changing policy roles have made a significant impact on the role of departmental heads. The contrast is strong between modes 1 and 3 in Table 4.2. The minister is responsible for decisions but also expects to be the policy leader, which may entail a range of activities: canvassing and gathering views and ideas from networks, being the policy initiator, and acting as policy arbiter regarding departmental advice. Ministers now expected to be involved in all stages of policymaking.

The following discussion of several dimensions of the changing role and continuities draws on interviews with department heads in Australia and Canada and how Westminster principles were being interpreted by these most senior public servants. The first was as follows: 'the key factor in the Westminster system is that ministers expect their bureaucrats to share information, and there are no rewards clearly for not sharing information' (A7). A more role-defining observation was that 'ministers will have a view that they make the policy and we deliver what is required . . . that's an important element in terms of the Westminster system' (A8).

What emerges is that ministers act as leaders on policy questions out of belief in their standing, and this is reinforced where governments provide charter letters to ministers at the start of their tenure, which specify responsibilities and provide a 'statement of expectations . . . on what you expect to be delivered over that period. And that drives also the cabinet process, and also the joint responsibilities.' Ministers 'adhere pretty strongly to their charter letters . . . and we track it closely' (A7). Under Canada's Trudeau, the similar 'mandate' letters to ministers are public documents.

Two different aspects of change follow, the first touching on contestability and the partisan context: 'the fundamental issue is that the public service gives good quality advice. What's changed is it's no longer the only source of advice. It's contested. Also, it's viewed through a partisan lens, much more than it was. The level of experience and maturity of both the offices and the ministers is not as good as it was' (A2). The second perspective addresses the nature of policy questions: 'you cannot land a complex policy now, without proper consultation and collaboration. As distinct from when we used to have a policy idea, put up an evidence-based approach to it, consult whatever that meant, and then put it through government to become policy. I can't really think of anything that can be done with that linear approach, because of other issues that feed into that' (A7).

There were continuities and significant changes in the provision of advice, which can derive from the minister, the department, or a fast-tracked variant in 'a fluid environment':

Typically, we're asked to provide policy advice on some development or issue, and that will be through the standard process. We will develop our briefs and put them up. We'll look at all the evidence available ... But quite often, the policy briefings might be generated out of the department, where we're seeing something which is occurring which the government needs to be aware of or needs to respond to. So, that's the traditional, conventional sort of policy function. But things nowadays are far faster and often more dynamic than that. Quite often, it's an interactive process. It can depend very much on the preferences of ministers, on how they like to get policy and how they like to deal with it. (A6)

A second secretary observed that basic advice had not really changed: 'You have a couple of mechanisms ... [T]he normal process would be a written brief developed around an issue that the minister may not be aware of, or an issue that is ongoing with the minister, which could have been initially a deep dive with the minister.' However, what is different from the past is with 'complex issues that move across many departments, where it is pretty standard to be doing oral briefings. But ideally, you always want to put it down on paper, obviously for decisions, because that's the way it gets actioned, and that's where the accountabilities lie' (A7).

Similarly, a Canadian deputy minister reflected on changes to policy development since circa 1990:

[T]he world presented itself as a much simpler place. Policy development was a kind of 'specialist' endeavour. Few people or organisations had a real opportunity to have their voices heard on individual issues. It was ... the responsibility of the public service to reflect the diversity of views in its advice to elected government on how to implement its policy direction. But today, because of the evolution of things like globalisation and ubiquitous access to information and communication technologies, public policy development is more challenging, more complex and arguably more important as the policy space has become a noisy and crowded space. (Fonberg and Fyfe, 2013)

Ministerial styles vary (as in the past: Halligan, 2020; Heady, 1974). A Canadian deputy minister made the distinction between different kinds of minister: 'sometimes they think from here down or sometimes they think from details up' (C3). Similarly, an Australian departmental secretary perceived a spectrum between two ministerial types, with one having 'an absolute need to build things from the ground up in terms of the minister's knowledge about all of the facts and evidence and, who was absolutely demanding around getting very comprehensive and rigorous briefing material about virtually everything that related to any issue' (A6). At the other end of the spectrum was the minister with 'a vision for an outcome that [he or she] wishes to achieve', who wants advice about 'how this would be presented publicly, or in the media, or in cabinet, or in interactions with other ministers around the country' (A6). Advice assumed many forms, ranging from the 'minister who likes to be given options, and he'll make the decision' to those who 'do want to know what my view is, and the department's view' (A8).

A UK policy leader highlighted how policy advice is designed to reflect ministerial style:

[P]olicy advice does vary a lot from minister to minister. So we've just gone from having a secretary of state who wasn't really interested in reading policy submissions. Liked to do things through meetings and talking ... [I]t was a very meeting way of doing decisions ... The new secretary of state prefers very concise but numerical and targeted submissions – economist by training and is operating already in a very different way. We have had two ministers one likes facts, figures, graphs; one is really interested in what are the personal stories. We deliberately tailored it to what they would want. (UK17)

A Canadian deputy minister commented on several dimensions of the job: 'We are political appointees, not partisan political ... [W]e are kind of in between the world of the department and the minister. We're the cusp ... [W]e can't be tone deaf to political realities, but we can't be co-opted. So that's a funny place to be in. As long as it's within the confines of the authority and it's all legal, et cetera, I don't care. I don't particularly like it, but it is within their prerogative' (C3). The deputy minister had to be responsive to the politicians' rhythm: 'We used to have a government that at 4 in the morning or whatever they'd pore over the newspapers and by 6am you'll be inundated with whatever was in the media. We basically changed the working hours of a whole bunch of our staff. Because that was the rhythm they were working on, you have to be adaptable to how your political side of your equation works' (C3). Officials may have the experience and skills to draw a line regarding fundamentals but are still tested by defining the public service role in the advice space: 'there's roles for political staff, and there's roles for the ministers. But it's really hard to do your job appropriately because you have to occupy your full space, even when your advice is not welcome, wanted, sought after, asked for. You should never shrink within your space, but you should not also overstep your space either' (C3).

Department heads were not necessarily sidelined: '[M]inisters will ask for advice on particular things, but we as a portfolio will look at our obligations under the legislation, what's happening in the environment, whether there are policy gaps, what's the data telling us, and we'll provide advice when we think we need to for either a new policy proposal, change in policy direction, legislation or where the minister needs to be aware of what's happening' (A8).

A Canadian deputy minister positioned the officials' role within the broader PAS context as 'maybe the most important source of policy advice but everyone is giving advice to ministers on policy issues. We are probably the only people who are providing advice consistently day in and day out to ministers and commenting on advice that ministers are getting from other people so, you know, policy-making is just not the domain of the public service (Craft, 2016, 151).

The conclusion is that there have been highly significant changes in officials' roles, but there are also continuities with the past. Department heads still seek to adapt to ministers' style, but the degree of adaptation is much greater.

Politicising Appointments and Professional Behaviour

Politicisation is often deemed to be about political appointments to either public service positions or the top layer of the bureaucracy, which is not the primary usage in anglophone countries. In the latter case, an institutionalised procedure exists for any incoming government to make appointments of their own choosing but subject to public service continuity. In the former case, which covers a variety of experiences, appointments may be from inside or outside government and more arbitrary, haphazard and partisan. In anglophone countries, politicisation centres on political appointments to ministers' private offices (Chapter 5), the greater influence of politicians over appointments of top officials and the more intense pressures exerted on how senior officials operate. The latter can take a variety of forms, ranging from command control through to subtle signals about acceptable behaviour. The implications for the policy advisory system can be significant in terms of what officials do (how they respond) and do not do. A distinction can be drawn between the appointments systems of the unitary and federal systems (Halligan, 2020).

The New Zealand and the United Kingdom appointment systems are differentiated by attention to a formal process that incorporates an independent element while providing opportunities for the political executive to contribute. There has also been provision for the resolution of differences and some degree of transparency. The New Zealand arrangements have a significant degree of independence because of the role of the State Services Commission, whereas the British formalities belie the role of informal influences and processes (Kellner and Crowther-Hunt, 1980; Richards, 1997; Diamond, 2019). There has been sustained pressure for enhancing the role of politicians in the appointment process, which has resulted in greater roles for the prime minister and the secretary of state.

Australia and Canada have more politically charged systems. There were political appointments in Australia dating from the 1970s, but this trend moved to a new level with the Howard government's sacking of six secretaries in 1996. The Abbott government in 2010 dispensed with two departmental secretaries and established a precedent by displacing the secretary of Treasury and making all three heads of central agencies external appointments. A procession of secretaries departed prematurely in the 2016–17 years, several because of differences with ministers. For a professional public servant, the most antithetical action was the sacking of department heads because it was 'highly corrosive of the culture of impartial service' (Varghese, 2016). There was also the readiness of successive new governments to appoint a new chief adviser (the secretary of the Department of Prime Minister and Cabinet).

In Canada, the prime minister has long appointed the numerous deputy ministers as well as the second-tier associate deputy ministers, and they can be dismissed 'at pleasure'. Deputy ministers have traditionally regarded the prime minister, not the minister, as the person to whom they are accountable. Deputy ministers' appointments have come mostly from the public service (although there was an increase in external appointments in the 2000s), and there have been instances of partisan political appointments (initially under Mulroney). In contrast to the other systems, and the mainstream administrative tradition, the public service and political spheres have been less separate in that there have been cases of deputy ministers moving to the lower house of parliament (Aucoin, 2010, 66–7, 74). The prime minister's power to appoint the top public servants has been enhanced with the increase in the number of positions: approximately six dozen serve 'at the prime minister's pleasure' (Aucoin et al., 2011, 121–2; Aucoin, 2012, 187). The appointments and tenures of deputy ministers are at the prime minister's discretion for open-ended terms with no guarantee of their retaining the position. The PM can also 'demote or transfer senior officials, since the power to appoint includes the power to dismiss'. Consequently, deputy minister appointments are 'essentially political', and the 'professional' public service is depicted as falling 'between the "career system" and the "spoils system"' (Bourgault, 2014, 314). The cross-over character of appointments was exemplified by the appointment of Mendelsohn, the author of part of the Liberal's election manifesto, as a deputy secretary in PCO, and one dealing with cabinet on the achievement of results (May, 2016a). Both countries have developed systems involving a high level of political control and a reliance on the prime minister's office. Canada has given more attention to an appointment process, but the concentration of power in the prime minister overrides its significance.

What effects do these changes and pressures have? The dismissals, high turnover and contractualisation of senior officials had an impact on behaviour. The lower use of contractual appointments in Canada and the United Kingdom did not preclude dispensing with top public servants; nor was it a prerequisite to attracting the full attention of heads of department. The incentives for Australian secretaries were communicated through political messages that dictated strong political control and the use of the contract system. This led them to 'hedge their bets on occasions, limit the number of issues on which to take a strong stand, be less strident, constrain public comments, limit or craft more carefully public documents and accept a muddying of their role and that of political advisers' (Podger, 2007, 144). The ultimate sanction on a secretary's behaviour is knowing that 'telling a minister what he or she does not want to hear will certainly result in being sacked – or not having the appointment renewed' (Burgess, 2017). These elements were also present in the other systems: backing off taking a stand with ministers, despite the adviser's professional judgement; consciousness of the career consequences if responsiveness to ministers was not strongly displayed; and changes to the nature of advice (Scott, 2010; Hallsworth et al., 2011; King and Crew, 2014).

Coordination and Collaboration in Government

Two dynamics have been operating: centralising tendencies at the centre of government within fluctuations in competence and direction under different political leaders; and expansive agendas for horizontal connectivity among departments of variable intensity and success.

Central Roles in Policy Coordination

The patterns of governing and coordination at the centre have been the subject of constant change in the reform era. Australia experimented with a prototype steering model in which central agencies' intervention and control over departments was reduced by focusing on strategic directions and being a catalyst and intermittent coordinator (Campbell and Halligan, 1992, 43). This attention to balancing departments and the centre was lost in successive phases of devolution and the revival of the centre (Halligan, 2006), but these reforms were overshadowed by the strengthening of political control and the prime minister's office, and the political management of policy (Halligan, 2020).

The New Zealand pattern was simpler. In the systemic overhaul under its public management model, devolution to departments was embedded so effectively that it was difficult to adapt and develop the public management system. Central agencies took a long time to recover roles or to adjust to new roles (Norman, 2008; Morrison, 2014). The nascent strategic centre focus evolved with more sustained boosts to the role of the State Services Commission. The new system has moved closer to a mix of corporate management and a form of strategic governance.

Canada inherited a strong centre in the form of prime ministerial leadership from Pierre Trudeau, which morphed into a central machine centred on the PMO that successive prime ministers relied on for several decades (Savoie, 1999). This form of political management reflecting corporate management (Bourgault, 2014) has been generally evident through whole-of-government requirements.

The United Kingdom's move towards devolution was overshadowed by the disaggregation to agencies and then by top-down performance management under the target-fixated Blair government (Pollitt, 2007). The UK centre has essentially been two central agencies, plus No 10, whose power and relations have varied. Moves in the direction of corporate governance were evident under the Cameron and May governments in the context of deficit management. However, given the system's ambivalence about its identity and potential (Haddon, 2016), and chronic capacity issues, the question remained as to whether a more strategic approach could be readily realised beyond the exigencies of Brexit.

The prime minister's department (the DPMC in Australia and New Zealand, PCO in Canada, and the CO in the United Kingdom) is one of two or three central agencies responsible for coordination across the national public sector, in this case coordinating policy for the whole-of-government. The PMD has varied in significance over time and between countries. It tended to acquire new functions before and during the reform era but was then outpaced by the rapidly expanding PMO. The extent to which the PMD has acted as the central coordinator has been contingent on the PM's leadership style and the level of reliance on the PMO. One response to complex policy needs was to build coordinating units within current structures, particularly within the Department of the Prime Minister and Cabinet (part of an Australian tradition: Weller, 2018).[1]

The Australian PMD had a major delivery role imposed on it and was affected by unstable government in the 2010s and a quick succession of departmental heads (four in six years for the most senior public service appointment is unheard of elsewhere). The Canadian Privy Council Office seemed to have lost more responsibilities to the PMO and earlier than other PMDs but has still managed to maintain distinctive coordinating roles (Savoie, 2011). The less-developed PMD in NZ is regarded as sufficient for the purposes of a smaller and low-key system that has been department-centric and presided over by a strong State Services Commission, although an agenda for rebalancing the responsibilities of centre and departments has been brewing for some time. The United Kingdom's Cabinet Office and No 10 have been fluid in terms of sharing responsibilities between them and in exhibiting ambivalence about their respective functions (Jones, 2016). Instruments have been lodged in the Cabinet Office that might otherwise be in Treasury. It is ironic that managerial functions are so strongly present in the Cabinet Office, which might otherwise have specialised in policy coordination. No 10 hardly compares with the roles of PMOs elsewhere, although its influence is often decisive when well managed.

The form of coordination at this level is inclined to be contingent on personalities and politics; cohesiveness is unusual where relationships among central agencies are shaped by their roles and power. The dominance of the two treasuries at different times is well documented, the UK Treasury often being the lead central agency as was the New Zealand Treasury's early role in public sector reform (Boston, Martin, Pallot and Walsh, 1996; Diamond, 2014). The reduction of treasuries' roles has been frequently advocated and occurred in Canada (1966) and in Australia (1977). The relative standing of central agencies and their level of cooperation has had a significant bearing on coordination. The ascendancy of the UK Treasury (Diamond, 2014, 171–3), its interventionist stance under Chancellor Brown, and the rivalry between Blair and Brown exacerbated coordination problems between the Cabinet Office and Treasury. The tensions between No 10 and the Cabinet Office were the most prominent of the systems. However, this passed, and the Cabinet Office has since acquired responsibilities in the 2010s, with relationships becoming more cooperative. The role of the UK Treasury has been termed 'controlled discretion' (Thain, 2010). It has continued to have a major policy role through its responsibility for spending reviews and the ambitious single-department plans.

An important difference derives from the roles of treasury on the one hand and the prime minister's department on the other. The prime minister's department is stronger in the federal systems, where the functions traditionally assigned to treasury, as in the two unitary systems, are divided between two central agencies. The treasury has been highly significant in New Zealand and the United Kingdom because it encompassed economic policy, the budget and resource management and may be used for ministers' agendas (e.g. Brown on social policy), although their once pre-eminent positions within the public sector changed during the reform era.

Australia, and particularly Canada, have tended to favour stronger centres compared to New Zealand and the United Kingdom, but all have been subject to centralisation and the strengthening of policy-making capacity following the fragmenting effects of new public management reforms (Dahlstrom et al., 2011). The prime ministers' departments in Australia and Canada have remained stable central agencies for policy coordination that may have policy-related functions added (or subtracted) as required by the prime minister. The trend has been towards greater responsibilities during the reform era, although central agencies remain prone to regulation and interventions in departments (Savoie, 2011; Halligan, 2020).

The United Kingdom's centre has been weak by comparison with other anglophone countries (Yong and Hazell, 2014) and derives from a conception of the role of the Cabinet Office that places emphasis on cabinet and collective responsibility whereas prime minister's departments focus on the prime minister (Weller, 2018). The United Kingdom has experimented with specialised advisory and policy delivery units in the Cabinet Office and the prime minister's office, which have tended to be short-lived. They include the Central Policy Review Staff in the 1970s and other variants including a PMO 'policy unit' and 'performance and innovation'/strategy unit in the 1990s (Fleischer, 2009; Smith, 2011a). These reflect the anglo tradition of providing flexibility for first ministers and cabinets in shaping government policymaking to suit their particular styles and needs (Halligan and Power, 1992; Esselment et al., 2014; Craft, 2016).

Ultimately the role and influence of central agencies is dependent on the prime minister and the power of the PMO (see Chapter 5). In Australia, Howard's mode of governing registered discontent at senior levels about the policy process and politicians' lack of strategic focus. The most telling development occurred when a key policy agency, Treasury, was bypassed by the government in the development of policy frameworks for water reform and climate (Henry, 2007, 6). The secretary of the Treasury (Henry, 2007, 13–14) observed in an election year: 'Our capacity to ensure that our work is "responsible", and not just "responsive", will be put to the test. How successful we are will impact on our . . . long-term effectiveness.' Under the Rudd government, the PMO acquired more comprehensive authority and power (Waterford, 2009) and the DPMC was strengthened to operate strategically (Halligan, 2011a), which meant greater intervention in departmental policymaking. Rudd's successor Abbott introduced arrangements that were highly centralised and authoritarian; yet policy making was ad hoc, and coordination and strategy were lacking (Patrick, 2016). Both approaches failed, and both prime ministers were displaced from office.

The concentration of power in the Canadian government has been frequently acknowledged (Savoie, 1999, Zussman, 2015; Prince, 2018). The combination of a powerful PMO and PCO has been sustained for several decades and remains more highly centralised than those of other countries. Under Harper the arrangements were 'regarded as the most centrally controlling governance system that has ever been devised in Canada' (Zussman, 2016, 56; Shepherd and Stoney, 2018). One result was that deputy ministers had 'fraught' relations with the PMO (Bourgault, 2014, 377). Much depended on the prime minister's style: compare the 'directive' approach under Harper with the 'facilitative' approach under Trudeau (C13).

The role of the centre was employed to pursue implementation with units being used in Australia, Britain and Canada. Reporting was directly to the prime minister or through a cabinet task force and ministerial oversight and with PMO responsibilities (Gold, 2014, 2017). A variation, largely unsuccessful, was the Cameron experiment with implementation task forces composed of ministers, to monitor and resolve issues with service delivery and crosscutting priorities (HC CPA, 2016a). Treasury's regular spending reviews have been influential. The most recent and ambitious has been the results and delivery agenda run out of the Canadian Privy Council Office (Results and Delivery Unit, 2016). Of other experiments, New Zealand did not use a delivery unit, although the BPS agenda arguably performed this function for government priorities.

The other relevant central agencies are those responsible for the finance and economic functions. Australia's Finance Department and Canada's Treasury Board Secretariat are hybrid agencies with different programs ranging from budget management to performance management of departments, including running austerity programs (but see Craft and Wilson, 2018).

Moving towards Collaboration

The focus of policymaking within government used to be the departmental hierarchy with an emphasis on vertical portfolios. Type 2 envisages a shift to broader horizontal internal cooperation through task forces, committees and groups, and the consideration here is to what extent this is apparent in anglophone countries.

The ministerial department has remained a central actor in policymaking, even if diminished under centralising prime ministers or because of loss of capacity and being modified by how external and internal roles are envisioned. There is however a stark contrast between understandings about the old and the new public service, and this is clear from five directions of change: the greater insistence on better quality and more timely consultation with internal stakeholders; the nature of internal networks and committees; the attachment to joined-up government and collaborative ideas; interagency activity; and cases of high intensity collaboration involving shared goals and accountability.

But first the changing environment and immediate contexts need to be noted. Horizontal government approaches have been developed to promote inter-agency coordination in order to pursue complex policy goals and joint implementation. A range of instruments reflecting horizontal and whole-of-government principles have been used to address 'wicked' and other issues that could not be handled within a functional department (Christensen and Lægreid, 2007). The new focus on coordination was expressed through: horizontality, a core value in Canada since the 1990s (Lindquist, 2014, 193); the United Kingdom's 'joined-up' phase (Bogdanor, 2005); Australia's 'culture of collaboration' in the 2000s (ANAO, 2010, 13); and New Zealand's experimentation at the same time (Boston and Gill, 2011, 213–14).

Apart from the collaboration movement, the internal environment has changed. Internal processes have become more open, with ministerial staff constantly interacting with public servants and being able to range and provide counterpoints across the policy process.

Networks have become a fashionable area of inquiry, but less so within the public service. Three forms of network are political, functional and professional plus interdepartmental committees (IDCs), the latter two being relevant here. IDCs were regarded as inconsequential and process-oriented fiefdoms that lacked productivity (see MAC, 2004); the critique was that they operated as permanent communities of interest and were not necessarily productive. Public service arrangements were affected by the growth of ministerial adviser networks, central interventions and the greater preference for short-term, task-oriented processes. Nevertheless, IDCs, informal interaction and networks continued to be significant and commonplace (Boston and Gill, 2011). Officials routinely worked across departmental boundaries to collaborate in formulating national policies through ad hoc and short-term IDCs, task forces, joint working parties and other cross-agency mechanisms (ANAO, 2010, 13). The IDC remains a component of interdepartmental interaction but without the rigidities and permanency that characterised its predecessors' domination of many internal advisory processes.

The second type of network is professional. New Zealand and the United Kingdom have given the most serious attention to resurrecting the policy function through mounting programs for developing the policy profession (discussed in Chapter 9). Interactions among agencies have expanded and are now extensive. Australia recorded over 1,800 inter-agency agreements for twenty-one departments (including two agencies), which indicated interdependencies and a breadth of activity (ANAO, 2010, 30). Of these agreements, three types of service were provided by one agency for another (delivery of public services; provision of advice or data to another department; shared services between two agencies); and relationships based on joint program implementation and border security coordination. These were concentrated at the lower to middle end of the spectrum of intensity. Unclear was the extent to which these arrangements gave centrality to policy processes. Of cases of coordination reported on by the audit office, relatively few addressed policy development (Halligan and Smith, 2019).

Horizontal coordination was inclined to reflect the influence of hierarchy (Peters, 2015), or simply the intersection of horizontal and vertical coordination, but this was predictable (and appropriate) where enlightened central agencies practised different shades of hierarchy. Horizontal coordination remained uneven and problematic (cf Europe: Lægreid et al., 2016), and the complexities displayed in the early wave of horizontalism were still evident, as were the weaknesses at the centre and in interdepartmental workings (Bakvis and Juillet, 2004). Cross-agency work was still dogged by silos (Robertson, 2018).

There continue to be constraints on types of collaborative arrangement that have minimised their use. The United Kingdom's public service agreements were created under the Blair government as a coordination tool and evolved over time to include joint targets, an 'ambitious attempt ... to re-engineer government along more collaborative lines' (Paun and Blatchford, 2014, 131). There were problems with joint targets because of difficulties with coordinating 'cross-departmental policy and resource allocation' owing to the siloed departmental structures in Whitehall (James and Nakamura, 2014), but they provided a foundation until terminated by a new government. Cases of departments working together were investigated by the Committee of Public Accounts, but it concluded that these 'practices rarely lead to formal funding or accountability arrangements, and only two formal joint bids were received by HM Treasury as part of the 2015 Spending Review' (HC CPA, 2016b, 5). Departments had sought to work together, but the obstacles were insurmountable: inter alia, 'disagreements between ministers; disagreements about who should fund policy areas; and insufficient flexibility within single departmental plans to enable departments to work together' (CAG, 2016c, 37; also Parker, Paun, McClory and Blatchford, 2010). The Spending Review process was unsuited to handling issues that spanned departmental boundaries because it was based on bilateral negotiations between Treasury and departments. Treasury's approach controlled departmental spending but prevented the tackling of difficult questions, including 'policy issues such as obesity' (CAG 2016c, 18; HC CPA, 2016b, 12).

New Zealand illustrated two approaches. There were early experiments with cross-department arrangements that entailed sector groupings in fields such as justice and natural resources, each with a sector leader. However, this approach was depicted as being forced to 'fit to an existing standard, using a work-around to combine a horizontal role with a vertical accountability framework' (Boston and Gill, 2011, 229). The Better Public Services review elevated the approach to a new level by addressing the problem of poor coordination under the NZ model, a defining characteristic being the concentration of 'decision-rights and accountabilities with the chief executives' (BPSAG, 2011, 21). The mode of coordination changed from inter-agency consultation to a more tightly coordinated and politically driven arrangement under which ministers had to agree to, and be aligned around, a small number of significant, measurable sector-wide results. With this structure and the focus on intermediate outcomes, there were successes with specific policy objectives (Scott and Boyd, 2016, 2017).

More generally most coordination has tended to be short-term, ad hoc and more informal. European surveys report that commitment to collaboration is too vague about meanings and practice to be of much assistance. Moreover, the European paradox may apply: 'while coordination and collaboration generally are seen as important contemporary reform trends, few executives see significant improvements in the quality of policy coherence and coordination over the last few years' (Lægreid et al., 2016, 251). There is a shortage of evidence as to the extent to which collaboration has become integral.

Overall, the level of coordinating activities has multiplied substantially. Yet calls are still made for greater coordination and modification of silo effects. The tension between coordination and specialisation remains a matter of balance. Like other fundamental questions considered in this study, coordination represents a story without an end. Despite the celebration of 'collaboration' during recent decades, the more committed, shared forms remained under-incentivised and under-used.

Externalising Focus and Engagement

Three dimensions of externalising are relevant here. First is the use of external units for policy advice in lieu of internal capability, such as outsourcing policy work to consultants and think tanks (see Chapter 7). Second is the use of external expertise through task forces and inquiries to augment internal capability (perhaps with an 'insourcing' character) (Chapter 6). The third is about the public service's focus on external engagement with actors in society and entails being receptive and accessible to them and promoting active interaction in policy discussions.

An enlarged policy advisory system can mean not only greater use of external sources, despite the public service, but the public service itself drawing on such units and shifting to an external focus in the policy process. Type 2 in Table 4.1 envisages an external, collaborative and open model of policy advising. The underlying conception is of a shared arrangement and a co-design with networks and coalitions. In terms of the locus of policy process, the public service employs consultants and other advisory sources. It engages with groups, research institutes, think tanks and lobbyists. Officials are participants in policy discussions inside and outside government. They may also manage policy networks. None of the countries could claim to closely reflect type 2. Specific departments and agencies will be actively interacting externally, particularly those with substantial service delivery programs, but not systems overall. Countries are at different stages of adapting to new environments and loss of capability.

A comparison of an early responder with a late starter is illuminating. The UK ran an active reform program in the 2010s with sometimes radical agendas. Open Public Services (HM Government, 2011) represented the push on thinking externally and commissioning services from outside the public sector, but the most directly relevant agenda was 'open policy making' (HM Government, 2012) which focused on improving capability. Open policymaking was articulated as an agenda for making the policy process more collaborative, in a myriad of ways: crowdsourcing, policy labs, co-design, involvement of experts and access to data. Other approaches included funding for contestable policymaking, matching resources to priorities, development of staff skills and expertise, a focus on evidence of what works, and horizon scanning (HM Government, 2012, 14–17). The United Kingdom has a great flair for generating imaginative ideas, but these are not necessarily enacted in practice. Nevertheless, there has been an impact on the civil service culture, 'what works' centres are useful, behavioural insight has become another UK export, and measures for improving capability of staff have been actively pursued (e.g. the policy profession discussed in Chapter 9) (HM Government, 2013, 2014). Undoubtedly, Brexit has played a part in that the active recruitment of policy workers was significant despite the lingering austerity policies.

In contrast, central leadership in Australia was slow to follow up on the diagnoses about the condition of policy capability, allowing it to deteriorate further under the austerity policies of the mid-2010s. The parlous position of the system was depicted by the head of the public service as the 'degradation of policy expertise', in part a result of the 'loss of capability in the outsourcing era' (Parkinson, 2018). The articulation of the issues and the need to adapt and respond externally (Parkinson, 2018; Woolcott, 2018) also reflected a new awareness of the imperatives of change. Contestability is not simply a matter of ministers wanting alternatives but also about the need to directly address an environment where challenges, backed up by competitive policy expertise, come from think tanks, single-issue groups, NGOs and lobbyists (Woolcott, 2018). Insiders have been well aware of how policy sectors often differ from those in the past with more groups contending for influence and requiring more extensive attention (A1, A3, A5, A7). A prerequisite was seen to be open dialogue and user designs that accord centrality to citizens' needs, which for public servants, 'means being connectors, interpreters, and navigators ... This requires a very different approach to collaboration from the traditional approaches ... The APS sometimes plays more of a "broker" role; as a strategic coordinator of policy inputs and helping to ensure that all components are fit-for-purpose and impartial in order to realise the best outcomes' (Smith, 2018, 13).

Policy Capability of Departments

Policy capability is an integral component of the public management system but has been identified in the twenty-first century as an ailing field not readily amenable to resuscitation. Managerialism had earlier pushed management to the forefront as both an activity and a primary responsibility of senior public servants (this relegation of policy is also attributable to the externalisation of activity and politicisation (Craft and Halligan, 2017; see Chapter 3).

The decline in the policy capacity of the federal public services is particularly clear in the Canadian case, where studies have documented shortages of policy analytical capacity (Peters, 1996; Howlett et al., 2017). In the 1970s, the policy advisory group flourished within the federal bureaucracy, but its fortunes declined from the 1980s with successive expenditure reductions and public management reforms (Prince, 1983; Zussman, 2015; Craft and Daku, 2017). The managerialist reforms of the late 1980s and early 1990s produced a decline in policy capability, a shift towards generalist managers, discouragement of engaging in inter-departmental policy dialogues and government bypassing the public service (Carroll, 1990; Sutherland, 1993; Fellegi, 1996; Lindquist, 2014). The federal public service's policy capacity declined with widespread shortages, particularly of policy analytical capacity (Peters, 1996; Dobuzinskis, Howlett and Laycock, 2007;

Howlett and Wellstead, 2011). However, studies reveal a more complex picture in which policy analytical capacity is 'lumpy' or unevenly distributed across policy domains, the public service, and non-governmental units (Inwood, Johns and O'Reilly, 2012; Howlett, Wellstead and Craft, 2014b, 2017). A few departments retained capacity because of their centrality to government agendas and the strength of their ministers, such as treasury, finance and foreign affairs, although some attrition to their power occurred where governments were seeking to reduce their influence.

An internal review by the New Zealand Treasury (Scott, 2010) found that considerable resources were being put into advisory work and capacity within departments, but often capacity was unavailable in key areas or was unaligned with government priorities. The Department of the Prime Minister and Cabinet's (DPMC) 'policy project' diagnosed a long-standing policy problem with multiple dimensions. These included variations in quality, skill shortages, evidential shortfalls, cross-agency weaknesses, and a series of contradictions and divergent goals resulting from the changing environment (DPMC, 2014, 1–2). Policy resources were 'under-managed', departments were making an insufficient contribution to the policy agenda, the big policy issues were not being responded to, there were gaps in 'policy advice leadership capability' at the chief executive level, an imbalance existed between the emphasis on process at the expense of analysis and advice, the quality of data was poor, and consultation was mishandled (NZ Treasury, 2010). The key issue was that policy analysis (i.e. the content of policy) was 'weakened in favour of a systemic focus on the process and presentation aspects of policy. Capability in basic policy analysis disciplines[2] was 'degraded across the public service in favour of increased expertise in risk and process management' (Scott, 2010, 37). The DPMC (2014) 'policy project' was established because of complex policy problems.

The Australian public service's policy role changed with the rise of managerialism as senior executives and department heads were expected to manage, and the centrality of the policy role within the advisory system was disbanded as political executives became more assertive (Halligan and Power, 1992). Studies have since reported that the policy capability of departments has been eroded (Edwards, 2009; Tiernan, 2011; O'Flynn et al., 2014; Carson and Wellstead, 2015; Tingle, 2015; Vromen and Hurley, 2015), and their policy expertise valued less (Head, 2015). An official review pronounced that the policy capability of the public service, particularly innovative and strategic advice, required strengthening (AGRAGA, 2010, 21). The ambiguous status of secretaries' policy role was such that it required legislation to revive it as a formal responsibility (Halligan, 2013).

Details about the loss of departmental policy capability provide insights about the extent of the Australian problem. Systematic assessments of departments' capability were undertaken (2011–15).[3] Departments varied widely in terms of the quality and extent of their policy capability, ranging from well-developed to laissez faire, but were generally weak on six dimensions: policy development; strategy; research and analysis; policy implementation; stakeholder engagement; and evaluation. There were substantial variations in departments' ability to offer choices, ground advice in evidence (particularly where they had a large database), draw on effective consultation internally and externally, and be forward-looking. Most departments lacked a strategic focus or made inadequate provision for it. Strategic policy was often ad hoc, siloed and unrecognised as a capability organisationally or in relation to departmental objectives. In addition to the disinclination to be forward-looking, departments were reactive, which was attributed to day-to-day pressures and issues, a culture of problem-solving, and the importance of tactical and transactional factors. The policy/implementation relationship was a perennial issue, with systematic feedback loops lacking between service delivery and policy development and program design. Departments generated rich intelligence from the interactions of networks with clients and service providers, but the evidence was insufficiently tapped and processed for relaying back to the national office. Stakeholder engagement on policy was a pervasive theme, but consultation was usually inadequate. Evaluation was usually patchy or under-developed. Overall there was a passive approach to policy, which was reflected in the lack of advocacy and leadership (Halligan, 2016).

Others have pointed out that there was simply a more competitive marketplace for policy advice given the on-stream of new advisory capacity from outside the public sector (Boston, 1994; Tiernan, 2011). The argument was that 'competition for the ministerial ear' increased the range of inputs and improved decision-making. However, this was only likely if ministers wanted it to happen, and it was not apparent that governments were open to a range of options

(MacDermott, 2008, 27). The new fashion for policy first and development of evidence later became more prevalent beyond the 'headline policy' of new governments in Australia and the United Kingdom with 'policy-based evidence' entering the lexicon (Varghese, 2016; interviews with UK civil servants, August 2018). Policy active ministers have implemented policy without evidence (e.g. Michael Gove while UK secretary of state for education) with policy initiated by hunch (or ideology) rather than by evidence (Bousted, 2017; Wilby, 2017; Rutter, 2018).

Interviews with senior Australian officials produced different takes on capability deficits, strengths and weaknesses, explanations, new capability needs, and how to respond. Departmental secretaries have options: some let capability slip in the face of resource shortages because of cuts or diversions to other purposes, while others sought internal ways of making use of what they had. One secretary observed that the quantity of expertise and capability was less: 'Departments which used to have extensive policy – critical mass – have lost much of that ... in the endless efficiency dividends and tended to move away from that sort of model.' Other departments attempted to retain central capability: '[Y]ou need that core policy capability there and when you're under the gun, being able to call on it really makes a difference' (A6). Another secretary referred to the need for 'centralising a lot of the data capability, centralising a more strategic area to look at the longer-term needs' (A1).

Capability was also viewed in terms of staff skills: 'The quality of the people today is of a level of education capability and skills, which is much better than the service I joined ... their analytical capacity on what they can do, particularly on data analytics' (A2). The question was posed about the type of capability that was needed: 'What we do lack is the analytic capability to really think about what's the problem we're trying to solve here? ... [T]here is an issue around capability, but we're in a bit of transition as to what is the best capability to help us deal with some of the complex issues.' In terms of public service evolution, there has been movement from 'the days of sitting in the engine room with treasury and dreaming up a policy, and not talking to your colleagues, to user-centred design. So, there's different methodologies' (A7).

Department heads reflected on the dilemmas resulting from lack of government interest in strategic matters. The question of capability, said one, 'was about demand and supply. You'll find there are different views but my personal view is that it's almost entirely a demand and supply issue. If the demand was there for a greater volume of higher-quality advice, the supply would be there pretty quickly. But the demand isn't there' (A1).

A secretary attributed policy problems to resourcing but emphasised the authorising environment's neglect of long-term thinking about policy: 'Policy advice to government may be different than some of the strategies and policies we need to pursue in the longer term, and I don't think the two are mutually exclusive' (A8). The public service must focus on government priorities but without losing sight of the sustainability of the system and outcomes over the longer term even though the willingness of the political executive to undertake 'longer-term thinking and scenario planning has probably been lost somewhat in recent times'. Work occurs within the constraints of avoiding: 'contradicting government policy or priorities either, or compromising them in terms of delivery ... Leaving aside the politics ... have we got people thinking about the longer term? Have we got the data analysts now? There's so much data in this portfolio ... but do we use it wisely? But will you necessarily have the resourcing given that often the priorities suck up a lot? This is what has happened elsewhere. It gets diverted, focusing on the short term' (A8).

This question of the long-term was linked to the role of the public service: 'That capacity is there in the staff – probably – and is improving. You've got to resource it to actually create the space for people, and you also have got to have a view which is much more than what is the next six weeks, two years. It's actually about what is the unique role of the public service. It's about the future. We're the only ones who care about life beyond the political cycle, one or two parliaments, because we are the continuity' (A2). The service has 'to worry about the next decade or the decades after, because the political process today doesn't tend to focus there. The media attention – the twenty-four-hour media cycle is reality. The political process tends to worry about Tuesday, not 2025' (A2).

Implications for the Public Service's Role in the Policy Advisory System

Thatcher is credited with triggering the shift in the 1980s away from ministerial reliance on civil servants among anglo countries. In the following decade, the United Kingdom was depicted as having a hybrid system of advice and declining internal capacity (Campbell and Wilson, 1995; Foster, 2001). The most agreed-upon dynamic in the Westminster cases became the shared erosion of public service policy capacity (Foster, 2001; Edwards, 2009; Painter and Pierre, 2005; Gleeson et al., 2011). Less clear is to what extent the position can be retrieved. Official and independent studies have continued to detail weaknesses in policymaking tied to deficiencies in advisory practices (Hallsworth, Parker and Rutter, 2011, 7; Halligan, 2016).

The second general trend has been the decline of substantive experience in favour of generalist and process-intensive forms of policy work (Howlett et al., 2014b; Page and Jenkins, 2005; Tiernan, 2011). This indicates the need to reappraise what the advisory system role is for the public service when it focuses more on being a broker and convenor of advisory inputs. The nature of the public service policy advisory role remains highly contingent on leadership style, minister's role conceptions, the significance of political advisers and the external environment. It can be taken for granted that the public service advisory role occurs within a pluralist, contestable, minister-driven context in which being responsive to others is more important than being the policy initiator.

The core work still entails the provision of advice to ministers. The traditional written form has been maintained as a necessary practice for putting on the record the formal actions and position of the department. A minister-centric conception that distinguishes twelve types of policy advice in Australia (Hamburger and Weller, 2012, 371) indicates the range of elements integral to the public service's role. The addition of the external engagement role being raised by officials (see type 2) will extend the policy work of departments. The emphasis on implementation can be beneficial to policy development but not if divorced from it.

Countering advisory system weaknesses has been attempted in all countries. New Zealand's DPMC has run a campaign in support of public servants being free and frank and in support of policy stewardship (Kibblewhite, 2015, 2018; Kibblewhite and Boshier, 2018), although the likelihood of providing such advice has declined (Eichbaum, 2017). There was the unusual exercise in the mid-2010s of senior Canadian officials undertaking, under the aegis of the PCO, a medium planning exercise involving departments and policy areas, which examined long-term issues in relation to policy advice and policy capacity (C4).

Historically departments in anglophone countries were inclined to be inward looking and external engagement was selective and more controlled. The poor quality of consultation with stakeholders reported by reviews within the last decade is relevant but also antiquated. The burgeoning external relationship role indicates the need to deal with an open-ended PAS. A public service role is becoming less about making use of sources of policy advice than about responding to the myriad of groups and interests active in policy fields. Given the policy pressures on the public service and the neglect of its capability, its policy expertise has been attenuated. The trend towards generalist and process skills will expand with the centring of the public service more directly in the policy advisory system.

From a policy advisory system perspective, there are interesting dynamics operating around the generation and circulation of advisory information. An open system means that much flows in that requires attention and bubbles round in societal discourse. Under a traditional PAS, much depended on the public service's dispositions. Under the open system, the processing of knowledge and ideas within government depends much more on how it fits with the mindset of ministers focused on the very short-term that emphasises their priorities and deprioritises strategic planning and long-term policy.

Underneath the carapace of political management, the senior public servant has remained committed to professional values, especially impartiality, provision of written advice to ministers and making clear where the line is drawn. Although the department head's roles have moved from guardian to policy adviser to manager (Bourgault and Dunn, 2014a, 437), and there is now a marketplace for policy advising, the continuing role for internal policy advice is integral for many purposes. Tensions are starkly present with the twenty-first-century ministers who want to be fully involved and have their priorities and preferences prevail but tend to be highly risk-averse and short-term focused. The institutional guidelines for public servants can be ambiguous, inconsistent or insufficient to cover all options, so they must exercise discretion wisely (Grube, 2015) and avoid the contradictory tendencies of either underperforming (yielding to demands that raise professional issues) or overperforming (crossing the line) (Halligan, 2020).

5 | Ministerial Partisan Advisers and the Politicisation of PAS

'Barbarians at the gate', 'junkyard dogs' and 'the people who live in the dark' are all terms used to describe the politically appointed staff that support ministers of the crown. These terms reflect their shadowy and at times aggressive advisory activity. In all four countries they were added to PAS for similar reasons: to shore up political control for ministers, address perceived deficiencies of public service policy advice, and increase ministers' capacity to address the 'big P' politics of policy work (Eichbaum and Shaw, 2010b; Craft, 2015a). Their effects have however been questioned on both empirical and normative grounds, having become lightning rods for debates about politicisation, but also flashpoints for concerns about the under-resourced nature of modern ministers' offices (Paun, 2013; Shaw and Eichbaum, 2018a, 2020). In a sense, they can positively and negatively politicise PAS. At their best, partisan advisers identify political risks and hotspots; they work on behalf of ministers and help governments avoid the derailment or watering down of their policy agendas. They serve as ports of call for officials, interested stakeholders and other ministers, and they facilitate the circulation of policy advice within and around government (OECD, 2011; Craft, 2015b). At their worst they have corrosive effects, over-stepping boundaries – both firm and soft – and throwing their weight around by falsely invoking their minister's name or attempting to direct public servants without the authority to do so. They can colour the professional policy advice of the public service before it reaches ministers for consideration or worse, exclude it altogether. They can serve as gatekeepers and prevent access to ministers and prime ministers (Rhodes and Tiernan, 2014a).

Partisan advisers are thus often portrayed as *the* politicising force of PAS. They are exceptional in that they are temporary public servants/ contract staff employed at the discretion of ministers, who serve as officially sanctioned 'political' advisers (Cabinet Office, 2010; Privy Council Office, 2015). They can speak explicitly to the values, political choices, resource allocations, intra-executive and legislative dynamics, and electoral and party aspects of concern to ministers (Craft, 2015b; Wilson, 2015). In some cases, they are subject matter experts or seconded public servants with experience in specific or varied policy domains (OECD, 2007; Shaw and Eichbaum, 2018a). In many ways, partisan advisers epitomise the contestation and policy coordination of contemporary Westminster PAS. They can offer ministers and prime ministers alternative views that are unavailable from public servants or externals but also engage on substantive policy matters *with* various other PAS actors, both of which may see the privileging of partisan-political values over evidentiary or public service perspectives.

There is considerable discretion in how governments and individual ministers organise and deploy these advisers, and within limits they are free to do so in the ways that best suit their policy and political needs. There is widespread agreement that partisan advisers, particularly those serving prime ministers, have become more prominent and influential (Savoie, 2008; Weller, 2018). Central political offices have become adept at using partisan advisers as systemic instruments to secure political alignment and coordination throughout government (Dahlstrom et al., 2011; Craft, 2016). Their growing numbers and the specialisation of policy functions within some ministers' offices have become important features for how ministers seek to exert political control and secure more contestable and coordinated policy. As one observer has noted, partisan advisers are one of the most significant examples of institutional innovation within Westminster political systems (Maley, 2011, 1469).

In this chapter, significant trends involving advisers are highlighted and comparative analysis is provided. It reveals important within tradition variation related to what advisers do, how they do it and with whom, as well as how governments use advisers to increase policy contestation, coordination and political control within and around advisory systems. Comparatively, Canadian and Australian PAS feature pronounced and systematic use of advisers, whereas the New Zealand PAS sees advisers play more constrained and selective roles. The United Kingdom falls in between, with more comprehensive involvement of advisers on matters of policy but clear constraints limiting their ability to engage in advisory work. Some PAS feature more formal engagement from advisers with cabinet policy processes and formal written briefings, but others see advisers involved predominantly with matters of political brokerage. Their advisory inputs are at times complementary and integrated with those of the public service, while in other instances they are separate and distinct. The considerable variance across the cases, and over time, reflects important differences in how ministers have sought to exercise control and purposefully politicise PAS.

Strengthening the Center: Political Control, Policy Contestation and Coordination

Partisan advisers were first institutionalised in the UK and Canadian executives, followed by Australia, and then much later New Zealand (Kemp, 1986; Maley, 2011; Craft, 2016). The pattern was consistent in the four cases with reforms first occurring in prime ministers' offices with partisan advisers partially or completely replacing seconded public servants. Ministers' offices followed suit, but here the patterns differ dramatically as discussed below. Table 5.1 illustrates the significance of the differences across the cases, with much larger PMOs in Canada and Australia but also larger complements of political advisers in their ministers' offices.

Australia, and particularly Canada, have tended to favour stronger centres over New Zealand and the United Kingdom, but all have been subject to centralisation and more prominent use of advisers (Dahlstrom et al., 2011). Two competing narratives have emerged around centralisation in Westminster systems, the first being the

Table 5.1 *Ministerial office staff in Australia, Canada, New Zealand and the United Kingdom*

	Ministers' Offices	Prime Minister's Office	Total
Australia	402	50	452 (2019)
Canada	490	91	581 (2018)
New Zealand	126	23	149 (2015)
United Kingdom	62	37	99 (2018)

Sources: Australia (Senate, 2019); United Kingdom (Cabinet Office, 2018); New Zealand (Shaw and Eichbaum, 2018b); Canada (Treasury Board Secretariat Canada correspondence with author).

displacement of cabinet, and traditional formal policymaking process, by courtier-like arrangements empowering first ministers at the expense of collective cabinet decision-making (see Savoie, 1999; Aucoin, 2012; Rhodes and Tiernan, 2014b). Alternatively, centralisation is claimed to be a natural by-product of contemporary governance, representing attempts by prime ministers to 'hold on' or 'reassert the centre' in an age of evolved prime ministership and fragmented and demanding governing contexts (Dahlstrom et al., 2011; Craft, 2017). Advisers assume major roles in both, but the forms they have taken on in PAS vary in marked ways. Further, leveraging political advisers for political control, increasing contestability and improved political coordination can mean walking a fine line. PMO advisers can protect and enable prime ministers but can also be detrimental to their leadership if they lack the political nous to understand their place within PAS and their reliance on others' policy and political resources. Comparative analysis of PMOs current and past is helpful to illuminate different approaches to PAS. The Canadian and Australian PMOs are much larger than No 10 and continue to feature a more partisan-political orientation to the policy unit. The United Kingdom and New Zealand feature a greater propensity for hybridity, with civil servants on policy matters and with PMO chiefs of staff being drawn from public service ranks.

United Kingdom

The distribution of advisers between ministers and No 10 in the United Kingdom has been consistent over the twenty-first century with a ratio of 2:1, with the exception of the coalition period of 2010–15 when the centre grew to accommodate junior coalition partners (Maer and McCaffrey, 2018, 7). Major changes in the contemporary era began with Blair's government (1997–2007) essentially doubling the number of advisers across the system, particularly increasing their use in No 10 for policy and communications purposes (Blick, 2018). Blair was innovative in his repurposing of central government wide supports, particularly Cabinet Office units and teams, for prime ministerial purposes. By 2005–6 there were approaching 800 staff supporting him including multiple policy units with direct reporting arrangements (Blick and Jones, 2010, 149–50; Jones, 2016). It has been difficult to return to previous arrangements, at least as far as the increased use of partisan advisers goes. Legacies remain, including the attribution of the title 'chief of staff', a first in the United Kingdom, for Jonathan Powell in 1997, and the continued use of the 'grid', a system to tie together communications and policy planning that persists to this day, though in modified form given the rise of social media. Centralisation of power was a characteristic of the Blair years, with harsh criticisms that he ran a 'sofa government' with key decisions taken by a 'kitchen cabinet' of select advisers, ministers and officials on a sofa in No 10, rather than in cabinet settings. Blair himself is on record as favouring centralised government, and his use of partisan advisers was a key resource for making that happen (Smith, 2011a; Blick, 2018).

The influence of No 10 advisers was taken to new heights when Blair controversially used an Order in Council to allocate formal executive authority to select senior advisers. In a major break from established practice and the Westminster administrative tradition, this provided these advisers with formal authority to direct public servants. This reflected a bigger role, policy included, for Blair aides who were well known to exert policy influence over a range of files and served to manage the competing centre of power coming from Brown leading the Treasury. Blair sought to build connective tissues with departments out of No 10 to drive implementation more forcefully but from the centre. As Smith (2011a, 186) succinctly puts it, 'Through targets, the use of personal advisers, bilaterals and the Prime Minister's Delivery Unit, the Prime Minister's Office became integrated into departments to an extent that is much greater than in the past.' New units and new roles for advisers, particularly around progress chasing and policy design from the centre, were hallmarks of the PAS during the Blair years.

Centralisation and the use of advisers for that purpose was, however, not guaranteed. Under Brown and Cameron, strong use of advisers at the centre was hampered by the global financial downturn and Coalition politics. In Brown's case (2007–10) as prime minister he quickly rescinded executive powers for No 10 advisers and restructured No 10, including appointing a civil servant as his chief of staff. The policy team was headed by a partisan adviser, one of about ten, who have been styled as 'mostly experienced policy experts, and unusually – most had experience as advisers in other departments' (Corry, 2011). Brown and the policy team were, however, affected by the response to the global economic downturn, and his own style of indecisiveness and overload were defining characteristics of what was perceived to be a dysfunctional PAS (Corry, 2011; Seldon and Lodge, 2013). Despite seeking to reduce the footprint of partisan advisers, the concentration of power, including key advisers at the centre, remained a prominent characteristic of the Brown years. Brown, like Blair, favoured the advice of select groups of loyalists and courtiers drawn from various quarters, including partisan advisers, but drew on more public servants than Blair (Yong and Hazel, 2014).

According to Sir Richard Mottram (a former permanent secretary), partisan advisers' growing influence at the centre has had profound effects on policymaking; as he put it, 'these are senior people and they are not simply there advising and offering a view and you can take it or leave it ... The way in which Government works now has a very significant influence from this process'.[1] Indeed, Brown himself would evoke similar sentiments on the influence of advisers, reflecting in his memoir that advisers 'may have had no power to make decisions but in practice they became among Britain's most important decision-makers ... [M]uch of what the Cabinet now does according to text-book constitutional theory is, in practice, done by these advisers acting as a kind of unelected Cabinet' (Brown, 2017).

The Cameron years (2010–15) saw a return to experimentation around the centre but with a prime minister who had publicly declared his intent to return to a more collegial cabinet in contrast to Blair and Brown's centralised operating mode. A coalition government further compounded the Cameron government's need to work collaboratively and through cabinet and – in a departure from the previous governments – to return to heavy use of cabinet committees in addition to strong Cabinet Office involvement (Paun, 2010; Hazell and Yong, 2012). Coalition also saw ministers from different parties create new dynamics, and interacting with No 10 required some strengthening of the deputy prime minister's office. Cameron had also made clear his intent to reassert political control over a civil service that was perceived as too large and unresponsive and had given the government's publicly stated intention to usher in a 'post bureaucratic state' (Diamond, 2017). While No 10 was clearly a key institutional driver of the government's policy agenda, the use of partisan advisers there, and in the system more generally, responded to the realities of the governance arrangement. As Hazell (2012) notes, the coalition saw the institutio-nalisation of a deputy prime minister's office that grew in partisan advisers and civil service supports as the junior coalition partner attempted to influence policy. While Cameron campaigned on a reduction of partisan advisers, the numbers grew as the coalition government continued, with sixty Conservatives while the Liberal Democrats employed twenty-five (Gruhn and Slater, 2012). Cameron's policy team at No 10 was initially almost exclusively civil servants, a strategy designed to mitigate the impact of a coalition government where the deputy prime minister would reject policy advice from Conservative partisan advisers (Hazell and Yong, 2012; Seldon and Lodge, 2013).

It was not long before criticisms of ineffectiveness and insufficient political oversight over policy led to additional special advisers being added to the unit. The government reintroduced an implementation unit after having scrapped the strategy and delivery unit upon taking office. Cabinet and cabinet committees that were revived to provide mechanisms for coalition policy and political bargaining became important institutional features within the government but did not increase the role of advisers, apart from a select group at the centre in both political offices (Hazell, 2012). In short, while advisers were important, they became more focused on political brokerage in lieu of policy advice, and those at No 10 were seen to have lost influence due to a weakened centre (Hazell and Yong, 2012; Yong and Hazell, 2014; Waller, 2014). The ability of the PAS, and advisers in particular, to adapt to meet the historic coalition circumstances under Cameron is a clear indication of how quickly advisers can be repurposed to support the needs of the executive.

Prime Minister May came to office by way of a party leadership change, not an election, and brought with her a group of partisan advisers, who had served her well as minister. The Brexit file she was saddled with from the start dogged May's prime ministership. She opted to have co-chiefs of staff at No 10, a departure from practice. There are legendary accounts of the aggressive and combative approaches of Nick Timothy and Fiona Hill, which saw relations sour with select senior officials, ministers and other advisers in No 10 and around government (Shipman, 2017). Interviews with senior No 10 staff under May confirmed such accounts, with staff sympathetic to the situation recognising the toxicity and difficult working conditions. The implications for PAS included the inability of partisan advisers and ministers to access the PM, either in person or through written briefs, and regular confusion and bottlenecks in disposing of policy matters (UK3, UK4). As in Australia, the United Kingdom's No 10 policy unit is large. Theresa May's policy unit consisted of twenty-four members, two-thirds of whom were civil servants and a third of whom were partisan advisers. No 10 is unique among all the prime ministers' offices in that its policy team features a hybrid set-up in a single office where partisan advisers and civil servants work in the same office within the same policy unit. The leadership team consisted of a partisan adviser as director and two directors, one of whom was a career official. Interviews revealed that civil servants and partisan advisers from the policy unit jointly authored the twenty to forty policy notes a week to the prime minister and that *both sets of views were integrated into a single note.* When asked how these inputs and streams of advice were reconciled, a No 10 adviser is worth quoting at length:

[T]here is quite close scrutiny of the Policy Unit from this wider civil service about whether it becomes overly politicised. In my experience, those guys are really professional in the way in which they manage that balance. And they [civil service deputy director] would always be quite good about pushing back and saying, no, you need to do this – if that's what you think the Prime Minister wants, then you're going to need to provide that piece of advice. Similarly, they would protect the civil servants within the Policy Unit by saying, I'm afraid [the partisan adviser] needs to do that piece of advice … [T]here was a kind of day-by-day management … There are obviously contractual and other mechanisms in place to try and ensure that people stay the right side of that line. But it just requires kind of professional working between the two teams. (UK1)

Interviews with May-era advisers suggest that the working relationships are governed by norms and conventions, which are largely left to public servants to enforce. That is, while advisers know what is and is not within bounds for the policy team's civil servants, it is the deputy civil servant head of the PMO policy team who ensures that public service politicisation is avoided (UK1). Whereas Cameron's PMO policy team was structured so that advisers were allocated to cover ministerial files, May's policy team was organised thematically, based on her main priorities, pushing out other matters to departments and ministers. One member of the policy team explained that they had found themselves engaged in all matters of policy despite trying to push out as much as possible to ministers. The role of the policy team has remained essentially the same. One adviser explained that, from a partisan adviser's perspective, the policy team was there to contest and ensure alignment with government policy objectives: 'the civil servants would work on data, facts, extracting things from other departments and so on, editing things. And the role of the special adviser was to say essentially, don't forget we promised in a manifesto to do this ... [T]he prime minister probably prefers this approach' (UK2). Several advisers noted the value-added nature of partisan advisers was to provide fresh perspectives and contestation for the prime minister. When asked about the added value of the No 10 policy unit, one former May-era adviser explained, 'Well, it is a massive filter ... [W]e add value by being a sort of funnel and quality control for incoming advice' (UK2). Senior No 10 staff interviewed explained that the policy team had three main functions, including analysis of departmental policy briefs and submissions before they went to the PM, coordination with the Cabinet Office and political oversight of inter-departmental or cross-cutting policy issues, and a third 'outward transmission piece' that involved policy creation with examples of mental-health policy initiatives or the gig economy being raised.

In July 2019 Boris Johnson assumed the office of prime minister. Initial signals suggested a PMO with a mix of new pro-Brexit blood along with a healthy dose of commodities known to Johnson: PMO chief Sir Edward Lister and No 10 policy director Munira Mirza were both aides from his time as mayor of London, and David Frost served as a Johnson adviser during his time as foreign secretary. Sheridan Westlake and Jean-Andre Prager, who served in the policy unit under Theresa May, were retained. Johnson tapped former Sky News executive Andrew Griffith to run his business advisory unit. Most controversially, Johnson appointed Dominic Cummings to No 10 as his senior adviser. Cummings was a high-profile SPAD to Education Secretary Michael Gove and served as campaign director for Vote Leave during the EU referendum. Cummings has several times expressed acerbic views of the UK civil service and openly suggested radical reforms, including the elimination of permanent secretaries in favour of a policy lead and an operations or management lead. He has publicly castigated PM May and attacked ministers for incompetence as well as senior public service leadership (BBC, 2020). The Brexit process was now being managed from the centre with a range of ministerial appointments, particularly Gove at the Cabinet Office, and with all ministerial partisan advisers now tasked with regular reporting to No 10 through Cummings (Gurr,

2019; Johnstone, 2019). A highly activist and adversarial tone had been set, with signals of continued turbulence flowing not only from Brexit but from attempts to exercise greater centralised political control from No 10. The resignation of Sajid Javid as Chancellor of the Exchequer, only eight months into his appointment, was reportedly caused by Javed's concerns about his ability to provide clear and candid advice to the prime minister and attempts by No 10 to control Javed's selection of partisan advisers (Payne and Parker, 2020).

Australia

Under successive governments since Whitlam (1972–5), the prime minister's office (PMO) has grown substantially in size, power and influence (Weller, 2018). The Australian case, is, however marked by significant instability featuring seven prime ministers in short order. This resulted in a succession of new personalities, organisational and stylistic preferences, and relationship building being required. The PMO in Australia is large, typically numbering over fifty and including a significant policy advisory component. For instance, advisers accounted for 75 per cent (forty of fifty-three) of the PMO staff in 2012 (Rhodes and Tiernan, 2014b). As with No 10, there have been greater tendencies towards experimentation regarding the use of partisan advisers and various advisory units to support the prime minister and cabinet than in Canada or New Zealand (Tiernan, 2006; Rhodes and Tiernan, 2014a, 2014b; Ng, 2018; Weller, 2018). For example, Prime Minister Howard (2003–7) created a cabinet policy unit (CPU) led by a partisan adviser who also served as cabinet secretary. The reorganisation allowed the government to increase its long-term and strategic policy capacity while freeing up the PMO and chief of staff to focus on tactical and day-to-day politics and policy issues (Tiernan, 2006). Functions performed by PM&C were relocated under the CPU with the aim of providing similar but politically supplemented policy functions to shore up advice and strategy at the centre (Rhodes and Tiernan 2014a, 2014b). Howard's PMO was also unique in that his decision to be primarily based out of Sydney and not Canberra meant that the PMO staff were split between the two. This served to further distance the political centre from public servants based in Canberra and necessitated a PMO whose advisory activity was now running from two central locations instead of one (Tiernan, 2006). Howard was explicit about his intent to innovate and institutionally embed greater contestability into the advisory system, including a strong assertion of the role of partisan advisers for political control (Tiernan, 2006). This complemented other broader public sector reforms seeking to increase responsiveness from the public service that some observers, including former Public Service Commissioner Podger (2007), publicly rebuked as politicising the public service.

When Labour returned to government in 2007 with the Rudd Coalition government it disbanded the CPU, reduced advisers by a third and introduced a code of conduct for political staff in 2008. A lighter touch with advisers was part of a broader suite of reforms that sought to loosen the perceived yoke on senior officials and return the equilibrium to a more traditional Westminster balance. However, adviser numbers would eventually climb back to their previous heights (Maley, 2018a). Like Brown, Rudd was consumed by the global financial crisis, and centralisation was the response. Rudd broke from long-standing practice by naming a minister to the cabinet secretary position and wanted strong contestation and idea exchanges. He was well known to have a large network of advisers as part of formal and informal kitchen cabinets that featured prominently ministers serving on the Strategic Budget and Priorities Committee (Tiernan, 2008). Uniquely, Rudd had served as a senior official and chief of staff at the state level and so knew the tricks, tactics and pitfalls of setting up and running government (Tiernan, 2008). Appraisals suggest both Rudd and subsequently Abbott (2013–15) were not well served, with Rudd's PMO labelled as 'kindergarteners' given their youth and inexperience (Maley, 2018a). The so-called warrior PMO chief of staff, Peta Credlin, took a heavy-handed approach in applying central controls and was a high-profile aberration in the chief of staff role, linked to the downfall of the Abbott government (Weller, 2018). Here there are some similarities to the UK experience under May's twin chiefs of staff who attempted to overextend their influence via aggressive central command and control on policy and political files.

From 2007 to 2018 the Australian PMO, and PAS more broadly, were chaotic and in constant states of transition. The exceptionalism of Australian circumstances was made plain by the spectacle of four prime ministers (Rudd, Gillard, Abbott and Turnbull) coming and going as the result of internal party factionalism. While Australian PMO staff are major players, recent experiences point to the clear constraints that exist regarding attempts to centralise and to discount both cabinet and the backbench, leading to disastrous outcomes (Weller, 2018; Maley, 2018a). Turnbull was on record as favouring a collegial cabinet-style leadership and used the PMO to attempt to deal with not only his policy agenda but also the politics of coalition management. Turnbull-era advisers were, however, clear that they sought to influence and control policy agenda. As one adviser put it:

> We have got quite a strong network between the PM's office, Finance, and the Treasury's office. Before cabinet meetings the three offices will have a page-turn; we sort of sit down and flip through each page of the cabinet papers, to collude as to how we're marshalling our ministers to direct the game. And if there are some decisions where we sort of say, here's the compromise package, then we'll get it cut up and talk with relevant other officers to sort of get it precooked before it even goes into the room, so the time is used efficiently for what are the real debates, rather than the little empty ones around the edges. (A10)

Turnbull also had the experienced hand of Arthur Sinodinos, the former long-serving Howard PMO chief of staff who sat around the cabinet table serving as cabinet secretary in 2015 and later as a cabinet minister from the Senate until his departure for health reasons. Turnbull's first three chiefs of staff were well-known public servants who brought gravitas and experience to the role, but in 2018 he opted for a more partisan operator, likely to attempt to quell internal dissent, only to ultimately fall at the hands of his own party in 2018. All of this points to a considerably politicised PAS but departs from traditional depictions of politicisation. The highly charged political nature was fueled not so much by public service interference or substantive 'colouring' of policy advice but rather by the party politics and leadership struggles of coalition governments.[2] Prime Minister Scott Morrison, taking office after another leadership spill, selected trusted hands with experience as advisers, with some moving from his office at Treasury and John Kunkel as his chief bringing strong business community bona fides but also experience as a Howard adviser.

Canada

Heavy political control over government and powerful advisers are a hallmark of the Canadian PMO (Savoie, 1999, 2019; Craft, 2018).

By comparative standards that office is less affected by the formal constraints of their counterparts. There are no formal party mechanisms to remove leaders, and there is a central agency structure designed to support prime ministers rather than cabinet as a whole (Craft and Wilson, 2018; Weller, 2018). It also features a PMO, a 'policy shop', that serves as the clearinghouse for all policy matters, which is led by a director of policy and typically staffed by six to ten partisan advisers. Partisan advisers are typically organised to shadow the relevant cabinet committees and a select grouping of government files (e.g. economy and justice, social policy). That unit averaged 8.1 policy staff during the Harper PMOs (2006–15) and a smaller Martin PMO (2003–6) employing 5.5 policy staff; the Chrétien PMOs (1993–2003) had an average of 9.6 policy staff (Esselment and Wilson, 2015). Recent studies confirm the ongoing unique role of PMO staff, both at the front end of policymaking and also on a more day-to-day basis, in working horizontally to give coherence to the shape, and help coordinate the pace, of governing (Savoie, 1999; Craft, 2017).

Contestation and coordination out of the Canadian PMO have become more formalised and systematic. The Chrétien (1993–2003) PMO featured knowledgeable and experienced advisers but operated on a verbal briefing basis, with most of the formal written advice generated by the PCO officers (Savoie, 1999; Goldenberg, 2006; Craft, 2016). The Canadian PAS saw fraught relationships, similar to the UK Blair–Brown battles, between the minister of finance and the prime minister, with staff serving as key brokers between the two offices (Goldenberg, 2006). The Martin-era (2003–6) government began as a leadership takeover followed by an election that returned the party to power with a minority, after which Martin ushered in a flatter more horizontal leadership style, which permeated the PAS. Accounts of these years emphasise the impact of the large group of Martin advisers known as 'the board', a close group of hardened partisans who had in many cases worked with Martin over several years in various capacities. The PMO and ministerial partisan political policy advisory process continued to be largely informal and oral. Senior public servants informally sought inputs and context from senior PMO advisers, but they provided their free and frank advice in writing supplemented with verbal briefs, as had long been the practice. The Martin PMO was assessed overall to be light on policy capacity. Its policy leads were seen as less capable than those of PMOs past, with its principal secretaries playing more limited roles (Jeffrey, 2010). The flat organisational structure also resulted in 'board members' weighing in on policy items, creating a loss of policy coherence and influence flowing from the PMO policy team.

Several clear changes to advisers' functions in the PAS were introduced during the Harper minority and majority governments (2006–15). Harper was well known to be a strong centraliser: he created both policy and communications processes to ensure high levels of discipline were put in place and respected given the minority parliamentary status (Esselment and Wilson, 2015). Harper was himself seen as a policy wonk who read all formal briefings and was actively engaged in the details of several files as chair of the powerful Priorities and Planning Committee of cabinet (Craft, 2016). The Conservatives returned with a clear and concise policy agenda and a distrust of the public service's loyalty and responsiveness. Combined with minority governments, this saw partisan advisers used to increase contestation and coordination in the form of alignment of policy development with the political direction of the government (Craft, 2016). The Harper PMO introduced a systematic written partisan-political advisory system that involved the PMO policy shop preparing written notes on policy issues that percolated up the system in lockstep with public service advice or in response to demands from the prime minister for advice on any given issue.

The PMO advisory process operated in very bureaucratic and systematised terms. Junior PMO partisan advisers, with their particular files and policy responsibilities, would typically draft their policy advice, which was then reviewed and formalised with the PMO policy director. The formal written partisan-political policy advice provided was described as concise – typically a one- or two-page document – providing a general partisan-political policy overlay, not in-depth policy analysis (Craft, 2018). In the Canadian case, partisan-political policy advice ensured: (1) appropriate political context was provided; (2) salient and contentious items were highlighted; (3) consistency with stated partisan-political policy objectives was adjudicated; and (4) a recommendation and rationale were provided for the prime minister (Craft, 2016).

Interviews with senior staff in the Trudeau government (2015–) have described the same process, with Trudeau perhaps characterised as less of a reader, preferring a greater mix including verbal briefs, particularly at the outset of his time in office (C7). Canadian advisers have thus seen a more formal, written advisory role emerge which has transcended changes in government (Craft, 2018). The Trudeau PMO adopted a so-called co-CEO format, with Katie Telford as chief of staff, dealing primarily with operations and the day-to-day, and Gerald Butts as principal secretary, focused on policy and strategy, though with the two overlapping often (Craft, 2018). While Butts's influence was well known in Ottawa circles given his long-standing close personal friendship with the PM, the PMO continued in the tradition of having a dedicated policy team. Mike McNair, who was known as a ministerial adviser in former Liberal governments, headed the PMO policy shop. The policy team was restructured, however, with the director of policy assuming the responsibilities for legislative affairs (planning not tactics) as well as cabinet and cabinet committee coordination. This was in addition to the responsibilities for managing the advisory process to the prime minister, including written and verbal advice flowing from the advisers shadowing policy areas.

The election of US President Donald Trump also saw a small unit struck in PMO to manage the issues flowing out of the Trump administration's chaotic and disjointed style. The significance was reflected in a later change in title from 'Director of Policy' to 'Executive Director of Cabinet and Legislative Affairs'. However, the majority of staff listed under that new title were 'policy adviser' or 'senior policy adviser', and it remained structured similarly to its predecessors, with partisan advisers providing written overlays on most policy briefs that make it up to the prime minister. The director of policy, however, also had a remit to deal with cabinet and legislation in the House of Commons, suggesting that the policy team's role was different from how it operated under Harper where there were separate leads for policy and legislative affairs. This is likely owing to the presence of Telford and Butts in the PMO, both considerable policy wonks in their own right.

Trudeau came to power promising a return to cabinet government – the empowerment of the *full* cabinet and end of governing from the centre. Officials interviewed suggested that the Trudeau had not only a laundry list of policy objectives but also a firm idea of how he wanted the machinery of government organised. In a televised interview, Trudeau remarked, 'One of the things that we've seen throughout the past decades in government is the trend toward more control from the Prime Minister's Office … Actually, it can be traced as far back as my father, who kicked it off in the first place … I actually quite like the symmetry of me being the one who ends that' (Delacourt, 2019). Early decisions to structure decision-making around the full cabinet rather than through a priority and planning subcommittee of cabinet supported the intention, but over time it became clear that command and control from the centre remained the standard operating procedure. Senior PCO officials confirmed that Trudeau's full cabinet met more regularly than Harper's and was used more regularly to deliberate on major policy issues of the day (C5, C7).

Senior Trudeau staff interviewed noted that the PMO policy shop still played a clearinghouse function to drive policy with the PCO priorities and planning unit remaining in place despite not having a formal committee of that name to support (C5, C12). One adviser, when asked about the reality of the return of cabinet government, retorted, 'I don't think you have the case at all and I don't think it's possible in the sense that the central agencies will always be very powerful in our system. It's just impossible. I think it's a good spin to say that cabinet has returned, but it's not what I saw' (C10). Others noted that, while the centre remained clearly the driver of policy and political priorities, there was discretion for ministers to develop policies and lead without central hand-holding (C11, C1). On the major files, however, it was clear the PMO was still driving the agenda.

The prominence and contentious role of the centre on advisory matters was put on full public display in 2019, with a disastrous cabinet shuffle and questions about the handling of the potential criminal prosecution of leading Canadian engineering firm SNC Lavalin. The events were historic – leading to the resignation of then Clerk of the Privy Council Michael Wernick, PMO principal secretary Butts and two of the most prominent Trudeau ministers. After resigning, former Justice Minister Wilson-Raybould alleged 'consistent and sustained efforts by many people within the government to seek to politically interfere in the exercise of prosecutorial discretion in my role as the Attorney General of Canada' (SCJHR, 2019a). Butts, after his resignation, shared a very different version of events. He insisted everyone was clear on the decision being the minister's alone; however, he said that the PMO and PCO had urged the minister to consult external advisers, given that the legal instrument available had never before been used (SCJHR, 2019b). The PCO Clerk too vigorously defended the 'lawful advocacy' approach taken by him and the government to ensure the minister was availing herself of all possible advice (SCJHR, 2019b). He would later resign for his controversial defense of the government's (and his) approach to the issue, stating, 'It is now apparent that there is no path for me to have a relationship of mutual trust and respect with the leaders of the Opposition parties' (Platt, 2019).

The incident put on full display both the fraught nature of advisory work – given how various other players can interpret PMO and PCO prompts to seek out advice in the system – and the dominant role of the centre on all matters of political salience to Canadian governments. Trudeau's minority government in the wake of the 2019 election not only saw a shuffling of some PMO and ministers office staff, notably the departure of Trudeau's long-time policy director Michael McNair, but also raised the spectre of constant campaigning (Craft, 2017b).

New Zealand

The NZ prime minister's department is unique, given that it was not until 1989 that it took on its modern form following a review by the State Services Commission. Prime Minister Palmer created a reorganised central agency based on professional public servants, the Department of Prime Minister and Cabinet and a partisan-political office, the Prime Minister's Private Office. This protracted period of institutional reorganisation was in part attributable to modernisation efforts but also represents the institutional expression of balancing the partisan-political and non-partisan public service advisory inputs in the New Zealand PAS. The Palmer reforms have proved long-lasting, with the explicit intention being to offer competing, complementary but distinct types of non-partisan professional public-service policy advice along with a partisan-political stream of advice to government through the private office (Hunn and Lang, 1989; Ng, 2018). These structural changes at the centre were part of a broader series of significant managerial reforms in the 1980s and 1990s which had important implications for PAS. The long-standing equilibrium of political-administrative relations via the traditional arrangement between politicians and public servants was 'punctuated by the reforms of the 1980s and early 1990s' (Eichbaum and Shaw, 2017, 28).

There is a paucity of research on NZ PMO advisers. One recent assessment suggests that the PMO has been weaker in comparison to the other Westminster cases and that its overall role in the policy process has been modest because it 'has been limited to a mere handful of political advisers, press secretaries, and administrative staff since it was separated from the DPMC' (Boston and Halligan, 2012, 213). Recent analysis of partisan advisers more generally is thin on PMO-specific policy functions and influence, particularly below chiefs of staff who are characterised as influential PAS players (Ng, 2018; Shaw and Eichbaum, 2018a; Weller, 2018). Interviews with former PMO staff from the Clark (1999–2008), Key (2008–16) and English (2016–17) governments suggest it has broadly stayed consistent in its organisation and advisory function under Prime Minister Ardern (2017–). When asked to explain what role PMO advisers played, a minister in the Ardern government explained, 'Someone has to manage the coalition arrangements. Someone has to manage political strategy. Someone has to manage policy, high-level policy advice. And someone has to be the literal chief of staff' (N2). The dominance of coalitions means that a high priority of the PMO is accorded to coalition politics and management, with advisers from all three of these governments noting a limited and select engagement in policy via a small team of generalists in the PMO, typically numbering three or four, and a heavy reliance on DPMC, particularly its Policy Advisory Group (PAG) (N10; N2).

Ministers' Offices: Contestation, Control and Coordination

In all four cases, PMOs do not operate alone but rely, in different ways and to different degrees, on ministers' offices. The United Kingdom and New Zealand cases feature the smallest ministerial offices, typically with only two advisers who are split between policy and communications or serve as generalists. The United Kingdom and New Zealand share a *hybrid* 'private office' arrangement for ministers that features both civil servants and typically two partisan advisers (Maley, 2018a). Australia and Canada feature *separate* ministerial offices, a significantly greater number of advisers, and a functional specialisation including dedicated policy teams, organised in formal hierarchies of seniority and 'junior' staff (Craft, 2018; Maley, 2018b).

In Australia and Canada, ministers' offices have seen staff numbers as high as fifty, rivalling the size of some prime ministers' offices. Like PMOs, most are not policy-specific staff, but these two cases do feature small teams with dedicated policy responsibilities. Their policy work is similar to the PMO, if decidedly more focused on their ministers' files with the exception of perhaps the finance minister's advisers (Tiernan, 2007; Wilson, 2015; Maley, 2018a). Ministers' offices have their own unique policy resources, for instance, where their more detailed knowledge of files and proximity to policy communities outside of government are particularly influential (Maley, 2015; Craft, 2016). New Zealand and the United Kingdom feature much smaller ministerial offices, often with only one adviser supporting ministers in a policy sense, and often that is constrained by other obligations to ministers.

A growing body of empirical evidence from all of the cases points convincingly to advisers as consequential PAS participants. Their salience as sources of policy advice and active participation in policy-making with an array of government and non-governmental policy actors within their respective PAS is well documented (Shaw and Eichbaum, 2010b; Gains & Stoker, 2011; LSE GV314 Group, 2012; Maley, 2015; Craft, 2016, 2018). From a PAS dynamics perspective, the impact of advisers has been most prominently linked to their role as a politicising force.

Australian Ministers' Offices

There is little doubt of the impact of advisers on the contemporary Australian PAS, as Tiernan and Weller (2010) note 'the emergence of ministerial staffers as central players within Australia's system of government is arguably the most significant change since 1981 when they barely rated a mention in *Can ministers cope?*' (Tiernan and Weller 2010, 253). The offices are large and stratified, featuring junior and senior partisan advisers, but in Australia more are tasked with explicit policy functions that can span departmental policy files, the core executive and outside of government (Maley, 2011, 2015; Ng, 2018). Ministers' advisers have been seen as influential policy players, in part because they are housed along with ministers in the Parliament House, which is physically separated from departments and DPMC (Tiernan, 2007; Maley, 2011). One key change has been the degree to which ministers are drawing on seconded public servants to help staff their offices. While Australian ministers' offices are often presented as partisan and separate, there is a long tradition of employing secondees from the public service. As Maley (2018a) reports, however, this trend has declined, with approximately only 20 per cent of advisers in 2016 being seconded public servants, down from 70 per cent during the Keating years (1991–6). This may reflect a professionalisation of available alternatives, namely partisan advisers, a reluctance of public servants to serve as secondees or shifting preferences for ministers.

Advisers interviewed pointed to a mix of written and verbal policy advice, but the emphasis seemed to be on verbal briefs. In sharp contrast to the experience in the Canadian case, some advisers reported that briefs went directly to ministers and were not quality controlled by the chief of staff. The logic was that it reduced bottlenecks, allowing responses to be generated from the ministers quickly, with clarification or supplemental briefs if required, and the chief of staff coordinating and managing items after ministerial input – on the way out rather than on the way in (A11, A12). Another PAS consequence for the larger ministerial offices in Australia is a greater role for advisers in dealing with key policy stakeholders and communities outside of government. Empirical evidence points to a greater coordination and brokerage function played by larger ministerial offices in both Australia and Canada (Maley, 2011; Craft, 2016). Whether this is still the case, however, remains unknown given the lack of systematic Australian data. In New Zealand or the United Kingdom, the empirical record is more mixed (LSE GV314 Group, 2012). One adviser explained that the work of advisers was about progress-chasing to a large degree and that relations with the public service soured when advisers had to step in aggressively to ensure departments were moving forward on key policy files. As the adviser put it:

You get some attitude from a lot of people in public service that goes, ministers' offices all interfere, they should keep their hands out of things. They should trust the public service. Most of the work we do is actually saving you from yourselves. We're making sure that you achieve what you're supposed to achieve. When the government announces something, they don't expect that four years later you're still working out how it might be delivered, which is where they'd wind up if they weren't pushed all the time. (A10)

New Zealand Ministers' Offices

NZ is distinguished by its much later adoption of ministerial advisers. It also differs in that it was more ad hoc and heterogeneous than the other cases, with some ministers opting to not use partisan advisers at all until the mid-1990s (Eichbaum and Shaw, 2007; Ng, 2018; Shaw and Eichbaum, 2018b). Minority parliaments and coalitions became the norm following the introduction of the proportional electoral system in 1996, which lead to more formal use of advisers to attend to the brokerage and coordination of policy and political matters. Partisan advisers have consistently been found to engage in more managerial and operational functions than those of their Westminster cousins, given the needs of policy negotiations and coalition maintenance within the legislative and executive arenas (Eichbaum and Shaw, 2007, 2008; Ng, 2018; Shaw and Eichbaum, 2018). A good deal of empirical research on New Zealand helps shed light on recent practice with advisers. Detailed analysis including interviews and surveys concluded that ministerial advisers 'provide a (healthy and appropriate) element of contestability into policy formulation. Advisers enhance the policy process by broadening the advice base, increasing ministers' options, testing officials' (Eichbaum and Shaw, 2007, 457). They however point to the potential risks that these new PAS actors pose – particularly for interfering with the ability of officials to provide frank and fearless advice to ministers. Initial analysis of a survey conducted in 2017 suggests that these risks have in fact become more pronounced. Respondents (all public servants) reported greater agreement that advisers did not promote free and frank advice within the system, and almost half of respondents agreed that in some cases they prevented that advice from reaching ministers (Eichbaum and Shaw, 2018, Shaw and Eichbaum, 2020). The New Zealand interviews we carried out indicated that ministerial advisers were performing a gatekeeping function. As one minister put it, this is '[b]ecause they both know what I'm not going to allow through. They are the first port of call: they'll look at what might be a draft cabinet paper before it even gets to me as a draft cabinet paper and say actually that's not going to work, you're going to have to change the language over there because our minister is not going to go for that' (N3).

Ministers use advisers for different purposes. Those interviewed in New Zealand in 2018 tended to either rely heavily on advisers for substantive policy advice or to play more of an active role in the intra-executive coalition management. Advisers were described as an important first set of eyes on cabinet papers and active players in the department files. Their political added value was in coordinating information with other advisers, particularly those in the offices of coalition partners to ensure political issues were identified and addressed before items went to cabinet, and in ensuring sufficient legislative support existed for policy work that required legislation. There was simply too much volume for advisers to be able to engage meaningfully on most cabinet papers. They caught what they could, but it was almost always a matter of a quick scribble, often on a sticky note placed on a document. Several ministers made it clear that their advisers were important sources of advice, particularly in terms of their ability to marry the political contexts with knowledge of the policy development within the public service. Many flagged the importance of the trust that existed with advisers, given their political orientations and appointed status that distinguished them from officials or those outside. As one minister from the Ardern government put it:

We have much more candid conversations, too-ing and fro-ing. To challenge my conversations with others, their advice gets more weight, more weight than my private secretaries, the department, anybody else inside this ivory tower really. They probably get more weight than my ministerial colleagues because they've got all the parts of the puzzle that I've got to try and think about to come to a decision. (N3)

That minister made it clear that her adviser was used to talk through and contest policy options and to work through cabinet papers. Other ministers stated that advisers were mostly engaged in the brokerage and coalition politics inside the executive. One partisan adviser with several years of experience in a variety of portfolios explained that policy advice was 'almost all from officials. And in my experience the adviser's role was certainly not about bringing your own views or experience but in helping be the conduit between the minister and those departmental advisers' (N5). The small size of the ministerial offices was a clear theme in discussions with both advisers and ministers. Senior ministers with massive portfolios might have two advisers and two press secretaries, with more junior ministers having a single adviser. The volume of policy work coming from the department was high, with advisers trying their best to flag and triage priority policy or political files with the rest getting whatever oversight advisers could muster. Partisan advisers in New Zealand, like their Australian counterparts and the Cameron-era advisers, also spent considerable time dealing with coalition politics. When asked to sum up what their role was, an adviser explained that it was:

A second pair of eyes and flagging it and just helping deal with the volume of stuff was really critical. With the political stuff, maybe like 20 per cent. And a lot of it is that coordination role, sorting out problems with other offices so that it doesn't become a problem for ministers because our role was to make their job as smooth as possible. So, if there was a problem between the two agencies, can it be sorted out before ministers have to get them to the cabinet committee room or the cabinet room and have an argument? (N5)

Canadian Ministers' Offices

In Canada, advisers have become more pronounced participants in formal cabinet preparations and processes, in some cases speaking at cabinet meetings themselves[3] (Craft, 2016). In contrast, while active in the cabinet papers process and cabinet committees, the New Zealand experience is that PMO advisers rarely attend, if at all, and it is unheard of for ministers' office partisan advisers to attend cabinet. Studies demonstrate Canadian advisers are actively engaged in PAS, often involving formal policy instruments around cabinet and its committee system. These offices are still dramatically larger than those of New Zealand or the United Kingdom. Contemporary studies have long identified advisers as influential policy actors who are able to influence policy administration. Analysis of Harper-era advisers suggests they were engaged in a full spectrum of policy work, increasing ministers' policy capacity and greater public service (Wilson, 2016a; Craft, 2017). Harper-era advisers engaged in policy advising in four principal ways: (1) working with officials during the development of their policy advice in an iterative and ongoing fashion; (2) providing formal written partisan-political policy advice as an overlay to formal departmental policy advice or that of stakeholders; (3) engaging with stakeholders during the development of policy advice and related to its partisan political and administrative-technical aspects; and (4) providing oral advice to the minister on any or all of the above (Craft, 2016).

While the Liberal Trudeau government elected with a large majority in 2015 was slow in staffing its offices upon election, they have seen modest expansions in numbers. They remain active policy players with policy teams structured in the same way as in the previous government. A chief of staff has overall advisory responsibility, but a director of policy takes the lead on policy matters, empowered by a few partisan advisers who typically manage and monitor a small number of specific policy files. There has been continued use of formal written briefing systems in ministers' offices as well, which, together with organisational continuity, suggests a stable institutional change to PAS after a change in party. From a PAS perspective, the Canadian case suggests a considerable reliance on ministerial partisan advisers not only to further ministerial policy goals but also to serve as coordination and policy relevant information feeders for the PMO. One adviser explained, '[T]tere's absolutely nothing that goes directly to the minister. Everything is reviewed before it goes up to him. Nothing goes to him if a staffer isn't able to talk about it' (C8). When asked to speak about advisers' work on formal policymaking, the adviser explained:

This has been done through basically any memorandum to cabinet [MC], which is the vehicle that we use in government to implement decisions or to bring some files to cabinet. The staff reviewed all the [MCs], and I mean we reviewed basically every word, every sentence. We changed the [MCs] quite often; we deleted paragraphs and all that stuff. We allowed ourselves to do it. I'm not sure it was greatly appreciated by the civil servants, but considering what they were sending us, it was needed (C8).

Others interviewed offered similar responses and echo essentially the situation under the Harper administration (Craft, 2016). The public service was seen as capable and professional, but at times advisers would push back either on questions of quality or on questions of the alignment of the policy work with the expected policy directions of the minister and the government. Relations between public servants and political advisers were for the most part appropriate, with exceptions and particular tensions around communications and message control, particularly under the Harper government (Robson and Wilson, 2018).

United Kingdom Ministers' Offices

The United Kingdom is the outlier, in part due to the hybrid nature of the ministers' 'private offices' that feature civil service and political appointees. These offices vary in size and complement, but typically they are headed by a career civil servant, a principal private secretary (PPS), and staffed by a number of other career civil servants, six or seven private secretaries, and perhaps a subject-matter expert on secondment from a department, plus a few administrative staff to keep the ship running. The political appointees are limited to two, three in exceptional circumstances (Paun, 2013). It is the latter category that is the focus here. The United Kingdom has demonstrated some variance and experimentation through ministers, like Brown at Treasury, who in 1997 created the Council of Economic Advisers to expand his preferred cadre of political appointees, including an expanded special adviser complement, who were widely known to exert considerable influence with Treasury on his behalf (Corry, 2011; Paun, 2013; Seldon and Lodge, 2013). Later, the Cameron coalition would see high-profile minister Francis Maude look to reform ministerial offices by increasing their capacity. This was sought through various initiatives designed to increase contestability in the PAS. These included the creation of expanded ministerial offices (EMOs) and a Contestable Policy Fund specifically designed to increase external advisory inputs into PAS for ministerial priority files, neither of which had much take-up in government (Diamond, 2017; Blick, 2018).

There is extensive empirical evidence confirming active policy advisory roles for UK partisan advisers. The Institute for Government *Ministers Reflect* series provides a comprehensive set of interviews with recent UK ministers and features several reflections on the important policy functions of UK advisers. A sample will suffice, with Secretary of State for Work and Pensions (2010–16) Ian Duncan Smith noting that 'good special advisers are worth their weight in gold' and offering great praise for the work of his senior special adviser in working through policy matters with the department, providing quality control and important shaping to policy with officials in the department and others across the PAS (Institute for Government, 2016). Other reports also note the heavy reliance on, and role of, advisers in, supporting ministers by providing a political lens, a second set of eyes on policy papers, and increasing contestability and coordination in the policy process (Hazell, 2012; Waller, 2014). A 2012 study based on surveys of just over 40 per cent of all advisers who served from 1997 to 2010 found they spent a considerable amount of time engaging in advisory and other policy design activity along with communications and to a lesser degree implementation and delivery activities (LSE GV314 Group, 2012). While they reported significant policy advisory and design activities, UK advisers also reported almost equal communications and political fixing activities, which were attributed by those interviewed to the small size and capacity of most ministerial offices, with only the larger ministers' offices benefiting from advisers with definitive specialisations (LSE GV314 Group, 2012, 9). The most up-to-date and comprehensive UK study of advisers depicts partisan advisers, who provide both advice and serve to increase contestation and coordination within PAS, as making a useful contribution, specifically to the policy process (Yong and Hazell, 2014). While some instances of gatekeeping and inappropriate overstepping are reported, their conclusion is that these are exceptions rather than the rule. This supports previous work highlighting the select but influential advisory system impact of UK advisers (Gains and Stoker, 2011; Gruhn and Slater, 2012; Hazell, 2012; Blick, 2018).

Interviews conducted with May-era advisers support such findings. As with the accounts from No 10 advisers, some ministers' offices supplemented short written briefs or comments on departmental submissions with verbal advising or used WhatsApp to skirt access-to-information regimes. As in New Zealand, the use of WhatsApp texting on matters of policy and politics was reported to involve ministers and their partisan advisers as well as interactions with No 10. Technology was seen as a way to improve convenience for busy ministers and save advisers time in chasing down diary time with ministers but also in providing encrypted and safe channels to have rolling briefs and updates with ministers. Advisers in the UK case reported uneven capacity for policy advice within departments, often speaking highly of individual civil servants but bemoaning the capacity of the department as a whole to provide high-quality policy advice in a timely fashion. One May-era adviser said:

[T]here are some very, very good civil servants and they're relatively far and few between, and I think there's a culture in this country ... [of] promoting people out of poor performance in the civil service. Which means there are often some very, very good civil servants actually at relatively junior levels, but there's layers of bureaucracy management, which can be very frustrating, and obfuscatory in the way in which they operate, rather than accountable and proactive. (UK5)

PAS seemed to work relatively well in terms of the interactions between ministers' offices and departments, and it was clear that, as in Australia and Canada, UK advisers were able to be gatekeepers and ensure quality control over what made its way to ministers. Advisers explained this was often to ensure volume was kept manageable but also that they performed a political triage function. One May-era adviser explained: 'In some ways my most effective lever was just to stop things going to the secretary of state. If something came up, a policy that I felt was perhaps, had its heart in the right place but would just be incredibly difficult to implement, and would cause an unnecessary political row I would just say no. I guess sometimes the civil service would push back and ask for reasons in which case I would kind of explain reasons but often I didn't have to' (UK6).

Conclusion: Comparative Analysis and PAS Implications

Westminster variation is quickly apparent when looking at how prime ministers organise and staff their own offices and their advisory functions. This is in part stylistic and reflects the preferences for individual prime ministers and ministers in how they want to use their advisers. It also reflects tensions in how the political office fits within the broader constellation of central agencies tasked with supporting prime ministers as individuals and cabinets as collective decision-making bodies (Craft and Wilson, 2018; Weller, 2018). In many ways the use of advisers helps to understand the flexibilities and rigidities around how political and administrative boundaries are drawn and enforced and how first ministers organise their support structures to suit their particular needs. In practice, the Canadian PMO is completely staffed by partisan appointees, while Australia, New Zealand and the United Kingdom have included a mix of public servants and partisan advisers in their policy units and in some cases have seen chiefs of staff seconded from both public service and political appointees (see Ng, 2018; Shaw and Eichbaum, 2018).[4] Comparatively, the Canadian PMO has been more centralised with the ability to command public service and political resources and levers, including the nearly exclusive support of the Privy Council Office (Dahlstrom et al., 2011; Craft, 2016). Australian PMOs are similar, often featuring internal policy capacity, and have been led by chiefs of staff who were at times seconded public servants, while in other times they have been partisans who take on a variety of roles depending on the prime minister and political contexts (Rhodes and Tiernan, 2014b; Weller, 2018). No 10 in Britain has featured the most institutional experimentation, with prime ministers using various combinations of civil servants and partisan advisers in specialised units dealing with policy, strategy, and 'delivery' or implementation units (Blick, 2018; Maley, 2018a). New Zealand's PMO is staffed exclusively by partisan advisers and engages much more selectively on matters of policy given its smaller complement but also given the importance of coalition politics and management.

Prime ministers' chiefs of staff are the most influential advisers in all four cases. With the exception of New Zealand, PMOs feature policy teams or 'shops' of various sizes and policy capabilities over time. On this front, despite the Canadian PMO being the largest overall, recent Australian PMOs have featured the greatest number of partisan advisers who are engaged on policy matters, followed by Canada and then the United Kingdom, with New Zealand featuring the least partisan-political capacity at the centre. The United Kingdom is an outlier in that it is a hybrid, including a mix of political appointees and career civil servants working within a single policy unit. PMO advisers' influence is positional and relational, flowing from their access to prime minister and cabinet, central agencies, and the unique policy resources and levers available to first ministers in charting the organisation and policy priorities of government (Craft, 2016; Weller, 2018).

Australia and Canada demonstrate more complex PAS interactions in part simply due to the greater number, policy-specific nature and hierarchical distribution of advisers, particularly in ministers' offices. In contrast, the United Kingdom demonstrates a much more constrained use, with some latitude having been experienced in prime ministerial preferences regarding how to organise advisers in No 10. This degree of constraint may explain why there have been other modes of change potentially driven by lower levels of discretion for ministers in interpreting the rules and practices around advisers within PAS, and stronger regimes governing advisers' functions within PAS. In particular, the granting of formal executive authority to advisers in No 10 represents a significant departure from Westminster tradition. In contrast, New Zealand features significant latitude for interpretation with a much later institutionalisation of formal rules governing advisers and, as noted in this chapter, a weaker contemporary regime governing their role as a force in the executive. New Zealand also demonstrates a much slower overall pace and a heterogeneous mix of advisers in ministers' offices.

The differences in the rules governing advisers' complements and functions along with how PAS have gradually evolved have implications for how advisers figure in PAS. Most are prominently related to their ability to provide contestation and coordination within and around the core executives. In all cases it is clear that prime ministers' offices have become influential players, though those of Australia and Canada seem to have the strongest partisan policy capacities while that of the United Kingdom features more variation depending on the prime minister and a uniquely hybrid mix of civil service and partisan advisers. The smaller ministers' offices in NZ and the United Kingdom suggest a more modest ability to cover policy files in ministers' offices and a more mixed functional use for advisers that consists of communications, policy and political functions on behalf of ministers. Australia and Canada's expansive ministerial policy teams and a more formalised advisory role through both written and oral advisory briefings suggest a greater propensity for advisers to engage in these activities and contribute to PAS that is more partisan-political in its orientation (Craft, 2018; Maley, 2018b).

6 | Alternative Advice from within Government

Government outside the core consists of congeries of organisations sharing some common features which contrast with those of ministerial departments. The difference between inner government – the home of the department of state and its minister and staff – and the rest of government is explicit in one organisational sense. The latter has been the location of an array of agencies that are either primarily concerned not with policy but with delivery, operations or regulation or are detached from the constraints of public service rules and ministerial authority. The several arenas within government but outside the core are defined by this insulation from ministerial control where professionals and technical specialists can work on matters usually outside the main policy mainstream that often have low political profiles. The organisations located here fall into three categories: arms-length authorities that exist as dependent appendages within a ministers' portfolio but are not a focus in this chapter; agencies designed to be largely immune from political influence; and ad hoc review arrangements for providing advice.

This chapter focuses on those units outside the core which are used for different policy advisory purposes. Some have substantial to high degrees of independence, while others may be at the beck and call of ministers. The spectrum ranges from bodies that are exclusively located within government with permanent standing through to those which exist under ad hoc arrangements that may include external actors and are transient. Alternative advice from within government is therefore distinguished by whether it is solicited or not, the former covering advice commissioned by government or ministers (e.g. task forces or tsars). The latter is about whether and how the unit is influential for policy. The distinction can be restated as between organisations according to the degree of direct or indirect influence on government.

For PAS, the main questions centre on which advisory units have been influential, in what ways they have been changing, and whether it is possible to generalise about trends that are evident. There are indicators that the use of alternative sources has been expanding. Governments have been looking for instruments providing timely expert advice that either incorporate wider interests and/or provide a means for canvassing and digesting a broader range of viewpoints. New clusters of advisory capacity have emerged, which are not dependent on governments and can therefore contribute to policy debate independently. This means that while governments can shift the sourcing of advice from one arena to another, it cannot necessarily shift it between arenas in the 'within-government category' apart from variations in the choice of instrument. A rationale for seeking advice outside the politicised core (covered in Chapters 4 and 5) is to depoliticise it. However, much depends on which experts are chosen and the extent of their detachment from government. This problem was solved by one of the most controlling prime ministers of the twenty-first century, Canada's Harper, who chose to have only one commission of inquiry in a ten-year period (Inwood and Jones, 2018).

This chapter analyses three categories of alternative policy advice within government. The first consists of policy advisory agencies that are largely independent of government. Second are agencies that report to parliament rather than the executive and are independent of the latter. Third, there are ad hoc entities that operate as extensions to government and comprise a spectrum of inquiry forms appointed by ministers and government often with public service secretariats.[1] Each of these spheres has experienced major changes with implications for the policy advisory system. The dynamics of change for the three are quite complex and not readily explicable, although depoliticisation and politicisation are factors. Arms-length bodies may expand and contract according to fashions (quangoisation or bonfires), political control processes or rationalisation under austerity. The focus here is on several non-departmental agencies with whole-of-government purviews and significant emergent agencies. The institutionalisation of several types of independent standing bodies specialising in fiscal analysis and productivity or law and human rights has also been of growing importance. Parliamentary committees or agencies responsible to parliament, such as the audit office and the budget office, have reflected the renaissance of parliaments in their greater activity whether through legislative reviews or policy investigations. A major trend with ad hoc inquiries has been towards freeing up governments from a reliance on highly formal and independent public reviews. Ministers and governments favour more flexible instruments of inquiry and review that operate in the medium term. The expansion and contraction of these sources of advice within PAS have occurred over time and have varied between countries and points in election cycles, but the broad trends have been similar and reflect patterns discussed elsewhere in the book, in particular politicisation.

Staying inside Government

A standard approach to political control is for the reach of ministers to be reduced or contained using agencies that are deliberately at arm's length. There are also other managerial reasons why authorities are detached. It became fashionable in the United Kingdom to depict the creation of quangos as being evidence of depoliticisation (Flinders, 2008).

Politicisation is being used in the sense of increases and extensions to the control and influence of the minister. The effect on ministers' departments was discussed in Chapter 4. This also applies to non-departmental organisations relevant here that are brought under ministerial control. The long-term trend has been towards merging them, absorbing them within departments or abolishing them, as well as extending them under austerity measures to include minor advisory committees of experts in Australia (Halligan, 2016). A case was the recommendations of the Uhrig inquiry (Uhrig, 2003) in Australia, which produced only two templates: ministerial control and board control for all non-departmental organisations. The reincorporation of the United Kingdom executive agencies in departments is another case (Talbot and Johnson, 2007; Elston, 2014). While these various bodies are not primarily policy advising, many do have a policy function.

The second application of politicisation pertains to the use of inquiry forms over which ministers have considerable control. These are short-to medium-term ad hoc investigations of policy issues with ministers appointing reviews or panels, and reporting may be direct to the minister. These can in some cases be regarded as depoliticisation, in the sense of venue-shifting of 'hot' policy issues to advisory committees and groups to provide government distance. More independent reviews still occur, but they are less often used except for specific inquiries into issues that ministers wish to keep at a distance and which may have little policy significance.

The third effect occurs by default. Because many central departments have been largely emptied of expertise, the capability must be found elsewhere, either beyond the public sector (Chapter 7) or in specialised agencies that undertake work previously done in departments. This can be regarded as a displacement within government, as external appointments to inquiries and reviewers take on work that public servants might have performed.

Ad Hoc Inquiries and Standing Review Bodies as Alternatives for Advice

Despite a common lineage – the historical forms used in the United Kingdom – and diffusion of principles and approaches to inquiries among anglophone countries, contextual factors still matter, and variations in terminology and practice abound. Disentangling the different types of inquiry and review that have operated as extensions of the core of government is therefore challenging, even more so in aligning them across the four countries. Others have observed that it is something of a quagmire, the most universal observation being that it is impossible to have clarity over the different types of inquiry (Prasser, 2006; Banks, 2015; Stewart and Prasser, 2015), although recent modernisation and rationalisations of terminology and operating principles in several countries has been helpful.

Different types of inquiry are involved, ranging from highly formalised and more independent to informal (and political) arrangements. Different uses may be made of specific forms of advice (e.g. the United Kingdom's policy tsars, where ministers operate in less formalised and accountable ways). There is, however, assistance with understanding the inquiry process from official sources. The New Zealand nomenclature is clear but still complex, with eleven options for a formal inquiry differentiated under six different 'mandates' (ranging from general government inquiries to reviews by specific agencies and parliament to the responsible minister). Public inquiries, below the most formalised, are where problems with classification and significance arise. There is provision for the 'ministerial inquiry', which requires the prime minister's approval, and for the 'independent working group', for experts reviewing a technical issue and for which the minister is responsible (DIA, 2018). The equivalents of these categories elsewhere are highly diverse.

The units of advice may be advisory or investigative, a basic distinction that has a broad application, and may be officially used for inquiries or applied to analysis of parliamentary committees. The mode of proceeding may be essentially retrospective, entailing a judgement about what has occurred, or prospective, involving an inquiry that is looking forward. A third feature is the degree of specificity: how narrow or broad is the inquiry? The powers and procedures vary with different forms, being most explicit for commissions of inquiry (Manson and Mullan, 2003a; Prasser, 2006; Caird, 2016; Cowie and Sandford, 2018).

In these days of many players, a one-to-one connection – i.e. a direct communication between the unit and minister – may be improbable. Determining the influence of advisory units is often difficult unless an explicit acknowledgement of their role can be established. Governments may or may not accept key recommendations of an advisory unit for political reasons (the bane of a productivity commission) or accept recommendations but not act on them (Banks, 2012).

These categories can be regarded as being located in different arenas with different expectations and patterns of influence. A key question is whether they are permanent or ad hoc bodies, although records on the latter are not necessarily available. Reviews and inquiries generally derive from government decisions. However, the origins of many are quite complex, including the creation of an officer of parliament. The parliamentary budget office (PBO) may derive from fallout from a corruption scandal (e.g. Canada's PBO was established following the Gomery report) or from a coalition deal between parties and independents (Australia).

The extent of political influence varies between the different arenas, being very high for government reviews, usually low for agencies of parliament (with the exception of some parliamentary committees), and variable for specialist agencies where they are required to accept commissions (although their reports may be quite independent) (Table 6.1).

The PAS in the four countries cover the three basic categories and most types within two of them, the exceptions being indicated in Table 6.2.

Table 6.1 *Types of review and inquiry agencies and accountability*

	Govt/minister commission advice	Independence	Responsible to
Government reviews			
Commissions of inquiry (incl. royal)	Yes	High	Govt
Government/ministerial inquiry	Yes	Mixed	Govt/Min.
Policy tsar	Yes	Variable	Minister
Independent review	Yes	Variable	Minister
Parliament			
Select/standing committee	Possible	Variable	Parliament
Auditor General	No[*]	High	Parliament
Parliamentary budget office (or IFI)	No	High	Parliament
Specialist agencies			
Law Commission (& other agencies)	Yes	Variable	Govt/public
Productivity commission	Possible	Variable	Govt/public

[*] Provision for 'requests' may exist.

Public Inquiries

The public inquiry instrument was inherited from Britain (Hoole, 2014, 335). Royal commissions followed by commissions of inquiry have topped the inquiry pyramid (Simpson, 2014, 317), the 'royal' signifying an inquiry of sufficient importance to be singled out for greater formality, 'reserved for the most serious matters of public importance', whereas the commission of inquiry has less prestige and is reserved for less serious questions (DIA, 2018). There are differences between countries as to whether they have a statutory basis (e.g. powers to require witnesses to attend). A distinction is also made between this top tier and a second focused on the ministerial level. Legislative modifications have occurred in some jurisdictions to recognise this preference for processes that are less encumbered.

Table 6.2 *Government reviews and specialist inquiry agencies: use by country*

	AU	CA	NZ	UK
Government reviews				
Royal commission	√	√	√	√
Commission of inquiry	√	√	√*	√
Government/ministerial inquiry	√	√	√	√
Policy tsar	–	–	–	√
Independent review**	√	√	√	√
Parliament				
Select/standing committee	√	√	√	√
Auditor General	√	√	√	√
Parliamentary budget office***	√	√	?	√
Specialist agencies				
Law Commission	√	–	√	√
Productivity commission	√	–	√	–

* Equivalent called a public inquiry.
** Independent reviews may fit into other categories.
*** Independent fiscal institution in the United Kingdom.

A distinction is made frequently between advisory and investigative inquiries that address events including crises. In Canada, the first has a broad mandate, and the second is more specific and focused (Privy Council Office, 2018) and between broad and narrow policy. UK royal commissions were normally used for advising on broad policy questions (Caird, 2016). Where ministerial inquiries and independent reviews begin and end can be hazy. The relationship with ministers may sometimes be direct, but the public service frequently provides a secretariat or other forms of support. It is standard practice for policy coordination departments to provide support at the centre because of their expertise and experience with oversight (e.g. the Canadian Oliphant Inquiry). Classification is problematic because of inconsistent use of titles,[2] a common problem being that different forms of inquiry are 'often indistinguishable ... with regard to the nature of the investigation' (HC PAC, 2005, 67).

The more formalised and independent advisory units are generally non-partisan (although this may be more tenuous where an inquiry has been established for political capital) and this may apply to reviews undertaken at the direct behest of a minister. The level of independence is also relative as the terms of an inquiry – even a formal commission – may be changed or its existence terminated (Manson and Mullan, 2003b), and/or the functioning of a body reduced through budget cuts or curtailed through the withdrawal of funding (e.g. Canada's Law Commission and the Parliamentary Budget Office). A related matter is whether bodies are reactive or proactive (i.e. able to initiate their own inquiries). Ongoing bodies may be subject to government agenda-setting and/or free to conduct inquiries as they see fit.

Commissions of Inquiry

The distinction between royal commissions and commissions of inquiry is largely one of importance, prestige and whether the governor general is a signatory. The traditionally important royal commission was typically constituted to confront longer-term policy issues and crises and offered focused attention on complex policy questions (e.g. in Canada, Indigenous peoples, official languages and economic policy: Inwood, 2005). Such commissions also had something of a reputation for being used historically 'in most Westminster models as a means of procrastination' (Seymour-Ure, 1987, 178).

Two to four years used to be the average length for UK royal commissions (Caird 2016). Complex investigations and broad policy questions may still need multiple years. For instance, the Australian Royal Commission into Institutional Responses to Child Sexual Abuse (2013–17) took almost five years.

The long-term view indicates extensive use of the two types of commission. Australia had 132 royal commissions from 1902 to 2014; Canada averaged one or two commissions per year from 1957 to 1990); New Zealand recorded 222 commissions from 1909 to 2013; the United Kingdom averaged one royal commission per year from 1945 to 1975 and appointed more than 600 UK committees of inquiry of 'various levels of importance' between 1945 and 1970;[3] both categories have declined substantially since (Hoole, 2014; Inwood and Johns, 2014; Prasser and Tracey, 2014a; Simpson, 2014; Starr, 2014).

Overall there has been a marked decrease in the use of royal commissions and committees of inquiry as advisory inputs for government. All four countries have largely dispensed with them since the 1980s, as a result of a preference for managerialist and political alternatives, although they are still used occasionally. The use of royal commissions in Australia increased in the 1970s and 1980s before dropping off, which was associated with a change from focusing on general policy advice to inquisitorial inquiries into corruption, impropriety and maladministration (Prasser, 2006, 253). The recent exception to the trends in Table 6.3 is the revival of the royal commission in Australia during the 2010s, with seven being appointed, the main focus being sexual abuse, detention of children, quality of aged care, disability neglect, and misconduct in the banking and financial services. While the type of issue and the scale of the problem are key factors in choosing the royal commission, the failure of government structures is credited with generating this need (Hayne, 2019). The public impact has been such that discourse routinely refers to the need for a royal commission as the means to address important issues. The use of commissions of inquiry and royal commissions for the four countries is listed in Table 6.3 (noting the difficulties with calculating the numbers over time – see Hoole [2014] – and more generally with terminology). The UK public inquiries take several forms, and one set of figures available indicates twenty (1990s), thirty (2000s) and sixteen (2010–17) (Norris and Shepheard, 2017), and while commissions of inquiry feature, the degree of comparability with the others is unclear.

The results of inquiries have not been subject to much comparative analysis, although numerous case studies exist (Prasser, 2006; Inwood and Johns, 2014; Prasser and Tracey, 2014b). A small sample was

Table 6.3 *Royal commissions and commissions of inquiry at national level, 1960s–2010s*

| | Australia | | Canada | | New Zealand | | United Kingdom |
	CI	RC	CI	RC	CI	RC	RC
1960s	0	3	13	15	14	5	11
1970s	8	10	20	5	25	10	7
1980s	1	12	11	6	7	6	0
1990s	2	1	6	4	3	0	3
2000s	2	3	5	0	1	2	0
2010s	0	7	3	0	1	4	0

NB: By date of appointment. CI: commission of inquiry. RC: royal commission.
Main sources: Riddell and Barlow (2013); Parliament of Australia (2018); Privy Council Office (2018); Simpson (2018).

shown to perform several functions, including agenda setting, issue promotion and legitimising government action, and more generally the impact of inquiries on public policy was substantial (Prasser, 2006, 246–7, 251). Types of policy change have been examined, which indicated that some policy advisory commissions were 'transformative and direct' and others were marginal and limited (Inwood and Johns, 2016).

Other Types of Public Inquiry

The broader concept of 'public inquiry' may be used for inquiries appointed under ministerial authority. There have been 600 in Australia (1902–2014), soaring to peaks in the 1970s and 1980s and dropping off greatly since then.

The Australian public inquiries' characteristics include that they are ad hoc and temporary bodies established by the political executive (cabinet, prime minister or minister) with clear and public terms of reference. Most members are drawn from outside government and exclude current politicians. The inquiry is actively promoted publicly, and participation is sought via hearings, submissions and special approaches to groups. A public report is produced for the government.[4]

The independent review is a standard approach to obtaining expertise from outside government. The review is led by an external expert and usually assisted by a small panel. It is commonly a focused exercise in topic and time frame, although there are exceptions, and the term is used for a diverse range of exercises that may not be directly comparable either within or between countries (Appendix B). The word 'independence' is used ambiguously and may pertain to using outsiders who may exercise independent judgement in reaching their conclusions. However, contrast two 2019 cases (unresolved as this book goes to press): Amyas Morse, the former comptroller and auditor general of the National Audit Office (NAO), lead an independent review of the policy on loan charges in late 2019; and the Independent Review of the Australian Public Service that was appointed under one prime minister provided a much delayed report in 2019 to a different prime minister, with the contents repurposed to reflect the changing political context. The Australian report ended up being insufficiently independent to attract the respect of external observers and too independent for a politicising government that proceeded to act in disregard of central precepts.[5]

The New Zealand 'independent working group' is defined as follows: 'A technical matter or issue is reviewed by a group of experts.' It is commissioned by the responsible minister, examples giving a sense of the advisory options: Treasury Tax working group (2017), a high-level eleven-member group of mainly senior corporate and consultancy executives and chaired by a former minister; and the MBIE Film Industry working group (2018), a diverse membership of fifteen (DIA, 2018). New Zealand has also used 'high-profile' working groups of varying degrees of independence, which are sufficiently distant for governments to be able to respond selectively to recommendations (Shaw and Eichbaum, 2011, 180–2). According to ministers, external taskforces were commissioned for big questions because it was possible to specify 'clear Terms of Reference, with deliverables and timelines; they can make use of expertise from outside the public service; their report can be published to gauge public reaction; and their recommendations are distanced from the government, which may or may not implement them' (Scott, 2010, 27–8). Former public servants were often appointed who were highly knowledgeable of public policy.

Australian governments have tended to favour working groups usually with close associations with a servicing department, but pragmatism dictates the mechanism used. White papers may be organised through the Department of the Prime Minister and Cabinet or Treasury, with clearer political oversight. There continue to be departmental and cross-agency task forces of public servants and reviews with external panels of experts or interests.

Policy Tsars as Hybrids and Political Appointees

An alternative to expanding the use of political advisers in the PMO or ministers' offices is the appointment of policy tsars (Smith, 2011b; Levitt and Solesbury, 2012, 2013a). Among the anglophone countries, they are identified with the United Kingdom because of the prominent use of them for two decades.[6] A similar type of appointment occurs elsewhere but is not so readily identifiable and may be less directly bound to a minister.

A definition of a tsar is 'an individual from outside government who is publicly appointed by a government minister to advise on policy development or delivery on the basis of their expertise' (Levitt and Solesbury, 2012, 4). They are ministerial appointments and have mainly been

Table 6.4 *Rate of tsar appointments in the United Kingdom, 1997–2012*

UK government	Appointments (N)	Government duration (months)	Rate per annum
Labour 1997–2001	14	49	3
Labour 2001–5	45	47	11
Labour 2005–10	130	60	26
Coalition 2010–12	93	26	43
Total	282*	182	19

* Total exceeds 267 because the Coalition renewed some Labour appointments
Source: Levitt and Solesbury (2012, table 4).

external experts, although some have been serving MPs or ex-ministers. There were 267 UK appointments between 1997 and 2012 (Table 6.3), the annual rate of appointment increasing across four governments (Levitt and Solesbury, 2012, annex 1.1).[7] The figure rose to more than 100 for the Cameron coalition and around 300 by late 2013 (Levitt and Solesbury, 2013b). Tsars have been ad hoc and temporary appointments, the majority of whom (70 per cent) completed their task in less than twelve months; one-fifth took less than six months (see Table 6.4). Their advice is made directly to ministers, 'unmediated (at least formally) by officials', thereby providing them with a direct source of policy advice, although there were other, sometimes political, reasons for making appointments. Most were termed 'reviewer', and the remit of 83 per cent of tsars was 'to review a policy question', although all remits entailed provision of 'advice to ministers on aspects of policy'. That one half of the reviews took between six and twelve months to produce a report was regarded as attractive to ministers and 'usually faster than most advisory committees or contracted researchers or consultants' (Levitt and Solesbury, 2012, 23–4, 41–2, 47).

Ministers have used these appointments for policy advice in preference to internal advice from civil servants or the traditional alternative sources such as advisory committees and commissioned research and consultancies (Levitt and Solesbury, 2012, 14).

Other countries regularly use the independent review process for a range of issues, but the institutionalised basis appears to be less explicitly identified with ministers' policy advice, and the adviser role indeterminate.

The tsar appointments have produced several kinds of action, although 'the labels should be interpreted with caution as they are inevitably imprecise ... because tsars' remits vary so much ... and because the amount of detail about outcomes in the public domain varies enormously'. Also, sometimes there was no public response from the minister. Among the results, over 40 per cent produced policy change and about one-fifth led to a new organisation. The conclusions were that 'a significant proportion of tsar appointments seem to make a difference to policy and/or practice and/or the terms of public debate' (Levitt and Solesbury, 2012, 58, 60–1).

Parliamentary Inquiries

The inquiries of the parliament invariably mean its committees, plus those of agencies or offices of parliament who report to it. The latter range from as many as nine for Canada to three offices for New Zealand, with variations as to how agencies are so designated. The consideration here is confined to the oldest, the audit office, and newest, the budget office. The focus is on those committees, and the activities of the offices, that are prospective although retrospective work may have policy implications.

Select and Standing Committee Investigations

The growth of committee systems has been the most significant institutional development in modern Westminster-style parliaments. The creation of departmental select committees has been argued to be 'the most important parliamentary reform of the second half of the twentieth century' (Norton, 2005, 117). These parliamentary committees have gained an increasingly positive reputation because they permit the detailed investigation of matters and encourage debate about public policy. This role in stimulating debate has, traditionally, been confined to committee deliberations rather than committee outputs. Increasingly, however, conflict and dissent became a part not only of committee deliberations but also of committee reports. This has been evidenced in the Australian context, with a decline in the tradition of consensus reporting by parliamentary committees (Halligan et al., 2007; Halligan and Reid, 2016).

The rising significance of committees has been the focus of increasing studies both in Britain and other parliamentary systems (Halligan and Reid, 2016). The interest in Britain has centred on assessing the impact of parliamentary committees on the broader political landscape, in particular select committees (for example Hindmoor et al., 2009; Benton and Russell, 2013; Russell and Cowley, 2016) and also bill committees. Since the chairs of House of Commons select committees became elective positions in 2010, the chairs of twenty-one departmental and several scrutiny committees are voted on by a secret ballot of the House at the beginning of each parliament (Priddy, 2018).[8] The committees have since acquired greater salience (Dunleavy et al., 2018) and greater engagement in policy work. They had minor roles in agenda-setting and new policy ideas and were somewhat active in reacting to government proposals and reviewing progress with implementation (42 per cent) (Russell and Crowley, 2016, 132). Case studies reported more exploratory or blue-sky activity and prospective inquiries took up one-third of their time allocation (White, 2015, 10). Select committees have been judged to be an area where there is an explicit parliamentary contribution to 'detailed policy-making' (Dunleavy et al., 2018, 169).

In Australia, the influence of committee inquiries and reports has also been addressed (Holland, 2009; Monk, 2012), and an explosion of 'policy' reports occurred across three decades, from the 1970s to the 1990s (Halligan, Miller and Power, 2007). Detailed analysis of the policy roles of the Australian parliament indicates their significance for different facets of the policy process and that the Senate has been an active upper house in contributing to policy debates. Of the two most relevant investigative policy roles identified, review (reports that were either broad and retrospective or a prospective and narrow focus on specific agencies) and strategic (both broad and prospective with two components: systemic reviews of major proposed policy and agenda setting with the intention of taking a lead) together produced 493 reports and increasing numbers and proportions of total reports across the three decades (Halligan, Miller and Power 2007, 64–5, 274–5). The Canadian and New Zealand committee systems have registered less of an impact as sources of policy but for different reasons. Canada has been overshadowed by the negative reputation of the Senate as patronage-based, which belies the work undertaken by a few committees over time. Policy studies work has been a notable component of committee activity and has been expanding (Lawlor and Crandall, 2013). There are numerous examples of influential reports on the energy emissions crisis, euthanasia, aboriginal governance and mental health (Schofield and Fershau, 2007; Kirby and Segal, 2016; Glenn, 2018). New Zealand's committees acquired enhanced responsibilities, but they have concentrated on legislative review because of the automatic referral of bills, rather than investigations and reviews. One weakness is the neglect of the long term (Boston, Bagnall and Barry, 2019).

Parliamentary Budget Office

A common dynamic has been the institutionalisation of specific types of independent fiscal oversight agencies, a development influenced by their growth in OECD countries in response to the global financial crisis (von Trappe and Nicol, 2017), which added capacity and improved accountability. The two main models of independent fiscal institution are represented: the fiscal council (United Kingdom) and the parliamentary budget office (Australia and Canada). The former is more of a hybrid as an agency of the executive but subject also to parliament. Apart from the analysis of long-term fiscal sustainability, their functions are quite different: the United Kingdom's Office for Budget Responsibility (OBR) has a role in macroeconomic or fiscal forecasts and in monitoring compliance with fiscal rules, whereas the two PBOs support parliament with budget analysis and have a role in policy costing (plus, in Australia's case, costing election platforms) (von Trappe and Nicol, 2017).

The work of the PBO is essentially prospective and focused on parliamentary support. Canada's first Parliamentary Budget Officer (PBO) was appointed in 2008. Mandated through legislation, the general purpose of this office was to provide independent analysis to parliament about the financial position and economic trends. In practice the PBO–government relationship was confrontational, with accusations of PBO policy advocacy on the one hand and the government withholding of essential information on the other (Page, 2015; Zussman, 2015). Australia has had a Parliamentary Budget Office since 2012 (Bowen, 2016; Watt and Anderson, 2017). New Zealand is expected to have a PBO in 2020.

The United Kingdom established an Office for Budget Responsibility in 2010, under the executive but nevertheless largely independent and with a board. There is a dual basis to accountability with the House of Commons Treasury Committee appointing members. Its functions are the provision of official economic and official forecasts. Unlike similar think tanks (e.g. the Institute for Fiscal Studies) and private sector organisations, it can access government data (OECD Journal on Budgeting, 2015, 243–4; Keep, 2018).

This pattern points to a new advisory capacity designed explicitly to serve parliamentarians but independent of traditional public service channels. The impact of their reports is somewhat indeterminate, although the work of the office is highly regarded for independent advice (Watt and Anderson, 2017).

Office of the Auditor General

The auditor general in anglophone countries is an officer of the parliament who reports to a public accounts committee. Most audit reports used to be retrospective and concerned with financial compliance. However, under modernisation, audit bodies in anglophone countries have become 'explicit instruments of public management reform with a key role in monitoring the activities of the state'. As a result of NPM pressures, 'auditing in its various forms became a policy instrument . . . extending its reach beyond the traditional mandate of verification to encompass and operationalise ideals of cost effectiveness, efficiency and . . . effectiveness' (Power, 2005, 329).

The growth of audits and the influence of audit offices has been associated with the addition of performance (or value for money) audits to the traditional financial fare. Prospective reviews with explicit policy implications may be regularly produced, the most active body being the United Kingdom's National Audit Office (an example being observations on the government's spending review, November 2018; see CAG, 2018). In some cases, an audit office may be requested to initiate an inquiry.

Standing Policy Advisory Bodies within Government

The experience of policy advisory bodies has been chequered and dependent on their statutory basis. Even this does not ensure independence. More prominent in the past, the longevity of these bodies is often dependent on changes of government, new priorities and the politics of advice. A standard tactic is to reduce or freeze funding and, in times of austerity, to abolish them or merge or absorb them in departments (Halligan, 2016). The variable pattern is apparent in the United Kingdom, with new bodies emerging (e.g. the Independent Commission on Aid Impact, which scrutinises spending and provides evidence-based advice), while other expert advisory bodies were abolished (Rutter, 2013, 41). A case in point is the Canadian National Round Table on the Environment and the Economy, which was shuttered in the 2012 budget after twenty-five years as an independent policy advisory agent to the government (Zussman, 2015). It was no longer required because it was unaligned with the government's aversion to a carbon tax.

Permanent bodies take on briefs (self-generated or otherwise) that might otherwise have to be referred to separate review processes. These bodies generate their own references, although they may also receive them from elsewhere. The bodies addressed here have a pronounced prospective character to their inquiries, as exemplified by the productivity commission.

Productivity Commissions

Special advisory bodies often combine official funding with an arm's-length relationship, and their advice is influential even if not necessarily accepted. Both Australia (from 1998)[9] and New Zealand (from 2011) have a productivity commission that provides independent advice to government on microeconomic policy and regulation. The Australian commission can initiate inquiries but, like New Zealand's commission, generally works on referrals from government. The impact of their advice is variable, although commissions responding to government briefs may be more influential.

The Australian commission's purpose is to contribute to improving policy of long-term benefit, and its significance derives both from its role in advising the government and informing parliament and the community, and from operating on an arm's-length basis through transparent processes (Banks, 2011), although a standing body. Its inquiries 'share the ad hoc and once-off character of royal commissions and other inquiries in relation to topics' (Banks, 2013, 13). The government regularly refers matters for investigation, an example being the Mental Health Review (2018). About two-thirds of its recommendations were accepted by government and 'more or less' implemented (Banks, 2012).

Regardless of their source, the NZ commission has addressed major policy issues. In contrast, Canada prefers to work through in-house institutions and advisory units, primarily the Department of Finance, and ad hoc committees of eminent Canadians.

Law Commissions

All four countries have had independent law commissions, the original being in the United Kingdom (1965) followed by Canada (1971), Australia (1975) and New Zealand (1986).[10] One commission has been subject to divided political preferences. The Law Reform Commission of Canada was dissolved in 1992, re-established as the Law Commission of Canada in 1996 and abolished in 2006. The commissions have independent standing as non-departmental agencies with the primary function of providing advice to government. Matters may be referred by the minister of justice (or equivalent) or issues identified, and inquiries initiated, by the commission. Recommendations are made to both the government and parliament.

The commissions monitor and analyse laws with regard to keeping them modern, up-to-date and accessible. They may conduct research, conduct public consultations, and publish papers and reports. Advice is provided on specific matters for law reform and how to respond to significant issues of the day (e.g. victims of family violence).

A range of other standing agencies conduct inquiries that produce policy advice, although that is not necessarily their primary or sole purpose. One notable case is the human rights commission, which exists in all four countries on a statutory basis, Canada's and New Zealand's being established in 1977, the others in 1986 (Australia) and 2007 (United Kingdom). Their operations are independent of government and are responsible for promoting human rights and enforcing anti-discrimination. Public inquiries are conducted by commissions from Australia on, inter alia, children in immigration detention and homeless children; the UK on the state of equality and human rights; and NZ on human rights.

The point has already been made that 'independence' is relative for these bodies, which may or may not have control over agenda-setting and depend on governments to implement their recommendations.

Comparative data does not appear to be available about the impact of their recommendations. The politics around many issues means that the recommendations of hard-nosed economists do not get endorsement of, say, tax reform proposals. Governments can simply ignore recommendations or propose another process that plays to the politics of an issue.[11]

Patterns and Variations: Advisory Units and Policy Advisory Systems

Looking across the four policy advisory systems the patterns are similar (Table 6.5). The trends have been towards reduced use of highly independent, formal ad hoc inquiries in favour of more flexible quasi-independent and often politically influenced reviews, plus selected new independent ongoing review bodies.

Independence is of course relative, with numerous inquiries carrying that name or assigned that quality, whereas independent agencies have more control over the review process and the release of reports to the public. Those associated with parliament have arguably the most independence, and the designation of officers of parliament reinforces this status, although the executive may still exercise influence through its control of funding (a notable case being the auditor general).

Within the 'internal' category there is a common pattern of deinstitutionalisation of types of advisory units: the royal commission is the best example although not yet extinct as an option (but note the spike in Australia in the 2010s). Similarly, use of the commission of inquiry has slumped since the 1970s, and it plays a negligible role today in several jurisdictions. The exceptions are clear with new specialised agencies.[12]

There are also variations in anglophone systems in the significance of advisory sources from within government. While it has been asserted that Australian public inquiries have become more extensive and acquired features that differ from other systems (Prasser, 2006, 254), there is considerable convergence with such inquiries.

In some cases, specialised agencies have displaced departments that no longer had research units or specialist analytical capacity because of cutbacks and the rise of the generalist. The Australian Productivity Commission is instanced as being able 'to extend its influence into

Table 6.5 *Trends in government policy reviews and inquiries and specialised bodies*

Government reviews	
Royal commissions	Decline overall since 1980s, more so in two countries
Commissions of inquiry	Decline with the exception of the United Kingdom
Government inquiry	Extensively used
Ministerial inquiries	Extensively used
Policy tsars	Confined to one country's active use since 1990s
Independent review	Prolific
Parliament	
Parliamentary committees	Of significance in two; lesser roles otherwise
Auditor general	Revamped extensive role with policy implications & impact
Parliamentary budget office	New type of review organisation; institutionalised
Specialised agencies	
Law Commission	Active roles in three; intermittent historic role in one
Productivity commission	New type of review organisation; institutionalised

areas of policy that in earlier years would have been jealously guarded by responsible departments' (Banks, 2014, 115). Many inquiries are extensions of government departments where they are involved in a process that accords legitimacy to policy directions. The capability loss experienced by departments is partially retrieved through the inquiry.

The use of commissions of inquiry has been subject to the preferences of prime ministers (Prasser, 2006), Thatcher's disinclination towards royal commissions accounting for the absence of this form in the United Kingdom in the 1980s. The Australian government revived royal commissions for complex social issues in the 2010s, but public utterances for using them as a preferred investigatory option appear to reflect lack of confidence in the capacity of government to make decisions (Hayne, 2019). New governments also prompt a flurry of activity: the numerous inquiries, reviews and working groups under the Blair, Rudd and Ardern governments providing examples. These activist governments, particularly those out of office for some time, want review instruments that are flexible, appropriate for short-term reporting on policy issues and extend beyond, although often grounded in, the public service. They receive legitimation of sorts through being termed independent or by the formal process and procedures adopted. These government initiatives have produced bulges in the inquiry activity and the shape of the PAS.

The expansion of public inquiries within the policy advisory system has played a fundamental role in shaping its twenty-first-century character. The upsurge in the use of newer types of public inquiry has been a mainstream dynamic in the reconfiguring of the policy advisory system. It is notable for the deinstitutionalisation of ad hoc advisory bodies through the decline of highly formalised and independent commissions of inquiry. There has also been institutionalisation of specialised advisory bodies in parliament and the executive, as well as new forms of ad hoc inquiries that are responsive to the requirements of government.

7 | *External Advice*

Governments have long had access to policy advice beyond that from the 'internal' PAS category. Policy advice is no longer, if it ever was, a monopoly of government. Policy professionals ranging from private sector consultants to think tank staff, university faculties and international agencies among others can all readily supply policy advice. If anything, ministers and department heads are awash with advice, of varying quality and from variously located sources, only some of which is solicited. External advisers are an important consideration in how PAS operate and figure prominently in analysis of their evolving nature, particularly in Westminster systems (Halligan, 1995; Craft and Howlett, 2013; Veselý, 2013). They also attract regular attention from parliamentary committees, government audits and reviews, and media scrutiny that questions massive government expenditures on consultants, and the privileged access they and select think tanks seem to enjoy in policymaking circles (Beeby, 2011; Auditor General, Australia, 2017).

This chapter does not focus on externalisation resulting from pressures for the public service to be externally engaged, nor advocacy by non-governmental actors, but rather the narrower displacement of public service advisers by those outside of government. This raises functional and distributional questions about who is advising government and on what matters, as well as potential shifts in influence from the public service to advisory units outside the public sector.[1] The nature of the external category – anything that is not public sector – is expansive, and this chapter is limited to analysis of think tanks and consultants, with some attention paid to lobbyists and international bodies. There is also some consideration of the nature of the external environment, as that has changed and is important as a source of pressure on governments to open up or integrate external advice. Preferences and context shape if and how governments seek out external advice. The various strategies and rationales for 'going outside' the public sector are detailed here, along with evidence about how they are manifest in Canberra, London, Ottawa and Wellington.

Comparative analysis reveals important differences in the prominence and types of externals present and draws attention to the elasticity of PAS as well as the Westminster administrative tradition itself. In neither instance are there hard or fast rules regarding the optimal balance of variously located sources of policy advice. Some governments favour using think tanks or consultants, while others tend towards greater insularity. This chapter documents variations in externalisation in these four countries, a theme returned to in Chapter 8. The United Kingdom, for example, demonstrates not only a long-standing and vibrant think tank community with clear links to government policymaking, but also a penchant for experimentation with the integration of externals into formal institutions and policy processes. The salience of Brexit in the United Kingdom and the 2008 global financial crisis in all four countries also reveals how major policy issues can dominate a PAS and compel recalibration, including a heavier reliance on externals (Corry, 2011; Peters, 2011). Australia's think tank community has evolved to become more competitive, but it is an enduring reliance on private sector consultants for policy work that is most striking.[2] New Zealand has seen consultants play significant roles in PAS and also serve as a rationale for government to claim that less or more public service capacity is required. Comparatively, the New Zealand and Canadian cases feature less prominent think tank communities, with episodic departures in standard practice. Interviews and secondary source data compiled suggest that externalisation has in some regards been overstated, with an uneven distribution of external supplies in the four cases, despite clear evidence that externals have become embedded and regular PAS features.

Externalisation often invokes a notion that ministers are *soliciting* advice from external supplies because they are dissatisfied with the views available to them. There is extensive evidence of attempts to limit or roll back the state because of ideological preferences for smaller or more efficient government. Precedents are provided by Thatcher and Mulroney in the United Kingdom and Canada in the 1980s or, later, Howard, Cameron, Harper and Key (in Australia, the United Kingdom, Canada and New Zealand, respectively), who pronounced on their efforts to run government more efficiently (Savoie, 1994;

Hazell and Yong, 2012). Alternatively, it is important to recognise that externalisation also functions as a pressure on government rather than being solely a decision to solicit non-public sector policy advice (see Chapter 3). These pressures derive from international agencies, agreements or contexts – for instance Brexit and the global financial crisis (GFC) – or from domestic proponents of 'open' government and 'open policy'. In the following sections, rationales for externalisation and their implications for advisory activity in the classic Westminster systems are examined.

Circumventing Unresponsiveness and Outsourcing the State

It has been argued that externalisation is in some cases a product of attempts by elected officials to secure greater political control over the administration. This involves, among other techniques, the increasing use of exogenous sources of policy advice to weaken a perceived public sector advisory monopoly (Rhodes and Weller, 2001; Peters and Pierre, 2004; Dahlstrom, Peters and Pierre, 2011). The logic, similar to that of increasing partisan advisers canvassed in Chapter 5, is that non-public service inputs facilitate the avoidance of policy capture by the public service and help to advance government policy and political agendas.

Ministers and prime ministers have at one time or another called into question the responsiveness of officials. Conservative leader Stephen Harper openly accused senior Canadian officials of being Liberal 'hacks' and noted that '[p]robably the most … difficult thing you have to learn as prime minister … is dealing with the federal bureaucracy … [I]t's walking that fine line of being a positive leader but at the same time pushing them and not becoming captive to them … I could write a book on that one' (Wells, 2018).

The United Kingdom and Australia too have seen the responsiveness of senior officials regularly questioned. The *Yes Minister* and *Yes Prime Minister* television series provided satirical caricatures, but recent experiences in the United Kingdom indicate how far ministers and prime ministers will push for greater political control. The Cameron coalition in the United Kingdom came into office on the back of a campaign manifesto which explicitly attacked the bureaucratic state, and one of its responses was greater contestability through more comprehensive use of externals. Francis Maude, a key architect of the manifesto and later minister for the Cabinet Office, and other key No 10 advisers favoured increasing contestability and bringing in external expertise to wake up the bureaucracy (HM Government, 2014, 19). It was not simply that the public service was seen as unresponsive and sluggish, but also that there was an attempt to relocate activities outside of government. Cameron's No 10 chief strategist went so far as to claim that 90 per cent of the civil service could be cut in favour of outsourcing to private sector consultants (Wright, 2012). New governments established after prolonged periods in opposition may come to power suspicious of the public service's loyalty and with plans to shake up perceived inefficiencies through privatisation and externalisation of policy work (Savoie, 1994; Tiernan and Weller, 2010).

Such claims are symptomatic of the frustrations of the political executive and emblematic of broader questions raised about senior officials' commitment to the austerity agenda and modernisation plans of the Cameron government (Tiernan, 2015b). New Zealand and Australia are no strangers to debates about political control and public service responsiveness. Successive public sector reforms designed to highlight responsiveness and performance and increase political control have been put in place. Clark's Labour government came into office with clear concerns about the dominance of the New Zealand Treasury and the quality of policy advice available to ministers (Lodge and Gill, 2011). Australia's Howard government adopted a hardline approach through extensive outsourcing and changing public service values to include responsiveness (MacDermott, 2008; Podger, 2007). Externalisation has been a feature, particularly in New Zealand linked to service delivery as well as 'purchase advice' and more recently to respond to public service capacity gaps (Boston, 1994; Tiernan, 2015c).

Filling the Gaps: Looking for Capacity Elsewhere

Another rationale for externalisation is to find alternative policy capacity that is simply not available from the public service. As surveyed in Chapter 4, all four cases have been found to suffer from public service capacity challenges, some more starkly than others. The issue of policy capacity is complex, with declines not universally distributed across the respective public services and arising for a variety of reasons (Tiernan,

2011; Howlett, Wellstead and Craft, 2017). These capacity challenges have consequences, with elites looking for capacity elsewhere. This is not a new phenomenon, with, for example, one British minister reporting in 2006: 'I am regularly frustrated by the lack of expertise in the department. People complain that we spend too much on outside consultants and others, but often we don't have a choice' (Lodge and Rodgers, 2006, 26). Australian Prime Minister Rudd publicly raised concerns about the ability of the public service to solve policy problems and a lack of strategic policy advice within government (Rudd, 2008). Crucially, it is not only ministers who are looking to externals. Officials and political advisers were quick to note, particularly in Australia and the United Kingdom, that outsiders were viable advisory suppliers who could bring to bear expertise or fill gaps as needed. Dent (2002, 11) lists the most common reasons managers employed consultants as including accessing specialist skills missing in departments, technologies or their applications, specialist skills that might be transferred to departments, and benefits from consultants' experience or practices that extended beyond specific projects.

Formal audits in the United Kingdom and Australia expose the significant issues at play regarding public service capacity and externalisation. Temporary staff or private sector consultants are hired to perform technical or in-demand analysis, for instance in financial modeling or tax policy areas, on an as-needed basis (CAG, 2006, 2010; Auditor-General (Australia), 2017). In other instances, there are signals that externals are serving as longer-term fixes for ongoing capacity gaps. In 2009–10 the British Treasury, the Department for Transport and the Department for Education all spent more than 50 per cent of their total staff cost on consultants. The Departments of Energy and Climate Change and the Home Office spent 40 per cent of their budget on consultants (CAG, 2010). These are not-insignificant allocations of staff expenditures that could be spent on permanent public servants. Figure 7.1 from the 2016 National Audit Office report points to an ebb and flow in the use and costs of consultants in the United Kingdom. This is in part a reflection of austerity reforms and the effects of the 2008 global financial downturn that led to reform efforts in the form of centralised controls on department expenditures and private sector consulting contracts.

It must be emphasised that analysis in each of the countries is significantly hampered by the reliability and specificity of data

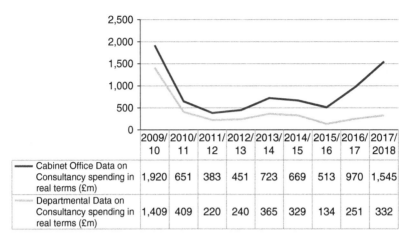

	2009/10	2010/11	2011/12	2012/13	2013/14	2014/15	2015/16	2016/17	2017/2018
Cabinet Office Data on Consultancy spending in real terms (£m)	1,920	651	383	451	723	669	513	970	1,545
Departmental Data on Consultancy spending in real terms (£m)	1,409	409	220	240	365	329	134	251	332

Figure 7.1 UK spending on consultants 2009–10 to 2017–18. Source: Adapted from UK CAG, 2019, 13; see original for data limitations & weighting.

regarding *policy advisory* consultants. This is due to differences in how departments and central agencies track spending and the vague categories used by countries to classify and describe work purchased (Howlett and Migone, 2014a). This makes it difficult to quantify how much consulting is specific to policy advice. Consultants in each case are often grouped into categories that can include policy advice, or at times data is discretely presented, while other categories typically include information technology, project and programme management, finance and other specialist consulting. Estimations of external advisory supply and influence are notoriously difficult to study empirically. For instance, Saint-Martin (1998, 320) noted in his comparison of Canada and the United Kingdom that 'there is no direct and simple causal link between increased spending and increased influence' of management consultants. A 2006 UK National Audit Office report found that over 100 million pounds in government consulting was spent for matters of 'advisory outsourcing' (CAG, 2006, 6). A decade later the categories had changed, and the biggest functional expense category reported was government contracting of consultants for consulting for 'multi-specialism' and finance and audit (CAG, 2016a, 19). Another key issue noted by Halligan (1995) long ago is that there is a clear domain variation in how PAS are organised and operate.

Intuitively defense, treasury and environment would be expected to involve different actors, policy issues, and advisory imperatives. This is also reflected in the use of consultants in all four cases. Here too poor data collection is problematic, Figure 7.2 demonstrates that in the United Kingdom in one year it was central agencies which relied the most on consultants, in contrast to some departments with negligible spending on externals.

This has most recently arisen under the massive impact of Brexit that has commanded most of the oxygen in the May governments (2016–17, 2017–19). A No 10 adviser interviewed indicated that the PM's chief of staff spent about 80 per cent of his time dealing with Brexit. The government response, in terms of staffing and consulting procurement, confirmed the urgency with frenzied recruiting in key departments, but that was not enough. Cabinet Office had to confront the reality that there simply was not the capacity at hand to address some of the technical matters involved, and as a result billions were spent on consultants to provide advisory work and other services that the public service could not (Owen and Lloyd, 2018; CAG, 2019). A 2019 report by the NAO also cited clear capacity gaps as a rationale for the significant growth in consultants set out earlier in Figure 7.1.

In 2018 the Cabinet Office also introduced a special 'call off' arrangement to ensure that consultancy firms could be quickly engaged to provide EU Exit services that were of a 'management consultancy' type. This essentially sees the Cabinet Office pay the firms for approved projects and then recoup the funds from the applicable departments. The Cabinet Office was again the biggest user of that advisory instrument, and, of the 151 times the instrument was used, the NAO noted that the vast majority were for substantive advisory work including: 18 times for 'Strategic support to assist departments with strategic consultancy in defining programmes'; 131 times for 'Strategic programme management consultancy services for EU Exit programmes', and only twice to 'Mobilise, manage and deliver' (CAG, 2019, 17).

Finding an equilibrium between internal public service capacity and that secured from externals creates an ongoing tension in all four cases. It has been vividly illustrated in New Zealand, which has a well-established track record of using consultants and purchase advice arrangements, particularly in implementing its original reform-era model (Boston, 1994). In 2009, the National government introduced a cap on core public service staffing numbers explicitly linked to

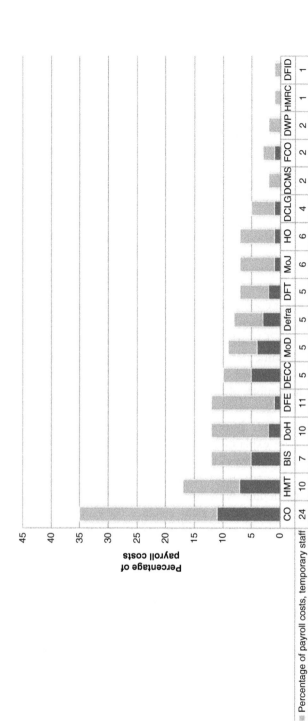

	CO	HMT	BIS	DoH	DFE	DECC	MoD	Defra	DFT	MoJ	HO	DCLG	DCMS	FCO	DWP	HMRC	DFID
Percentage of payroll costs, temporary staff	24	10	7	10	11	5	5	5	5	6	6	4	2	2	2	1	1
Percentage of payroll costs, consultants	11	7	5	2	1	5	4	3	2	1	1	1	0	1	0	0	0

Figure 7.2 Consulting and temporary staff costs by UK department, 2014–15. Source: Adapted from CAG (2016a), 18–19. Notes: CO = Cabinet Office; HMT = HM Treasury; BIS = Department for Business, Innovation & Skills; DoH = Department of Health; DfE = Department for Education; DECC = Department of Energy & Climate Change; MoD = Ministry of Defence; Defra = Department for Environment, Food & Rural Affairs; DfT = Department for Transport; MoJ = Ministry of Justice; HO = Home Office; DCLG = Department for Communities and Local Government; DCMS = Department for Culture, Media & Sport; FCO = Foreign & Commonwealth Office; DWP = Department for Work & Pensions; HMRC = HM Revenue & Customs; DFID = Department for International Development.

attempts to reduce expenditures, secure efficiencies and emphasise front-line service delivery functions for the public. With incremental adjustments over time, the government maintained the cap but was heavily criticised for its expenditures on consultants and the perceived 'hidden' bureaucracy that was hired to do what was previously public service work. Not long after forming government, Prime Minister Ardern's Labour coalition announced a lifting of the cap in 2018. The government made a clear argument that the cap had resulted in significant expenditures to consultants and contractors. In a press release entitled 'Government to reduce reliance on consultants', Minister Chris Hipkins stated: 'In removing the cap, this Government wants to see the public service rebuild their in-house capability and invest in permanent and long-term staff rather than spend millions on temporary contractors' (Government of New Zealand, 2018a). In 2017 a parliamentary select committee received reports from twenty-two of twenty-nine departments indicating a total spend of $546 million, an increase of nearly double since the 2009 capping was introduced, with the same departments then reporting expenditures of $272 million (Government of New Zealand, 2018a). Despite issues of disentangling how much of this is for policy advice versus IT or project management the comparison remains striking. The government's position on the matter is now on the public record with a published cabinet minute explaining that cabinet 'agreed that the State Services Commissioner conveys the Government's expectations that State services agencies invest more in building government core administrative capability in line with the Government's vision of a stronger public service, and reduce their reliance on purchasing external capability where this is appropriate to deliver value' (Government of New Zealand, 2018b).

New Zealand is closer to the traditional Canadian PAS than to that of Australia or the United Kingdom. When asked about using external advisers in general, those interviewed referred to stakeholders, largely professional or industry associations or community-level groups. The characterisation was more about political management of how these groups might react to policy changes or to providing opportunities for them to provide feedback more generally rather than as key advisory engagements. Many interviewed from across the political and public service spectrum were frank about a lack of think tanks and the reluctance to use consultants given the optics or costs. One New

Zealand minister, when asked about how frequently consultants were used versus the public service, said: 'There is always a little bit. I mean, you can never totally generalise because, of course we have got the big four consulting companies like everywhere else. But it would be 80/20 or 90/10. I mean, of course there are some things that they are involved in but they are not at all dominant' (N2). Another seasoned political adviser replied: 'Very minimal. So, the extent that we would use consultants here, in fact, ironically, we used them a little more in opposition than in government because we'd do internal policy work and then we'd go, bloody hell, I hope we get this right' (N9).

Australia too has seen the issue of externals use versus public service capacity rebuilding play out. As in the other cases, notably the United Kingdom, there has been a strong push in Australia to contain costs and to rationalise government. A public service cap was put in place in 2015, fixing average staffing levels to 2006–7 levels. Questions have been raised about the trend of increased consultant use at the expense of a hollowed-out public service, most recently following the Auditor General's broader review of the procurement practices of government. Figure 7.3 reveals the different trend lines in consultant spending versus public service staffing levels. It supports claims suggesting 'governments increasingly turn to private sector consultants for policy advice, to undertake programme reviews and increasingly to manage public consultations' (Vromen and Hurley, 2015, 175–8).

Interviews with ministers, officials and political staff frequently noted the pronounced role of consultants in matters of policy development and evaluation. Department secretaries too recognised that consultants had come to replace some of the institutional knowledge and advisory capacity that departments once provided (A2; A5). Then head of the APS Secretary Martin Parkinson put it bluntly in a speech stating 'a number of departments, a number of agencies, abrogated their core responsibility and have become over reliant on consultants', and while acknowledging that there were appropriate situations that warranted consultant use, he went on to say: 'But if you get to the space where you basically hand over thinking about policy development, policy prioritisation, to consultants, then you've actually given away your core business. And then you should ask yourself, what are you doing here?' (Easton, 2018).

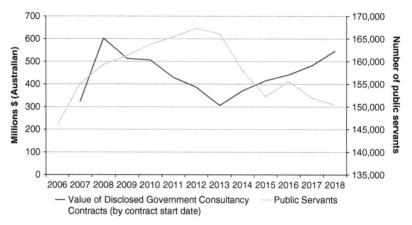

Figure 7.3 Public service staff versus consultant spends in Australia (2008–18)
Source: Authors created with raw data from AusTender and Australian Public Service Commission.

These figures are aggregate procurement numbers including various kinds of consulting services from IT to project management to policy. The tender-tracking system AusTender provides advice in specific categories but relies on public servants identifying and classifying their expenses correctly. Officials, in following finance procurement policy rules, are required to state whether consultants are engaged for advisory services due to: 'need for specialised or professional skills; skills currently unavailable within the agency; or need for independent research or assessment' (Auditor-General (Australia), 2017, 21). Recent analysis by the auditor general and leading observers of Australian use of consultants has found that there is a clear and growing need for specialised/professional skills not available from the public service but also a considerable use of consultants for independent research or assessment (Table 7.1).

Canberra interviewees observed that the use of consultants had become so pronounced that they were now institutionalised and public service capacities had been worn down. As one partisan adviser put it in explaining the value added by consultants, 'they'd be able to run comparisons that the department just doesn't have the data [for]. A lot of people are whining about how public service is being devalued and ministers' offices are going behind our backs. We're not being used, and we should be used. It's a case of, you don't have the data, you don't have the skills, you don't have the knowledge and the awareness, and

Table 7.1 *Consultant contracts by stated reason, 2007–17*

	Number of contracts	%	Value of contracts ($)
Need for specialised or professional skills	24,947	64.75	3,359,402,024
Need for independent research or assessment	10,082	26.17	1,242,772,767
Skills currently unavailable within agency	3261	8.46	432,062,421
No selection	237	0.62	21,070,103
Total	38527	100	5,055,307,315

Source: Adapted from Howard (2017).

we need people that are networked, who can bring the knowledge in' (A10). One study reflecting on some thirty years of Australian consultant use by government indicates that the patterns of growth are clear, particularly when juxtaposed against in-house capacity cuts, but more importantly that 'very strong growth in spending on contracts that bear the signs of relevance to, and possible influence over, the development of policies and programs' (Howard, 2017, 30). Howard is careful not to suggest that consultants have completely supplanted the roles of political and public service elites on policy matters, but his analysis is clear in suggesting consultants' policy relevance has grown over the 1997–2017 period (van den Berg et al., 2020).

Australian think tanks are also a viable avenue for a government looking to shore up policy capacity. Analysis suggests they have become more numerous and engage in a range of generalist or specialist advisory activity. Marsh and Stone (2004) argued in their comprehensive review that the Australian think tank community was comparatively weak, that they 'have not consolidated as a strong policy advice industry as in the USA' (2004, 262). In contrast, a more recent comprehensive assessment of the Australian think tank community by Fraussen and Halpin (2017) identifies fifty-nine active think tanks in Australia. Strikingly, 70 per cent of them had been established since 2000, indicating the massive growth in this advisory system component compared to earlier stocktakes of Westminster PAS (Halligan, 1995). Fraussen and Halpin (2017) also characterise the landscape as consisting of both specialist and generalist think tanks. Their assessment is that Australian think tanks tend to provide policy advice dealing with longer-term issues and that most are not decidedly aligned with the government in office. They conclude that Australian think tanks are 'proactive, anticipatory policy actors who are keen to move into new policy spaces' (Fraussen and Halpin, 2017, 120).

Canadian analysis is perhaps the most comprehensive and empirical in examining the specific functions and policy analytical capacity of private sector consultants and non-governmental policy actors. The findings are that policy and management consultants continue to be active within the PAS and remain attractive for ministers and public servants seeking specialised or quick expertise as replacements or substitutes for public service capacity that has been lost (Macdonald, 2011; Howlett and Migone, 2014b; Speers, 2018). Comparative analysis however points to a smaller role both in terms of spending and the perceived advisory influence of consultants compared to their Westminster cousins (Saint-Martin, 2004). There are persistent challenges with the data in Canada too. Attempts to get a better grasp of spending patterns have met with frustrating results given muddied figures including IT, technical and defense related contracts that are not clearly associated with specific policy or advisory work (Perl and White, 2002; Howlett and Migone, 2013a). Significant use of contract and temporary workers is common, but the categories are broad and underspecified, preventing attribution of that work to policy roles but pointing to similar dynamics where temporary staff and consultants are regularised stopgaps for public service capacity deficiencies (Public Service Commission, 2010). For Canada, consultants are comparatively well educated compared to public service counterparts but engage in similar process-heavy forms of policy work (Howlett and Migone, 2013b).

Scrutiny of the most likely policy-heavy category of 'management consultants' reveals an oligopolistic demand pattern with the distribution focused on a few key departments, not central agencies as in the United Kingdom. Two departments, Public Works and Government Services Canada (PWGSC) and Human Resources and Skills Development Canada (HRSDC), accounted for approximately half of all management consulting contract expenditures from 2003 to 2014 (Howlett and Migone, 2013b). There are also some examples of high-profile consultant use, with the Conservative government under

Harper paying Deloitte upwards of $90,000 a day to advise 'senior and elected officials on public and private sector best practices in improving productivity and achieving operational efficiencies' as part of the Deficit Reduction Action Plan (DRAP) (Beeby, 2011). The Trudeau government looked to McKinsey to advise and develop policy around Canada's first ever infrastructure bank. The firm has close ties with the government, with its global managing partner emeritus, Dominic Barton, chairing the minister of finance's Advisory Council on Economic Growth.

Canadian think tanks appear to be moderately active PAS participants. They do not enjoy the status or linkages of Australian and UK think tanks as key suppliers of policy advice to government, but their number and prominence appear greater than those in New Zealand. Attributions of influence to think tanks are complex and typically unsatisfying (Abelson, 2016). The concentration of power in the executive and the strong party discipline present in Canada has been highlighted as reducing the number of access points for think tanks (Abelson, 2016). However, research has found that officials can and do use think tanks to legitimise policy advice given their, at times, perceived independence from government (Abelson and Lindquist, 2000; Abelson, 2016). Overall assessments are less than sanguine with claims that think tank influence is often greatly exaggerated (Abelson, 2009). The most recent assessment by the leading authority on Canadian think tanks suggests they are policy relevant but that many are more active in trying to shape public discourse through the media, and presenting to parliamentary committees, and are engaged in profile building rather than advising governments directly (Abelson, 2018).

In the Canadian case, there is a discernable think tank community that is regularly trying to bring up policy solutions and offer analysis. The government has at times sought to invest in the think tank community through direct funding. Several think tanks in the early 2000s were forced to close due to a lack of stable revenue streams and fiscal restraints as the federal government reduced funding (Abelson, 2018). Analysis of funding changes from 2005 to 2010 for instance found a 'politically patterned structural opposition between conservative think tanks, funded by donors and centrist think tanks that are not funded by private donors' in addition to a general decline in state funding of centrists' think tanks which typically received the greatest proportion of state support (McLevey, 2014, 69). The Harper Conservative government cut funding to advocacy non-profits and increased regulation of their charitable tax status for perceived excesses in their allocated 10 per cent advocacy thresholds to maintain charitable tax status. In 2018 the Trudeau government raised eyebrows in the think tank community by providing $10 million in new funding to the Institute for Research on Public Policy for a centre of excellence on Canadian federalism with the explicit objectives of not only conducting research but also convening and engaging decision makers (IRPP, 2018).

Several interviewees, particularly ministers and senior officials in Canada and New Zealand, pointed out that there simply were not a lot of think tank options. Looking to Canada, there is not as elaborate an ecology of think tanks as is the case in Australia and the United Kingdom. There are well-established and emergent examples like the C. D. Howe Institute, the Canadian Centre for Policy Alternatives, the McDonald-Laurier Institute and Canada 2020, but there is nowhere near the number and depth to them that is found in the United Kingdom and to a lesser degree Australia. Asked to comment on the thesis that external advisers are more prominent and influential than in the past, both a long-serving Privy Council official and a senior PMO official were quick to respond that there was a clear lack of supply and bemoaned the absence of a vibrant Canadian think tank community (C5; C12). However, there were some close relationships, with Matthew Mendelsohn from the Ontario Mowat Center for public policy, a former deputy minister who had worked with Trudeau's co-CEO Butts in subnational government, being brought into the Privy Council Office to run the PCO results and delivery unit. Others included Tyler Meredith, former director of policy for the Institute for Research on Public Policy, who joined the PMO as a policy adviser. The Trudeau government has deep ties to Canada 2020, with Trudeau serving on the board and other interconnections with senior Liberal advisers attracting attention because of its influence with decision makers, but academic assessments have suggested it's more of a convener than a substantive policy player (Kingston, 2017; Abelson, 2018). Recent analysis confirms that Canadian think tanks tend to be limited in their formal representations to government, representing only 3 per cent of lobbying contacts from 2008 to 2015 (Boucher, 2018, 325).

Adding Contestability: Searching for Alternative Views

A further possibility is that externalisation is the product of a search for greater contestability. This rationale is distinct from the two previously mentioned in that it implies less that the public service is unresponsive or it has no capacity, but that government or ministers simply want additional *alternative* views. For ministers, where political staffs are small as in the United Kingdom and New Zealand cases, externals can represent a key vehicle to increase contestability and broaden the perspectives on offer. Here there are tremendous variations in the cases, with the United Kingdom experimenting with institutional reforms to facilitate formal avenues for externals to engage on matters of policy. The Contestable Policy Fund (CPF) was set up in Britain in 2012 with 500 million pounds to facilitate the commissioning of 'external' sources of policy advice from think tanks, academics and community organisations. The aim was to 'commission high quality advice from outside the civil service on ministers' priority policy areas; draw directly on the thinking, evidence and insight of external experts; and achieve a potentially broader and more radical range of options than ministers would receive internally'.[3] Evaluations of the initiative were tepid, with limited take-up and funds unspent; the intent was clearly to diversify available supplies and to weaken public service monopolies on advisory matters or fill perceived gaps in its advisory capacity. The UK experimentation with extended ministerial offices (EMOs) represented an attempt to onboard external experts by empowering secretaries of state to appoint external (non-public service) 'experts' on contract to ministerial offices. EMOs were intended to perform expanded roles not currently carried out by private offices: providing policy support, progress chasing and strategic advice (Paun, 2013). There were of course a number of restrictions that served to make them unappealing, such as the requirement for a No 10 representative in each, leading to only five experiments with EMOs which were abandoned in 2016 (Maley, 2018a).

Of the four cases, the United Kingdom presents the closest regular ties between government and think tanks. There has been a long tradition of Conservative association with think tanks from Thatcher on. Under New Labour, Demos and the Institute for Public Policy Research were seen as highly influential, not only as key sources of policy advice but as sources for advisers who would go on to work in No 10 policy units, as special advisers or consulting for government departments. Bentham (2006) goes as far as to characterise them as architects of the 'dominant political common sense of the current era in British politics'. Cameron-era Conservatives also had deep links with think tanks which were instrumental in refashioning the policy and brand of his conservativism (Pautz, 2012). Policy Exchange in particular, founded by conservative MPs and eventual Cameron ministers Michael Gove and Francis Maude, saw several of its staff also assume roles in the No 10 policy unit. Perhaps most convincingly, Cameron himself is on record saying that 'without Policy Exchange there would be no Conservative revolution' (quoted in Parker, 2008, 4). May's No 10 employed former think tank staff such as Policy Exchange's Will Tanner but also crossed party lines in contracting former Labour policy unit head for Blair's No 10 Matthew Taylor to produce a report on the future of work and the gig economy. As one No 10 adviser explained, Taylor was appointed 'as a kind of person with enough distance from government to have a genuinely independent view, and he's always a very smart guy and who's interested in this ... [W]e worked closely with him on what his recommendations might be, and that was a sort of brand-new thing that started life not in the DWP but in Downing Street' (UK2). However, another No 10 staffer suggested that this was the exception rather than the rule and that the May government had lots of policy ideas and Brexit to deal with, so think tanks were not major players. Diamond's (2017, 2019) recent studies of Whitehall suggest the same, with a private secretary on record explaining that '[t]hink-tanks tend to over-estimate their importance; they rarely produce genuinely new ideas. Also, they cannot produce detailed or really rigorous thinking about policy. Most new thinking is actually internally generated in the civil service' (quoted in Diamond, 2017, 10).

Officials, ministers and advisers in Canada all noted the growing practice of the Trudeau government of bringing in 'thought leaders' rather than consultants or think tanks. These were explained to be academics, international professionals or community activists who may have specific expertise in particular policy areas. The government would then ask them to sign a non-disclosure agreement and get them to provide advice on policy in development. Several interviewees indicated that this was a departure from practices of the previous Conservative Harper administration. One political adviser explained they wanted ministers to get a mix of formal and informal advice from externals, so 'very early on, we had an informal network of leading thinkers, informal channels, connecting with influencers in the research community, and in many cases, they became sort of a signals check on priorities, directions, etc. That was really relied on to get the balance right' (C11). Another adviser explained that his minister asked for formal ways to get views from those outside the department to be established through regular meetings or informal committees. The rationale was that the minister wanted fresh and alternative perspectives, despite feeling comfortable that the department was high-performing and had its own capacity. Deputy ministers were quite aware that ministers and their offices could talk to a range of externals, and so could they, all of which served to inform and better prepare policymakers for their decisions. When asked about externals, another deputy minister replied:

We encouraged it. We created multi-stakeholder groups to try and bring different people together and test ideas for that very reason. For the system to work, it needs to get forged in that arena of the different interests out there, and so it doesn't undermine our role of privileged relationship with the minister. I mean, that's anchored on the trust and the nature of the advice we provide, but it strengthens our ability to provide better advice, their ability to fully understand the issue and ultimately to implement with success. (C4)

Department officials and partisan advisers commonly reported stakeholder management and engagement in all four cases. This supports recent research that points to the significant role of stakeholders in contemporary Westminster policymaking (Maley, 2011, 2018a; Craft, 2016; Shaw and Eichbaum, 2018a). When pressed, much of what respondents described as stakeholder relations involved managing relationships to soften the blow of unpopular policy directions, identifying risks and issues to manage going forward, or seeking to gain credibility with stakeholders on preferred policy directions rather than engagements aimed at soliciting policy advice per se.

International Advice and Pressures for 'Open' and Democratic Policymaking

Early PAS thinking acknowledged an international component to the external category of advice supplies. Debates about the relative influence of international agencies over domestic government were important to broader questions about the decline of state-centred government in favour of modes of governance (Craft and Howlett, 2012). Early PAS thinking was deeply affected by the diffusion of managerial reforms that was spreading throughout Westminster systems and compelled reconsideration of how policy advice worked within government and global trends for public management reform (Aucoin, 1995; Halligan, 1995). More recently, the global financial crisis and UK Brexit issues have been two prominent policy issues that have highlighted the internationalised nature of policy, the constraints of international agreements and the prominence of international governmental organisation (IGO) policy advice. It has been suggested that policy ideas are increasingly generated at the global level through IGOs such as the OECD, the World Bank, the International Labour Organization (ILO), and the Group of Eight or Group of Twenty (G8, G20) and serve as key resources for domestic policymakers via policy transfer and diffusion (Pal, 2012; McBride and Merolli, 2013; Stone and Moloney, 2019). Despite recognition of the importance of international considerations, they have received the least focused analysis as aspects of PAS (Schlaufer, 2019; but see OECD, 2017).

It is common to see prime ministers from each of the Westminster countries on the world stage. Governments have long worked with and through IGOs, giving speeches and meeting counterparts for trade, defense and various policy matters. Behind-the-scenes elaborate policy networks often exist, in various states of formalisation and influence, where senior officials, political elites and select others engage on policy matters that span geographic boundaries and exclusive domestic authority (St. Clair, 2006; Coleman, 2016). Stone (2015) suggests that 'in contemporary world affairs, the Group of 20 (G20) has become a pre-eminent venue of policy deliberation' (Stone, 2015, 794). From a Westminster perspective, she also points to the prominent roles of domestic think tanks, including Australia's Lowy Institute for Public Affairs and Canada's Centre for International Governance Innovation.

Many IOG and non-governmental organisations hold policy preferences and seek to influence policymakers and outcomes in a range of jurisdictions and policy domains. Several, particularly those with finance and trade lines of activity, such as the World Bank, the WTO and the IMF, have faced harsh criticisms for ineffectiveness, predatory lending conditions, interference in domestic affairs and one-size-fits-all policy solutions with deleterious effects for member and user countries (Clift, 2018). In contrast, others point to the coordination functions and benefits of these organisations and the continued vitality of international arenas and organisations to sort out crisis and trans-boundary policy issues (Pal, 2012; Drezner, 2018).

Examining PAS implications from an international vantage point is challenging given the lack of systematic treatment, but existing accounts do raise some considerations. For example, Tiernan's (2015b) analysis of Australia's ability to weather the GFC and avoid recession and significant job losses credits the economic policy decisions of successive Australian governments and PAS to significant specific expertise around the PM and Treasury, but also the infrastructure and advisers of the Australian PAS. The comparatively high levels of policy capacity within the Treasury department combined with a significant number of partisan advisers (some seconded from the public service) with economics expertise and experience who had served previous governments in times of recession. These advisers were able to use their personal international networks of contacts to facilitate policy advisory work and ultimately the Rudd response.

As in Australia, the UK and Canadian responses to the GFC were informed by the Washington G20 meeting where decisions were made for a coordinated response. Domestic responses in both the United Kingdom and Canada involved a range of policy actors both within and outside of government, including a range of legal, financial and international advisers. In the case of the United Kingdom, the GFC experience has likely provided some measure of experience and procedural familiarity with procuring technical forms of policy advice. Post-mortem analysis by the government itself suggests a range of key players were crucial to providing timely and technical advice and in identifying clear gaps in capacity in the Treasury that required continued attention.[4]

Others have pointed to the constraints and binding effects ushered in by IGO policy positions and preferences that shape domestic policy choices on issues ranging from finance to trade, labour and environment policy (McBride and Merolli, 2013). For example, van den Berg (2017) highlights the European Union's role as a supranational body that has impacted European PAS and points to policymakers' reliance on international policy experts and consultants as a source of advice for domestic policy as key externalisation dynamics in PAS. The international aspect of PAS is not simply what is occurring within the IGO community or the pressure they can exert by way of their published advice or international agreements, but also the internationalised nature of think tanks and consultancies as well. Similar patterns for the big four consultancies can be gleamed from looking at the consulting contracts awarded throughout the Westminster cases (van den Berg et al., 2020).

While only an issue for the United Kingdom, Brexit raises the implications of how international policy issues can reshape PAS domestically. Radical changes to internal organisation and capacities, hiring of externals, and the political and technical constraints that have shaped the government's position on Brexit have played out before a global audience as Prime Minister May's domestic agenda has been vastly overshadowed by political defeats in the House of Commons and the questionable readiness of the government. Analysis by the Institute for Government suggests that the political and public service effects of Brexit have been significant, internally in terms of reconfiguring the PAS to meet the complexities and technical nature of advisory development but also because responding to Brexit has commanded significant resources, resulting in diminished abilities to tackle domestic policy issues (Lloyd, 2019).

Beyond the isolated incidents of an unparalleled global financial collapse and Brexit, a final international PAS implication is of the regular and established networks for exchanging best practices and policy advice. The similarities in the anglophone administrative tradition have also long been noted to prompt diffusion of practices, including those pertinent to PAS. For the small countries, it was standard practice to follow the activities of other systems: new British and US reforms received particular attention. Australia, Canada and New Zealand were more externally oriented because of colonially induced reactions and an inclination to emulate the experience of larger kindred systems (Halligan, 1996; Halligan, 2003). The propensity of countries to look externally and their preparedness to borrow the innovations of others shaped diffusion patterns. Newer waves of reforms on matters of open government and digital government have also seen the United Kingdom's digital government services unit and policy lab copied, as has been New Zealand's policy project, to improve the state of policy-making (see Chapter 8).

A final pressure to externalise may also be exogenous but domestic, in that governments increasingly face pressures to 'open up' policy-making and governance processes. Across all four cases there have been clear drives for more open, interactive and participatory forms of policymaking that can challenge the fundamental norms and practices of generally internal and public-service-centric advisory activity (Mulgan, 2014; Wanna, 2014). Government has long had stakeholders to manage, but there is a sense that the Westminster PAS has seen external actors able to exert greater demands on policymakers for access to the policy process (Scott and Baehler, 2010). Governments are responding, in some cases well and in others quite unsuccessfully, with various strategies and concrete programs and services aimed at consultation, open data and various forms of 'co-' policymaking (e.g. co-production, co-design), but there is a sense that the digitally driven open-government expectations of many of today's citizens run counter to the very fabric of Westminster PAS (Clarke, 2019). Tensions are clear, with, for example, continued calls for improvements to the access-to-information regimes that exist in Westminster systems or for more care in allowing governments to apply the secrecy provisions of cabinet to all matters of policy and advice. The historic contempt-of-parliament vote on the May government in December 2018 was linked to the government's unwillingness to release the full legal advice given to the Cabinet on the Brexit deal, underscoring enduring tensions related to transparency and selective disclosures at the heart of Westminster traditions.

Conclusion: Comparative Analysis and PAS Implications

External advice attracts considerable attention in part because of the costs associated with using consultants but also because it can be interpreted as leading to a weakening or decline of the public service influence as adviser. The implications from this chapter's review support the greater contestability of PAS. Clearly in some PAS this is linked to attempts to make the state more efficient or to shore up contestability to ensure ministers have a variety of views to inform their thinking. There is a sense too that the basic contours of PAS and the policy landscape within which it operates have become increasingly subject to pressures to open up and engage a variety of actors in the private, non-profit and citizen spheres.

Importantly, while the broad trends of externalisation continue to dominate the perceived PAS change and evolution, interviews with a range of elites – including ministers, senior PMO and ministers' office staff, and senior officials – revealed that the supply side is not always as robust as is assumed. As noted, the Canadian and New Zealand cases in particular saw some elites bemoan the lack of options for rigorous policy advice from think tanks, and reticence about relying on consultants was clear in all four cases, though clearly a necessary reality for many.

There has been a growth in the number and type of think tanks across most of the cases, though Canada and New Zealand continue to demonstrate a smaller number of think tanks with a less prominent role, comparatively. Consultants too are key external advisers to government who are brought in for technical and acute needs, such as the GFC and Brexit, but they have also become embedded PAS features as is clear in the Canadian, and particularly, Australian data examined in this chapter. However, close analysis points to further comparative differences, for instance the distribution of consultant contracts suggesting a strong departmental reliance on consultants in the United Kingdom, Canada and Australia, with a greater propensity for consultants use at the centre in the United Kingdom.

Data shortages and accounting changes complicate attempts to examine consultancy spends, particularly comparatively across the cases, let alone attributing policy influence to consultants. Based on available spending figures, however, there seems to be a greater tendency for Australian and Canadian consultants to be used in departments, while the Cabinet Office is a major purchaser of consultancy services in the United Kingdom. Brexit may intensify this in some ways but may also see select departments engage more consultants to deal with technical matters outside the typical remit of departments. This all raises an important issue in that there needs to be more careful discussion of the types of externalisation (e.g. to consultants or think tanks or to international agencies) and which policy domains or units are in fact onboarding externals.

New Zealand most vividly demonstrates how changes in government can lead to important shifts in how externals are utilised. The United Kingdom demonstrates the same but for different reasons, namely the huge capacity-building and consulting costs associated with Brexit after years of public service retrenchment and austerity. Another clear implication is the use of consultants and temporary staff as replacements for public service advisory supply. In New Zealand and Australia, the use and disuse of consultants evokes more fundamental questions about the role of the public service and alternative models of PAS featuring 'on demand' policy advice from outside of government. While the latter can be an attractive proposition, the realities of Brexit make clear what happens when there is insufficient capacity to respond to pressing policy challenges: consultants are used to fill clear capacity gaps.

If there is agreement amongst observers, and practitioners, it is that contemporary advisory systems are now more populated. There is, however, less agreement on how many, or how influential, so-called outsiders are within them. Externals speak to several issues linked to the composition and operation of advisory systems. Looking at four Westminster cases, there is tremendous variation in how think tanks and consultants engage in advisory activity with government, and there are distinct patterns regarding the use of externals. There are also well-documented differences related to ministerial preferences and their own personal networks. Some are more able, or more connected to externals, while others prefer to rely on the public service or political advisers (Savoie, 2003; Scott, 2010; Tiernan and Weller, 2010). In all four cases there is greater fragmentation of the PAS due to externals. In some cases, this fragmentation is more acute given the greater availability and access to externals. The implications for PAS are important, because it suggests a much more distributed system with dispersed influence, as Prince (2018) argued, one with many voices sharing influence. This was well captured by one Australian department secretary:

There are no organisations that have the authority that [department mandarins] used to have. That's part of the reason why I think government's so much more difficult nowadays, because just like everything else, it seems in our community, influence and capacity is more diffuse and it's much harder to assemble a strong coalition of support in favour of anything that's got a degree of difficulty to it. (A1)

It is clear too that international and domestic contexts can also put considerable pressure on PAS to externalise. Attention to externalisation also reveals that how that dynamic has unfolded in the four cases does not conform to consistent patterns. In Chapter 8 the theme of change in PAS is revisited to help broaden and deepen understanding of how externalisation contributes to PAS change.

8 | Understanding Westminster PAS Change

The argument from the outset of this book was that advisory systems are adaptable and change, particularly those following Westminster traditions. Understanding this change necessitates asking questions about the parts, the whole and the environments within which these systems operate. One approach to understanding PAS change is to focus on the institutionalisation and deinstitutionalisation of advisory units and practices. Some are added, others repurposed and some decommissioned. Many concrete examples have been presented, such as the addition of parliamentary budget officers, the near disappearance of royal commissions, and the changing advisory roles of the public service and political offices. However, not all PAS changes are created equal, nor do they always unfold identically. This chapter outlines the key characteristics and main properties of PAS changes in the four countries.

The analysis draws attention to the nature of PAS and differences in *type* of change by using a modified version of Hall's (1993) three 'orders' of change. First-order PAS changes involve routine adjustments to existing practices or units within the PAS. Second-order PAS change involves the ascendency and decline of particular categories of advisers or significant shifts in advisory practices. Third-order change involves system-wide macro-level changes. These distinct types of change help depict and analyse PAS change more accurately. It better recognises that change may be transformational or rather involves fine-tuning of existing advisory practices, or the rebalancing among the various advisory units within the system. The logic is intuitive: the addition of a handful of partisan-political advisers is not the same *type* of change as doubling their numbers and increasing their functions across government as happened under Blair. Localized policy capacity decline in one department is not the same as system-wide, or sustained, public service policy capacity decline over many years. Changes are not always so stark, with adjustments made to more routine matters as to how PAS operate being regular features of these systems. In part this is a product of their elasticity and flexibility. Operational functions include how policy briefs are written and delivered, how ministers use their partisan advisers, and how central agencies go about briefing cabinet or prime ministers, or ensure sufficient contestation and coordination of policy advice working its way through government.

Another question pertains to the trajectories of PAS change. These can be distinguished by differences in tempo and sequencing. Some PAS changes are gradual and long-term, such as the erosion of public service capacity sketched in Chapter 4. Others are more abrupt or transformational, for instance the responses to the 2008 global financial crisis (GFC) or New Zealand's PAS adjustments subsequent to its adoption of a proportional representation system in 1996 (Shaw and Eichbaum, 2018a). Further, some countries have been 'early adopters' of PAS-related reforms while others have been slower or completely resistant to reforms (Aucoin, 1995). The cases feature differences in sequencing of when (de)institutionalisation has occurred, such as when partisan advisers became established PAS features. Additionally, some changes are the product of directed or intentional changes, while other changes are not. This is partly linked to the differences in discretion that may exist over how advisory components or practices are set up. Cabinet committees are given prominence and concomitant advisory support, or they are marginalised by PMs who favour working bilaterally with select ministers, advisers and central agencies (Savoie, 2008). In contrast, other changes are foisted on PAS in response to the policy imperatives of crises or other non-discretionary transformations in their operating environments (Peters, 2011; Craft and Howlett, 2012). Recognizing these additional considerations helps expand and deepen the frame of reference for Westminster PAS change.

What is it specifically that has changed, and how did that change unfold? This chapter examines these questions as they pertain to the four PAS. The leading dynamics of externalisation and politicisation are reappraised. Drawing on the analysis in preceding chapters, subtypes of both are elaborated that depict more fully the breadth of these dynamics. Using the three orders of change perspective also draws attention to the systems-level changes. As noted in Chapter 1, there is a sense that PAS systems as a whole have been subject to adaptations, as various governments have engaged with them differently but also given the particular environmental factors in each country that have pushed and pulled the systems in various directions. The flexibility and adaptability inherent to PAS and the stylistic preferences of new governments, along with environmental pressures and developments, are likely to motivate continued PAS change, prompting the need for more comprehensive approaches to understanding the nature and type of these changes.

Types of PAS Change

First-Order Change

First-order PAS changes involve routine adjustments to existing practices or units within the PAS operation. These are typically the least controversial, for instance when departments reorganise their respective advisory practices to better brief ministers who prefer weekly meetings or on-demand clarification, written or verbal advice (Tiernan and Weller, 2010; Paun, 2013; Craft, 2016). The intent here is not to catalogue exhaustively all of the potential changes but rather to underscore that change occurs to the day-to-day advisory system operations and practices. At a basic level, each PAS has seen a professionalisation of public service advisory practices and massive increases in advisory volumes from the public services alone (Weller, 2016; Craft and Wilson, 2018). Ministers and prime ministers are at the end of never-ending streams of policy briefs, and there are more opportunities for external advice too, both solicited and unsolicited. Ministers have always faced challenges of capacity and bandwidth, but these have grown as the resources required to manage and circulate advice have decreased (Savoie, 2003; Tiernan and Weller, 2010; Weller, 2015).

Another first-order change has been paradoxical, in that some policy advisory practices have become more accessible while others are more opaque. In all four cases there has been significant discussion of the tendency of the public service to be more guarded in what it provides in writing. Formal written advice is still provided and signed off on for ministers, but verbal exchanges skirt access to information or allow for more frank discussions without leaving paper trails. Ministers and officials are more guarded about what is provided in written advice and, perhaps more importantly, what is not (Savoie, 2003; Tiernan and

Weller, 2010; Worth, 2017; Prince, 2018). Conversely, in three of the four cases there has been a general trend for ministers' offices to increasingly provide policy advice in written form, with the practice more ad hoc in NZ. Additionally, there are nuances in how policy advice from political or public service units is coupled and reconciled. A clearer separation of both streams is discernable, at least in terms of written briefs, in Canada, with a more mixed integration and separation as in Australia and certainly in the United Kingdom. New Zealand advisers persist with the strongest continued use of oral briefings, written advice being more the exception rather than the rule. This is linked to organisational practices in the four PAS regarding whether public servants are part of the minister's 'private office' in a hybrid arrangement, as in the United Kingdom and New Zealand, or if partisan advisers exclusively staff those offices as in Canada and Australia. Other important first-order changes involve some ministers preferring direct briefs from more junior political advisers directly responsible for shadowing particular policy files as in Australia, while in Canada all briefs are typically routed through the chief of staff or director of policy for clearing first (Craft, 2016; Weller, 2016).

Technology has been a massive driver of first-order change. There are basic features of PAS change that are now common but are stark developments in comparison with previous practices. There is widespread 'desk' fatigue, as complex policy issues and their associated policy advice are now communicated via PowerPoint presentations, ministers can now obtain information themselves much more readily via internet search, and information communication technologies have seen WhatsApp and similar secure direct message applications become preferred ways of organizing group and one-off exchanges on policy and various other governance matters (Massolla, 2016; Cole, 2017). The public services in Australia, Canada and the United Kingdom have all experimented with digitising cabinet documents, the most formal of policy advice, as well as briefing books and systems for prime ministers and ministers to varying extents that are 'digital first'. Briefs in Canada are now routinely tracked via an internal public service system, with ministers' offices often running parallel systems to track and coordinate their own advice to ministers (Craft, 2016). No longer are ministers' aides or senior executives carting around briefing binders; rather, ministers in some cases access advice via secured tablet interfaces, with opportunities to see real-time updates being made to their briefing material (Bushell-Embling, 2017; Marrando and Craft, 2017; Samojlenko and Boots, 2018; Tiernan, Holland and Deem, 2019, 24). These developments further advance the movement towards more 'on-demand' PAS.

Second-Order Change: From Public Service Predominance to Advisory Mixes

Second-order PAS change extends to the ascendency and decline of particular categories of dominant advisers or significant shifts in advisory practices. Returning to the original categories of public service, internal and external, set out by Halligan (1995), there are clear patterns of change. The cases feature a shared relative decline of the public service category, expansion and contraction of internal alternatives, and a general expansion of externals. Here, though, there is a clear variation in the patterns of externalisation. Chapter 4 makes clear that comparatively the public service has seen a decline in its predominance if not influence within PAS. Policy capacity in many of the cases exhibits lumpy or uneven distribution, with an overall trend line towards decline (Scott, 2010; Lindquist and Tiernan, 2011; Howlett, Wellstead and Craft, 2017).

Some of the more striking second-order changes include widespread patterns of movement towards more generalist and procedural advisory work by public services (Page and Jenkins, 2005; Scott, 2010; Head and Crowley, 2015; Howlett, Wellstead and Craft, 2017). There are strong arguments and evidence to support a generalist public service tradition in Westminster, particularly in the United Kingdom (Page and Jenkins, 2005). The high levels of executive churn and continued struggles with policy capacity suggest all four PAS are increasingly predisposed to more procedural forms of policy work, particularly short-term 'firefighting' advisory work, at the expense of evidence informed policy development and particularly longer-term strategic advisory work (Page and Jenkins, 2005; Head, 2015; Howlett et al., 2017). One result, especially clear in the Australian case, is the longer-term replacement of public service advice by that of consultants or other external suppliers. This is clearly attributable not only to public service operating cultures and traditions but also to the fact that some ministers and prime ministers clearly do not value the public service capacity to provide advice, expecting the public service primarily to implement government decisions rather than be the key source of policy ideas and analysis (Tiernan and Weller, 2010; Rhodes and Tiernan, 2014b; Craft, 2016).

This change has been reflected in a shared attempt to emphasise service delivery and implementation. Politicians have always wanted to be able to claim 'promise made, promise kept', but the rise of delivery units, implementation teams and progress-chasing units, while not new (see Lindquist, 2006a; Richards and Smith, 2006), has certainly been a shared hallmark of all four Westminster cases. It is second order in nature because it suggests a movement of the public service from advisers on matters of policy formulation (what to do and options on how to do it) to questions of how to make it happen or to implement (Lindquist, 2006b; Zussman, 2015). The rise of implementation focused policy work is second order as it includes both a refocusing of public service policy advice and a strengthening of the use of the centre to drive policy coherence and results. As Chapter 4 presents, these initiatives were popularised under Blair in the United Kingdom, but subsequent units in Canada and Australia have been set up, with mixed success (Gold, 2017).

Additional second-order changes pertain to the rise of the center of government more generally. Centres of government in each case have remained important loci of influence and resources in PAS. All four cases demonstrate tendencies towards centralisation of power around prime ministers, with Canada having the fewest constraints (Weller, 2018). There is also an ongoing tension between the centre and departments. This is by design, with contestability produced by central agencies able to vet, contextualise, and push and prod departments for better advisory offerings, and the particular coordination functions undertaken at the centre (Weller et al., 2011, chapter 11; Craft and Wilson, 2018). Yet, the centres have developed distinct characters which have been attributed to the more PM-centred supports and command in Canada and Australia, whereas the United Kingdom and New Zealand involve more whole-of-government supports (Dahlstrom et al., 2011; Weller, 2018). The United Kingdom remains attached to a relatively weak department to support the prime minister, despite repeated calls for the Cabinet Office to be replaced by the stronger model of Australia's DPMC (akin to Canada's Privy Council Office). The lack of cross-government policy initiatives has been critiqued (NAO, 2015), but the intricacy of the policy landscape suggests that the complexities require attention to the fragmentation of Whitehall, government steering capacity and institutional fit (Matthews, 2013). Conversely, the intensity of centralisation in Canada surpasses that of the other cases, as does its earlier adoption of partisan advisers, but these have occurred through an incremental tempo featuring occasional bursts of centralisation and, much less frequently, attempts to flatten or decentralise (Savoie, 1999; Craft, 2016).

Second-order change is also pronounced in terms of the use of the internal alternative category in all four cases. Here we see a widespread propensity to discontinue or more infrequently use longer-term policy advisory mechanisms like royal commissions in favour of shorter-term parliamentary committees or bespoke inquiries. In the latter case, governments can exert greater control over duration, cost, terms of reference and even who is appointed to do the work. One advantage may be that they better meet the needs of compressed policy processes, where policy advice must be generated more quickly if it is going to feed into responses to policy pressures driven by media or technology cycles (Peck and Theodore, 2015; Höchtl, Parycek and Schöllhammer, 2016). The addition of budget office/officers across the cases points to the unique characteristics of the internal non-public service category. It can be seen as being arm's-length or sufficiently distant from the governing party's command of the public service but also more legitimate given its proximity and government underwriting. It also highlights cost realities, where opposition parties – who have long had much less access to comprehensive policy advisory resources, other than typically modest parliamentary research budgets – can be supported without compelling them to engage external advice.

One of the clearest manifestations of bespoke internal PAS is the use of partisan advisers. This is an indication of second-order change more generally, with the use of advisers representing a clear departure from the previous practice of public service dominance towards a more complementary (and in some cases conflicted) multipartite advisory relationship. There has been the overall growth of the unit within the category but also country-specific growth, particularly in Canada and Australia. Visible distinctions based on relying on stronger PMOs, particularly in Canada and Australia, represent one track of second-order change, together with central agencies and often with the complementary function of stronger ministerial offices.

The cases also reveal that reversals in these patterns are possible but difficult. For instance, the capacity erosions and the rise of consultants in New Zealand and Australia were linked to the capping of public service staff levels. However, changes in government in both cases led to reversals to this sort of practice, some not yet tested by time. Whether this is merely a job creations scheme by swelling the public service ranks or is actually intended to deepen policy capacity remains an open question. In the case of partisan advisers, the United Kingdom and New Zealand have seen constrained and limited growth. In part this reflects differences in how public servants and ministers' offices are integrated or kept separate. There is a greater willingness to deal with the hybridity of advisers and seconded civil servants working for ministers in all cases except for Canada, where stricter separation continues to see an expansion in the number of partisan advisers rather than more use of seconded public servants.

Additional second-order changes can be seen with the formalisation of codes of conduct for partisan advisers, some seen as more effective than others (Wilson, 2016a; Ng, 2018; Shaw and Eichbaum, 2018). These codes can be argued to be second-order as they, to varying degrees, clarify and formalise expectations and boundaries around advisory practices and broader political-administrative relationships in each system. New formal parliamentary actors like budget officers, ethics and integrity officers have also seen formalised codes and other measures that add some degree of formality and clarity to advisory activities, for example lobbying codes. As Chapter 4 suggests, there have also been attempts to alter the practices of remuneration for senior officials, in part as a measure of increasing performance management and other techniques used to incentivise senior officials and make them more responsive. In all four cases there has also been a growth in the influence of audit offices, in many cases because of increased powers to conduct value for money audits. The reports of auditors are often consequential. Recent examples are those on procurement practices, including those of consultants, in Australia that led to parliamentary reviews, or the Canadian audits which led to the Gomery Commission investigating the 'sponsorship inquiry' of the early 2000s (Savoie, 2008). In both cases, audits raised red flags about purchase advice or about advisory arrangements and practices amongst political and administrative elites.

Third-Order PAS Change

Third-order change involves system-wide macro-level changes. These have been ongoing matters of concern across the Westminster systems. The reform period of the 1980s is an obvious place to begin analysis of third-order or more transformational PAS changes. While reform is not dwelt on here as it has been well covered elsewhere (Savoie, 1994; Aucoin, 1995; Halligan 2020), it points to the significant transformations that can be brought to bear on PAS. These transformations had lasting effects on the separation of operations and policy (particularly in New Zealand and the United Kingdom), experimentation with advisory supplies and processes outside of public service norms (Boston, 1994), and legacies including performance management contracts for senior officials and greater reliance on political aides for ministers and prime ministers (Eichbaum and Shaw, 2008; Lodge and Gill, 2011).

Echoes of this debate have played out, though with important differences, during the perceived shift from government to governance. From a PAS perspective, the issues are reflected in the arguments by authors such as Radin (2000), Prince (2007) and Parsons (2004) among others that the well-known older 'speaking truth to power' model of policy advice (Wildavsky, 1979) has given way in many policymaking circumstances to a more fluid, pluralised and polycentric advice-giving reality that has been characterised as 'sharing truth with many actors of influence' or 'weaving' policy knowledge (Parsons, 2004; Prince, 2018). This dispersed advisory capacity combines technical knowledge and political viewpoints in ways that differ from the way advice was generated, and conceived of, in early thinking on advisory systems based on producer-broker-consumer or autonomy-control considerations. The impact, from a PAS perspective, is creating expectations around transparency and participation of citizens, stakeholders, or affected communities and requiring governments to engage in greater resource exchange (Bingham et al., 2005; Mulgan, 2014). The diminished viability of traditional mechanisms for securing political control has not resulted in a complete absence of the state. Rather, it has seen the state reassert itself and necessitated new strategies and tactics, including concerted attempts to centralise, introducing performance management regimes for senior officials, increased reliance on partisan advisers, and various forms of network management and 'steering' (Dahlstrom et al., 2011; Halligan, 2020).

There are indications that further third-order changes may be in progress. PAS has implicitly been predicated on the notion of a strong and stable executive that can rationalise PAS units and practices to ensure it benefits from optimal (or proximate) advisory conditions (Wanna, 2014; Veselý, 2017). However, the proceeding chapters point to significant turbulence in executive politics, particularly in Australia and the United Kingdom, which calls into question that assumption. The ability of parties to generate enough legislative support to tip balances of power, frequent leadership changes, and intra-party and intra-executive tribalism have major impacts on PAS composition and operation. Where the transition periods between governments are perpetual, a less stable PAS emerges.

Lastly, general societal changes are putting pressure on PAS to adapt as well, including those prompted by rapid technological changes and the so-called post-truth environment. In some cases, these amplify known pressures and introduce new questions to the fundamental principles and arrangements that undergird how PAS work (Pierre, 1998; Marrando and Craft, 2017). One set of pressures is linked to technology, with artificial intelligence and machine learning producing potentially game-changing algorithmic advisory scenarios. Even at this stage there are signs that penchants for user centrism and emphasis on implementation have taken on new energy with service design and digital user-centric approaches (Clarke and Craft, 2018). The impact is that PAS becomes further conditioned to downstream implementation questions and concerns to the detriment of thoughtful and rigorous formulation activity.

Other more fundamental challenges to the nature of contestability, which is a central animating force within PAS, have surfaced, with tensions around evidence-based policymaking but more acutely with issues of 'post-truth' realities where the basic veracity and credibility of policy advice are now matters of highly politicised debate. While some are confident that trusted and traditional policy approaches and committed academics will help raise issues and clarify perceptions (Perl, Howlett and Ramesh, 2019), there is less certainty about how post-truth politics will reshape how PAS operates. Some argue there is an epistemic crisis, or a crisis of epistemic authority, characterised by a diminished ability to distinguish or vet quality policy ideas and inputs (Hernando, Pautz and Stone, 2018). Just maintaining current Westminster PAS standards and norms may require considerably more state resources to sift and sort advice. It may also prove challenging for external advisers who will need to invest more significantly in ensuring that their credibility can be defended and that decision makers are willing to take their advice.

The Diversity of Westminster Externalisation and Politicisation

To date there has been little or no qualification (or expansion) of PAS externalisation or politicisation within the PAS literature. As sketched in Chapter 3, most treatments present them as a blanket phenomenon or narrowly associated with particular sets of advisers (Craft and Halligan, 2017; Veselý, 2017). 'Externalisation' involves the displacement of public service advisers by those outside of government; and 'politicisation' the extent to which partisan-political aspects of policy advice have supplanted non-partisan public sector sources of policy advice (Craft and Howlett, 2013; Hustedt and Veit, 2017). What does the experience in Canberra, London, Ottawa and Wellington indicate about these two dynamics of PAS change? It is clear that there is more going on than simply pronounced use of partisan advisers or greater use of consultants.

Politicisation

Concern over the politicisation of PAS has often focused on the functional impacts of ministers' office advisers and, to a lesser degree, on the politicisation of senior public service appointments (Eichbaum and Shaw, 2008; Craft and Howlett, 2013). Partisan advisers are important and increasing focal points for PAS analysis because, as argued in Chapter 5, they are direct and institutionalised manifestations of attempts to increase partisan-political policy inputs within PAS. Even within the adviser cadre, diversity is apparent, with Chapter 5 outlining distinctions based on how systematic and how formalised the use of advisers is, as well as how partisan adviser inputs are reconciled with others circulating within PAS.

It is clear that politicisation can take several alternative forms, as set out in Table 8.1. Chapter 4 details the impacts of more activist ministers who can politicise the policymaking process by more actively engaging in department policymaking activities and being more direct in asserting and monitoring the advancement of individual or collective

Table 8.1 *PAS politicisation*

Forms of politicisation	Description
Appointment-focused	Politicisation of senior appointments to ensure politically favourable advice
Reorganisational	Departmentalising or bringing agencies and other arms-length bodies under more direct political control
Substantive politicisation	Partisan advisers or other actors colouring the content of public service policy advice
Procedural politicisation	Actors constraining ability of public service to provide free and frank policy advice (e.g. ministers or advisers preventing advice from being considered)
Activist ministers	Ministers engaging actively in policy and administrative matters beyond traditional Westminster divisions of labour
Purposeful erosion of internals	Funding cuts for public service and oversight agencies
Purposeful erosion of externals	Eliminating funding or access to non-politically favoured advisory bodies outside of the public service or government (e.g. NGO groups, watchdogs)
Strong centres	Domination of the centre by political office (e.g. PMO); using central agencies or political offices to extend political reach
Partisan advisers	Using advisers for countervailing advice, for process management; systematic use versus focused use (e.g. centre versus departments)
Intra-party or intra-executive conflict	Politicised contexts due to coalition politics or party factionalism (e.g. advice rejected or favoured for its intra-executive or party effects)
Accessibility	Creating/reducing more veto points for opportunities to (re)frame or (re)define policy problems; mobilising stakeholders to create advisory pressure. Redacting documents or abusing cabinet secrecy provisions
Venue shifting	Politicising by moving advisory activities to new venues (e.g. public committees, courts, other orders of government)

ministerial policy goals. Other concerns have also materialised, notably via debates around powerful prime ministers and more generally the displacement of cabinet, but also growing attention to permanent campaigning (Aucoin, 2012; Boston and Halligan, 2012; Craft, 2018; Weller, 2018; Marland et al., 2018; Diamond, 2019). The four PAS also draw attention to the purposeful attempts to shrink or constrain public service policy capacity through budget cuts and advisory marginalisation. Arguments can be made that the public service caps in Australia and New Zealand and the austerity programs of the Cameron and Harper governments in Canada all not only aimed to reduce costs but were associated with pushes to politicise the public service in the sense of securing greater political control (Zussman, 2015; Diamond, 2019). Similarly, as discussed in Chapter 4, the politicisation of public service appointments and use of contracts and performance management regimes for senior officials have been well explored as politicising techniques but not well integrated into studies of PAS. There is also the activist minister form of politicisation, which involves more aggressive and active engagement by ministers over policy matters. This latter form strikes at the heart of debates about 'positive' politicisation, overly technocratic and elitist policymaking, and those who see the public service as a 'platonic guardian' of the public interest (Rhodes and Wanna, 2007). In a similar vein, there is the reorganisation of previously arm's-length or independent bodies to subject them to greater or more direct political control, as seen in departmentalism in the United Kingdom, Australia and New Zealand (Kavanagh and Richards, 2001; Flinders, 2002).

Alternatively, politicisation could be driven by heightened intra-executive and intra-party factionalism. Politicisation occurs when coalition maintenance dynamics result in political motivations conditioning the substance or processes by which policy advice is generated or consumed. This is common in New Zealand coalition governments but has also emerged in Australia and the United Kingdom. There is also a question of factionalism within parties as evidenced by the corrosive effects of the Blair/Brown, Chrétien/Martin and Abbott/Turnbull/Morrison periods, each characterised by intensive advisory conflicts and debates, particularly when challengers were in finance/treasury portfolios.

Other forms of politicisation of PAS can relate to stronger attempts to manage or control external advisory inputs. To date, politicisation has centred on endogenous governmental issues with insufficient theorising or empirical study of how externals or environmental changes may lead to *system* politicisation. For instance, a government can cut funding to organisations that engage in advisory work perceived to be hostile to the partisan/policy interests of the government of the day. Harper, for example, tightened the controls on the advocacy thresholds allowed to Canadian registered charities in the tax code. Opening up or closing the advisory process and thereby changing the nature of its accessibility to other actors is another form of politicisation which serves to broaden or restrict participation in advisory work. Finally, venue shifting is similar but involves moving the locus of advisory activity or decision-making to arenas that feature additional or preferred veto point arrangements, result in new decision-making dynamics, or serve to reduce public service control over advisory processes (Boucher, 2013; Pralle, 2006).

Externalisation

One distinction involves supply or demand types of externalisation. There can simply be a greater array of available external alternatives or clear potential preferences in the types of externals that are used by government. Chapter 7 for example detailed the comparatively more regular and pronounced use of consultants in Australia and more marginal roles for think tanks in New Zealand and Canada. On the demand side distinctions are apparent too, with prime ministers, ministers or senior officials all being potential sources of demand for external advice – for example, the differences in the Key, English and Ardern governments in New Zealand with respect to the use of consultants as outlined in Chapter 7. Similarly, the UK Brexit conditions have seen officials reaching outside the confines of the public service for consultants to assist with various advisory matters that the public service simply lacked the capacity to deal with internally. A final point on supply forms of externalisation relates to the unsolicited versus solicited nature of externalisation. There is a myopic consideration of externalisation as always driven by solicited requests for advice. There are various PAS actors engaged in unsolicited advisory activity seeking to advocate and promote their policy advice in government decision-making circles. Each of the four PAS includes pronounced external communities of lobbyists, consultants and non-governmental organisations who readily push policy advice into the system. Externalisation can then be a matter of outside initiation or pressure by which exogenous advisory inputs advocate and agitate.

Table 8.2 sets out a range of other forms of externalisation, for example, *building capacity* through government externalisation. Through direct funding or use of particular externals government can create capacity – for instance, Trudeau's $10 million allocation to the Canadian IRPP for a new centre of excellence in federalism in 2018. In contrast, procedural forms of externalisation pertain to how advice is generated with distinctions here being about preferences for a non-public service/internal process or effects. This could be because 'traditional' processes are undesirable or unsuitable or be a matter of wanting to engage (or be seen engaging) in more open and 'co-' forms of policymaking. Co-design, co-creation and various other modes of policymaking may necessitate policy advice being uncoupled from internal processes or being driven or managed primarily by externals (Mulgan,

Table 8.2 *Forms of PAS externalisation*

Forms	Characteristics
Supply-specific	Consultant, think tank, non-governmental
Demand-specific	Driven by specific actors in the system (prime ministers, individual ministers or senior officials)
Content-based	Externalisation for substantive content purposes
Process-based	Secure political control; democratisation or satisfy participatory imperatives for more civic or public participation in advisory process
Capacity building	Promote policy capacity growth in externals by providing funding/non-material benefits (e.g. legitimation) to external suppliers
Credit claiming or legitimation	Seeking external validation of existing policy problem definition of preferences for solutions
Depoliticisation/ politicisation	Depoliticising contentious issues by moving them outside of government; disempowering public service institutions by removing authority over advisory development
Blame/failure shifting or avoidance	Distribute or deflect blame, to hedge against or avoid policy failures through greater integration of externals advice

2014). As canvassed in Chapter 7, 'open' government and 'participatory' policymaking are real pressures on PAS, and official 'open government' plans have become a common feature of contemporary Westminster-style governments (Clarke, 2019). Alternatively, procedural forms of externalisation could be linked to politicisation in the sense that they serve as a means to increase the direct control of ministers or governments over the advisory process by uncoupling it from traditional public service processes.

Legitimation forms of externalisation centre not on the content or process per se but on an outcome – validation – in this case from 'expert' or other external PAS actors including citizens (Pierre, 1998; Salacuse, 2018). This type of externalisation would be likely in scenarios where there is already a firm policy goal or preference and governments or elite policy actors use externals or external processes simply to confirm or legitimate their preferences through pro forma advisory processes. Similarly, externalisation of policy advice can take the form of *policy failure or blame avoidance* when the government seeks to externalise to generate plausible deniability in case of policy failures or to muddy the attribution of blame for highly contentious policy issues (Hood, 2010). For example, venue shifting of a policy issue to an affected community or stakeholder group may serve to bind them to advice that is generated if they have been active in its development. Both of these forms of externalisation underscore the connections that can exist with (de)politicisation as well. Actors within and outside of PAS can seek to politicise or 'depoliticise' issues by moving them in or out of focus or changing the arenas in which advisory activities are undertaken or who is providing the policy advice (Flinders and Buller, 2006; Beveridge, 2012). One example of this would be the use of management consulting and audit firms for austerity reviews and budget-cutting exercises, like those of the Cameron coalition or Harper-era cuts in Canada where 'consultants' provided their professional determinations of 'efficiency' gains and optimal cuts.

Comparative Analysis and Implications for PAS

To suggest Westminster PAS has changed is uncontroversial and less helpful than being clear about how and why it has changed, along with the implications of those changes as set out in Chapter 9. Many PAS adaptations are minor, with calibrations of existing practices to suit personalities and shifts in policy priorities. This remains a strength of these systems that are able to bend and stretch to meet the needs of a David Cameron or a Theresa May, a Bill English or a Jacinda Ardern. What has been more controversial are second-order changes relating to the balance of public service and other sources of policy advice, as well as the basic practices of policy advising which have seen norms and practices develop that are at times in conflict with traditional public service norms.

From the institutionalisation side we see shared additions of budget officers, expanded remits for auditors general and clear growth of partisan advisers, though constrained in two of four cases. The types of second-order change reflect the nature of advisory work to some degree as individual governments seek to reform and mould PAS to suit their needs, with, for instance, greater or less use of consultants or think tanks. On the deinstitutionalisation side of externalisation, there has been the decline of highly formalised and independent royal commissions. The near monopoly of the public service has been jettisoned in favour of a distributed ecology of advisory inputs that are on demand and supplied, and a lack of institutionalisation is also apparent for external consultants where their use is subject to government advisory preferences and fashions, including cost and capacity issues.

The major catalysts for early PAS change were the pluralisation of supplies, changing demands and the widespread prevalence of managerial reform thinking during the 1980s. Halligan's (1995) chapter was penned against the backdrop of successive assaults against the public service and questions about how it was coping and where others may now have emerged as influential policy advisers. The continued use of the 'government control' variable was pertinent and to a degree remains so, as it captures areas where governments have discretion. Ministers and prime ministers will continue to have opportunities to refashion the machinery of government and their own advisory preferences. Much of PAS is, however, not under direct control, and this is precisely where understanding how changes in non-discretionary aspects of these systems can help shed light on their compositions or operations.

Finally, there are signs of important third-order changes linked to technology that governments are just on the cusp of addressing. Machine learning and artificial intelligence are moving from the realm of science fiction to controlled experiments. While in many cases these are still innocuous or early-stage pilot projects, the notion of algorithmic policy advisers is not too far off. This raises significant implications for how democratically elected decision makers will deal with these inputs amongst the others they will have to consolidate. A number of ministers and political advisers interviewed reported using messaging applications like WhatsApp for policy and political matters. This illustrates the ways that technology can promote information exchange and asymmetries but also circumvention of transparency and accessibility provisions.

The cases examined here provide a richer and fuller perspective on PAS change. The benefit of hindsight is that more is known about how PAS can change in both gradual and abrupt fashions. Some of these changes are directed and internal, as with government reforms that modernise public services and the political arm of government. While politicisation and externalisation have dominated how we think about the nature and evolution of PAS in these four Westminster systems, that is only a partial account. Thinking about each of these dynamics of change can be broadened as can consideration of how the systems themselves change, the ratio and balance of their advisory units, or the very ways in which advisory work is undertaken. PAS has become more contestable both with respect to the internal and external locational considerations and in the basic advisory processes. There is more volume, more players and more perspectives on offer. Comparative analysis also reveals that there are some shared properties to the changes and some differences in the pathways of evolution that have marked these systems.

Lastly, there are powerful currents of change in the context within which PAS operates related to pressures for opening up PAS to citizens, and as international bodies remain important centres of coordination and best-practice generation. Concerns over the rise of a post-truth world amplify many long-standing tensions around the use or discounting of evidence-based, techno-cratic and elite policymaking. A post-truth context also casts doubts on the credibility and legitimacy of previously unquestion-ably credible sources. Nothing is uncontested; there are no facts, just more or less well-argued (or believed) partisan positions. A cynical view would see clear shifts in the speaking to sharing truths models sketched out in Chapter 4 to a post-truth advisory world which is more about constructing and verifying truths than sharing or speaking them in a world where no one is willing to listen. Chapter 9 now turns to look at the conditions of each PAS and reflects on them comparatively, along with what has been done to better manage how these systems serve government and their broader communities.

9 | Trends, Tensions and the State of Neo-policy Advisory Systems

This concluding chapter reviews the positioning of the individual policy advisory systems in comparison to each other and within the framework of the anglo administrative tradition. A particular focus is the directions in which PAS have evolved and the implications of the trends for the quality of public policy. It also reflects on what learning has occurred with managing and optimising these systems. The book has shown that the Westminster PAS has been significantly transformed over the last forty years and that its elasticity has been enabled by an administrative tradition that is pragmatic and highly instrumental. Several dimensions of PAS distinguished in Chapter 1 are returned to here and reappraised comparatively. These provide complementary insights regarding the state of the general Westminster PAS and help situate the country-level developments.

Westminster PAS, like Westminster itself, is not defined by a single static model. Rather, comparative analysis in this book has demonstrated the extensive *within*-tradition variation that exists. PAS can be organised and operated in a variety of different ways while still subscribing to the general principles of Westminster. Each advisory system is therefore a version of Westminster PAS – a product of different interpretations of the basic administrative tradition along with the country-specific traditions and developments that have shaped and reshaped it over time.

There has been remarkable change in the four PAS since the 2000s in terms of supply and demand of advice and the overall systems. Some advisers have become more influential, while others have been relegated to lesser roles or their relative influence has fluctuated because of the changing needs of ministers, competition from other suppliers and the turbulence of policymaking. The practices and work of policy advising have also evolved within the public service, where they were largely developed and honed, and through the increasing professionalisation of advisory activity outside of government. Comparative analysis helps us better understand not only the evolving architecture of PAS but the art and craft of advising Westminster governments.

Contemporary Westminster PAS

What is the Westminster model of PAS in the twenty-first-century environment? Distilling the main elements that are common across the countries, several components stand out (Table 9.1). First are the prime ministers who set the tone for the core executive, with differing governing styles and propensities to exercise types of control but with variable degrees of success. Ministers can play central roles in PAS as leaders and decision makers who drive policy agendas and work, supported by a ministerial office featuring politically appointed and often partisan advisers. The public service has retained a core function of providing policy advice, but it is a function which to a considerable extent has been converted to the role of digesting and processing internal and external inputs and focusing on downstream implementation work. The political-bureaucratic relationship is closer to that of an enforced partnership rather than the interaction between political and professional peers, signifying the level of engagement (or intervention) of ministers and their advisers in the policy process.

External consultation is more routine except when the policymaking process is curtailed by ministerial fiats. PAS is more accessible, both as pressures for government transparency and 'open' forms of policymaking and governing are in demand, and as PAS draws from various sources within and outside of government. Different types of advisers are extensively drawn on, and commissioned policy work is standard for Westminster countries. Inquiries are regularly used for drawing on internal and external expertise and for joining up government better, the less formalised ad hoc review being the most favoured instrument.

PAS has been able to expand within the principles of the Westminster tradition to display more features of 'governance' while retaining a state-centric focus but one tempered by greater responsiveness to external actors and a franker recognition of the limitation of the state's modes of command and control. PAS continues to be impacted by the broader international cut and thrust of policy issues, and the interconnectedness of global political economies results in needs to harmonise or mitigate advisory responses from other global players.

Table 9.1 *Emergent dimensions of Westminster PAS*

Dimension	Traditional	Emergent
Focus	Centred on core public service and ministers	Issue-driven and PM-/minister-centric; multiple actors & networks
Politicisation	Limited	Pervasive, a central dynamic of PAS
Externalisation	Limited	Central but contingent dynamic of PAS
Capability	Concentrated	Dispersed
Advisory sources	Formalised and narrow	Flexibility in choice; broad
Contestability of advice	Limited	Standard practice
Accessibility	Closed	Selectively open
Coordination of advice	Routine, narrow confines	Multifarious and highly demanding
Commissioning	Confined	Diverse range: consultants & reviewers
State centricity	High	State focus, responsive to society & international pressures
PAS interlocking	Tight	Loose, interacting & bespoke
Elasticity of PAS	Circumscribed	Expandable
Time frame	Short-, medium-, long-term	Short-term emphasis with episodic and ad hoc longer-term focus

The boundaries of these systems are now further out in terms of the relevance of the external actors and third parties of different types. The centre of gravity has in many respects shifted from being microcosmic at the core of government to embracing more actively and committedly the society that it represents. This represents major shifts from being relatively closed to more open, from being internally fixated to externally sensitive, although these changes should not be exaggerated, for governments have not become society-centred to the extent of being suffused by network governance. The core executive remains important and has continued, albeit with some difficulty, to seek greater coordination and coherence in policy advice that is generated internally and managing the flow and uptake of advice circulating within and around the core executive.

Politicisation is pervasive and a central dynamic of PAS, but it is also multifaceted and variable. It involves an attempt to reassert the primacy of politicians most overtly through influxes of political appointees working for ministers and public service politicisation with an impact that is pervasive and dominant. Ministers routinely turn to performance management techniques and partisan advisers to shore up responsiveness and drive policy through the machinery of government. Furthermore, politicisation of PAS has flowed from developments in society more generally when even basic facts and evidence are now regularly called into question.

Contestability has become standard but now regularly takes multiple forms: political, market, professional expertise and oversight. Commissioning is much more extensive, ranging from different types of independent review to employing consultants. The levels and intensity of public engagement and open government remain highly variable.

Externalisation has remained an important feature of PAS, but its extensiveness varies over time and context. So too is its rationale with important differences in available capacity across the PAS but also of differences in motivations for the use of externals, be it to fill clear gaps in capacity, legitimise existing policy preferences or ramp up contestability of public service advice. The trends are clearest where it has become fashionable to outsource or where lock-in and path dependence has made it an institutionalised feature of how PAS operates.

The great virtue of the anglo tradition is that a variety of governance arrangements and PAS configurations can operate within its principles and still be regarded as one of the family. The flexibility inherent in the tradition is conducive to the elasticity of PAS. This can be observed in the different PAS approaches, including preferences for high politicisation and centralisation through ministerial advisers and a dominating PMO or for heavy reliance on externals like think tanks and consultants.

The bespoke ability to fashion and manage advisory sources is a distinctive feature. Various advisory inputs are brought to bear for specific issues or based on the priorities and particular stylistic preferences of ministers or prime ministers or the capacity of departments or externals. The interlocking of advisory bodies is now looser and networked.

The time frame has become overwhelmingly determined by the short-term focus of politicians in an environment that expects immediate responses and action. Occasional exercises extend over the medium to longer term but on an ad hoc basis.

The regeneration of the policy function is occurring in the anglophone countries despite the attrition of the traditional role, although there are no absolute evaluations about progress across the several dimensions. There is a sense that all anglophone countries have experienced systemic weaknesses, previously identified by inquiries into policy capability but still not remedied, which have variously covered content expertise, policy analysis, new techniques, process skills, internal coordination and coherence and external engagement.

There are clear signals that PAS is being stretched in ways that are testing not only the orthodox assumptions around how these systems have typically been organised and operate, but also the highly debated pushing at boundaries around conventions and norms associated with Westminster more generally.

Within-Tradition Variation

Part of the rationale for this study was to examine the similarities and differences that characterise country PAS, as well as how they have developed and the implications for policymaking. The examination of the PAS experience of the four countries needs to recognise both administrative and country traditions. The four Westminster cases have had similar experiences characterised by the dynamics of a decline in public service policy capacity along with the general externalisation and politicisation of PAS. Closer inspection points to important differences in how these systems have evolved, when and why, which provides insights into the variations possible within the same administrative Westminster tradition (Table 9.2).

The variations between the policy roles of countries' public services are partly dependent on whether there has been a system-level program for resurrecting a significant role, what form that has taken (an overall augmentation, targeting the policy advice better or upgrading the quality of advice) or whether the political leadership has relegated officials to implementation. At the department level it depends on the ability of leaders to retain a core capability, particularly for long-term strategic work, and

Table 9.2 *Comparing Westminster policy advisory systems*

Components	Characteristics in PAS
Prime ministers	Pivotal in setting governing style, ministers' roles & PMO power
Ministers	Policy leader engaged in a range of policy roles. Role styles vary from domination to partnering to modified traditional
Departments	Secondary, responsive
Prime minister's office	Highly influential in AU & CA; variable role in NZ & UK
Political advisers	Highly influential in AU & CA; significant in NZ & UK
Central agencies	Policy coordination & leadership dependent on issue, PM's style
Formal inquiries	Drop off since 1980s, with occasional use for public issues
Ad hoc inquiries	Extensive roles (plus policy tsars in the UK)
Parliament committees	Committee reports influential (AU, UK); lesser roles elsewhere
Permanent bodies	New PAS bodies PBO (AU, CA plus fiscal cousin in UK), productivity commissions (AU, NZ), law commissions and growth of auditors' general influence (especially the UK)
Consultants	Range from high policy advice role (AU) and implementation (UK) to lesser activity elsewhere
Think tanks	Prominent in AU & UK, less so in CA & NZ

to protect them from being constantly diverted into short-term issues.

A pivotal factor for PAS has been the role and style of the prime minister, the type of impact being illustrated by highly distinctive cases: Harper closed and narrowed the Canadian PAS and strengthened partisan advisory inputs; Rudd promised strategic government but provided centralised policy processes and a disorderly Australian PAS; Ardern reduced a reliance on consultants, which was offset with increased investments in public service capacity; May's PAS was dominated by Brexit and the need for compensating policy capability.

While politicisation has been sustained and often relentless in anglo-phone countries, there have been ebbs and flows in the intensity as well as variations in the use of instruments. The intensity and form of politicisation has significant implications for policy advising by public servants. In comparative terms, the federal countries have embraced and elaborated the role of the centralised political machine, emphasising politicising features more strongly through their use of political advisers, the role of the prime minister's office and the handling of appointments (and terminations) (Bourgault, 2014; Halligan, 2020). The unitary systems display similar trends with their political executives but also have more institutional constraints, which partly accounts for the erratic use of instruments of political control in Britain, while being more proactive in some respects in engaging with capability declines.

A further source of variation occurs at the ministerial level. While ministers are much more inclined to be directly engaged in policy roles their propensity to be involved in policy processes varies substantially (Tiernan and Weller, 2010; Rhodes, 2011; Di Francesco, 2012).

Australia

The condition of the Australian PAS in the 2010s has been one of volatility, high politicisation, and relatively high centralisation and externalisation. It has been increasingly responsive to pressures for greater transparency and public engagement. At the core, political actors dominate. A beleaguered public service in the 2010s has been overshadowed by the parlous condition of national government with the rapid turnover of prime ministers, a 'coup culture', continuous electioneering, knee-jerk decision making (referred to as captain's calls when made by transient prime ministers) and variable use of evidence and process in policymaking (Head and Crowley, 2015; Evans et al., 2019). There is a three-year electoral cycle, as in New Zealand, but – unlike Canada's four-year cycle and the United Kingdom's fixed term parliament of five years – this places greater pressures on governments to advance their policy agendas quickly, contributing to the need for constant relationship rebuilding between ministers, officials and other PAS actors, and, given the short governing runway, compounds the tendencies for constant campaigning (van Onselen and Errington, 2007; Craft, 2017b).

Departmental policy capability overall has continued to be poor with a succession of reviews and reforms aimed at shoring up departmental capacity, particularly to confront long-term and strategic policy needs of government (Lindquist and Tiernan, 2011; Head, 2015; Halligan, 2020). The public service has been undermined by politicisation and the volatility of government and ministers. Partisan advisers are numerous (second only to Canada) and influential at the departmental level and in the PMO (Tiernan and Rhodes, 2014a; Maley, 2018a). The continued prominence accorded to partisan advisers as important sources of contestability and political inputs into the Australian PAS is unique given the greater number of public servants taking leave from the public service to join ministers' offices as so-called 'temporary partisans' (Maley, 2019). This is a novel feature of the Australian system, whereas public servants continue to sit beside ministers' partisan advisers in the hybrid minister's offices found in the United Kingdom and New Zealand PAS, while Canada features a stronger tradition of partisan-adviser-only ministerial offices supported by a departmental liaison.

In the outer public sector and beyond, extensive use is made of independent ad hoc inquiries, substituting for both the commission of inquiry and the public service. Australia arguably has had the heaviest reliance on consultants for policy advisory work. The evolving state of the Australian PAS suggests that consultants have become entrenched features and that a strong consultancy presence is linked to the challenges of public service capacity. The most detailed empirical analysis has found that spending on consultants in 2017 was 5.5 times higher than it was during the 1995–6 period (van den Berg et al., 2020). A comparatively robust think tank community further heightens externalisation, providing contestability and further advisory supply outside of government. There are also established linkages to parties as well on specific policy issues that contribute to an influence within PAS not found in Canada or New Zealand.

The Australian PAS, like the UK PAS, has therefore become more chaotic but for different reasons. It has faced near-constant disruptions due to frequent changes in government and a public service grappling with capacity building in the wake of austerity measures, but has also become increasingly reliant upon external capacity and alternative advisers. Its evolution has therefore consisted of both incremental and abrupt changes: a sustained rising influence of partisan advisers and consultants but abrupt transformations owing to the rapid succession of government changes since 2010. Like its New Zealand counterpart, it is inward-looking regarding concerns over the state of the PAS. Major public service reviews have raised questions directly pertinent to PAS matters but with largely inconsequential results. For instance, the 2010 Blueprint for reform touched on matters of capacity and responsiveness, and the hapless 2019 Independent Review of the Australian Public Service, which reported privately to a different government from that which appointed it, nominated the provision of high-quality policy advice as one of many objectives, and commissioned papers on relations with ministers and partisan advisers and using evidence to inform policymaking. This attention to components of the advisory system, and its optimisation for ministers and the public interest, is also found in New Zealand and the United Kingdom but is virtually absent in Canada in the 2010s. These reviews point to the need for political leadership to be engaged and to facilitate sustained and concrete implementation of recommendations, which is best exemplified in New Zealand.

There have been echoes of Richardson's (2018) argument about 'impositional' government because of the preoccupation with austerity and regaining a surplus. The public service's role within the Australian PAS has been further diminished at the end of the 2010s by the prime minister strongly asserting that it exists to implement government wishes and having engaged in a blame game by identifying public service weaknesses with loss of public trust in government (in contrast to New Zealand's approach). This is at a time when trust in Australian democracy has plunged in absolute and comparative terms to become the 'distrusted country' (Evans, Halupka and Stoker, 2019, 19).

Canada

The Canadian PAS is arguably the most stable of the four PAS, featuring less dramatic departures from the classic Westminster PAS in some respects but displaying striking boundary-pushing in others. The strong reliance on central advisory units, both political and public service, has seen Canada continue to exhibit high politicisation and centralisation, the latter attributed to the comparatively fewer restraints on the centre (Weller, 2018; Savoie, 2019). Canada has the strongest tradition of a powerful prime minister's office and the largest complement of political advisers of all four PAS. The prime minister's role continues to be pivotal for shaping the Canadian PAS given extensive discretion and limited constraints. The Canadian PAS continues to see prime ministers who favour disciplined, centrally led governments (Chrétien, Harper) but also those that have sought, with varying degrees of success, to implement more decentralised approaches and empower Cabinet and individual ministers (prime ministers Martin, J. Trudeau). Martin's government was plagued by coordination issues owing to the prime minister's decision-making style and attempts to involve a greater number of actors in decision-making (Jeffrey, 2010; Craft, 2016). Despite Justin Trudeau's planned return to more collective decision-making and 'cabinet government' model, recent experience suggests that while the full cabinet may meet more frequently and play a more extensive role in discussing key policy files than in the Harper government, the standard operating procedure remains a strong centralised mode of command and control (Prince, 2018; Savoie, 2019). The lack of strong individual ministers is now the rule rather than the exception in the Canadian PAS. A return to minority government status following the 2019 general election has the potential to amplify pathologies of PAS, reinforcing permanent campaigning tendencies and incentivising short-term and highly partisan advisory inputs. Government will likely impose considerable discipline on its ranks and govern from the center while recognising the need for parliamentary partners to legislate and maintain confidence (Craft, 2017b).

The public service remains an important, if diminished adviser – a 'fixer upper', to use the term of a recent Clerk of the Privy Council (May, 2016b). Yet, it remains a relevant PAS actor given its implementation functions and because of the comparatively weaker set of advisory alternatives. The contestability within the Canadian PAS tends to be generated by inter-governmental policy pressures or localised to the national government itself, with partisan advisers supplementing the continued dominance of central agencies in performing the challenge function in the policy process (Craft and Wilson, 2018; Prince, 2018).

The demand for the public service to provide policy advice and analysis has varied with governments, as has the willingness to ensure it is adequately resourced to do so. The distribution of policy analytical capacity has well-documented challenges and is unevenly distributed across departments and agencies (Howlett, Wellstead and Craft, 2017). Introspection in the Canadian case is more limited with ongoing reform initiatives present but featuring much less attention to matters of the quality of policy advice and especially the needs of ministers. Concerns about capacity gaps persist in Canada and have been subject to internally led reviews and efforts to develop the policy community partnership office, along with several targeted recruitment programs such as the Recruitment of Policy Leaders and Advanced Policy Analysts programs (Craft and Daku, 2017).

The Canadian PAS is most similar to New Zealand's in that it is insular or closed with less frequent and intensive use of consultants and think tanks, although there have also been indications of counter-tendencies. The modest level of externalisation is presumably the result of the restrained impact of NPM, as it was only a partial adopter of managerial reforms (Aucoin, 1995; Halligan, 2020), but also due to lack of alternative supply. The think tank landscape has contracted, with a few remaining key players and a smattering of emergent upstarts (Abelson, 2018). Consultant use, while not insignificant, is not as pronounced as in the United Kingdom or certainly Australia. It has involved predominantly process expertise rather than substantively focused advisory work (van den Berg et al., 2020). Parliament's policy role through committee reports has been somewhat limited, but effective use has been made of parliamentary officers, such as the PBO. Party government is showing signs of instability in Canada too with Harper and Trudeau having to navigate minority parliaments.

Canada continues to feature a strong role for the centre, which was established early and reinforced over time. Comparatively, it has been more impervious to some international trends and less experimental, and it was a late adopter of both the 'open government' movement and the results and delivery agenda (Aucoin, 1995; Zussman, 2015; Clarke, 2019). The then Canadian Centre for Management Development (CCMD) produced several significant works on advisory activity and contexts (see Halligan, 1995; Peters and Savoie, 2000). The CCMD's transformation into the Canada School of Public Service saw a significant decline in research capacity and presence. Renewal efforts like the 2016 launch of a Policy Community Project are now led out of the PCO and supported by pockets of departmental work (Shepherd and Stoney, 2018).

New Zealand

Once the country with fewest constraints on a government (immortalised as 'unbridled power': Palmer and Palmer, 2004), New Zealand then undertook the most radical reform of public management. An unintended consequence, electoral reform entailing mixed-member proportional, produced a system subject to minority and coalition governments (which, unlike most Australian cases, are negotiated after the election). This led to horse trading and a form of 'negotiated PAS' where government bargains on priorities, with policy advice constrained and informed by the exigencies of party negotiations. It has since been seeking to occupy a middle space that avoids some of the excesses of its counterparts (and its own past) with fairly centrist governments, while maintaining a reform agenda that has implications for the relative influence of the centre on policy. Despite its early reputation for radical change, there have been attempts across three decades to blunt the dysfunctional dimensions of the public management reform model. Public service legislation in 2019 is designed to strengthen the role of the centre and reaffirm primary Westminster-type values.

At the core, the ministers' role has been strengthened and their priorities have dominated, but New Zealand has been slow to develop a ministerial advisory system, which has remained comparatively small and with a mixed composition. The hybrid mix of partisan-political appointees and public servants working in ministers' offices is closest to the British system, but the sense was that there is a stronger capacity and influence in the British system and a much larger network of advisers to draw on, particularly given the New Zealand PMO is by far the smallest of the four systems. The PMO has a much more modest advisory capacity of its own and is reliant on the Policy Advisory Group (PAG) within the DPMC. The small size of government, and indeed the Wellington policy community, has produced a flatter and more informal advisory tradition, with several prime ministers known to have regularly exchanged text messages and calls with PAG advisers, in contrast to the other PAS where such interactions typically are restricted to senior officials.

Issues about public service responsiveness have picked up as the system has gradually become more politicised and with the extended official campaign regarding frank and fearless advice (Eichbaum and

Shaw, 2008, 2019). There are more protections for senior appointments through the role of the State Services Commissioner, and the
values of the administrative tradition have greater influence than elsewhere. The political arm has been more like that of the United Kingdom
with respect to advisers and being subject to the constraints of tradition, particularly on policy matters and dealings with officials. This is in
part a product of the shared hybrid structure, where public servants
work in the same offices as partisan advisers and the system has been
inclined to tread carefully to moderate real or perceived politicisation
of the state service's advice to ministers (Boston and Halligan, 2012;
Eichbaum, 2019).

The unicameral parliament was invigorated by the reform to the
electoral system, but this has not extended to an active policy inquiry
role as its committees focus on legislation because bills are automa-
tically referred to them. The government has a clear hierarchy of
inquiries, which are actively used. Other notable internal actors outside the public service are the Auditor-General and the Productivity
Commission, although the latter is dependent on government
referrals.

NZ adopted a radical form of NPM featuring a strong divide
between policy and operations, with implications for how policy advisory activity worked, but this has been reduced with agency integration. However, the adoption of NPM led to an early experience with
using external advisers, particularly consultants, as part of the larger
market-based approach that sought to shore up competition and contestability in the PAS (Boston, 1994). This has however ebbed and
flowed, as some governments have favoured looking inwards and
rebuilding foundational public service capacity while others have
looked to the consultants to provide a greater share of policy advice.
New Zealand occupies the middle ground on the use of externals. It is
not as prolific as others but shares more in common with Canada with
a limited think tank community but an established footprint for consulting firms, particularly the big four.

Comparatively, NZ has been relatively more introspective in
approaching PAS. It has maintained a sustained focus on addressing
policy capability, including leading on the development of a strong
internal policy community. It has launched serious systematic exercises
to examine and appraise the quality of policy advice and how well
ministers are being served. Overall, New Zealand is closer in spirit to

the United Kingdom in terms of relationships, and politicisation has been the most restrained of the four. However, two potentially contradictory processes have been occurring. Recent findings suggest partisan advisers are contributing towards greater pressures on the public service to become more responsive (Shaw and Eichbaum 2020). At the same time, the government has committed to changes to the State Sector Act 1988 that will provide for a more unified service, more strategic leadership of the public service, and potentially strengthen the role of the public service within PAS. New Zealand at the end of the 2010s is the only system that is tracking towards a renewed public service within a modified public management framework that will consolidate in legislation the constitutional role of the public service and a set of values that are given scant attention elsewhere (political neutrality, free and frank advice to ministers, merit-based appointment, open government and stewardship) (Eichbaum 2019; Hipkins 2019).

United Kingdom

The UK PAS is unique in that it features both stability and disruptive innovation. It has recently best exemplified the susceptibility of PAS to both austerity measures and to single-issue domination (Brexit). The United Kingdom is frequently depicted as a 'federated system', which presumably denotes the standing of ministerial departments and the relatively weak centre (both the Cabinet Office and No 10) and also signifies the scale and complexity of the machinery of government.

Politicisation has been highly significant, with ministerial roles enhanced greatly, and the United Kingdom has the best documented studies of ministerial behaviour and active policy roles. The use of instruments of politicisation indicate country-specific features. In terms of ministerial advisers, there is not the same centrality and influence as in the two federal systems. According to one study, the United Kingdom with four had the smallest average number of advisers per minister in 2015. The highest was Canada (nineteen), followed by Australia (twelve) and New Zealand (six) (Ng, 2018, 51). The United Kingdom has usually been less reliant on special advisers than elsewhere, although the policy tsars provide ministers with another source of advice. The hybridity of ministerial offices remains significant, particularly No 10's practice of having a PMO policy unit staffed by partisan appointees who work *directly with* public servants. However, with chief advisers to the prime minister there is a long history of highly influential, and often controversial, individuals playing pivotal roles in No 10, most recently exemplified by Dominic Cummings in Boris Johnson's PMO (Bennett, 2019; Greenaway, 2019).

It also needs to be noted that Thatcher initiated the enforced change in relations between the British civil service and ministers that was to reverberate in the other three countries, and Blair extended politicisation to new levels by both expanding substantially the number of ministerial advisers and centralising policy control through political instruments that were also influential elsewhere (Halligan, 2020). Francis Maude, the minister for the civil service under Cameron in the 2010s, funnelled prevailing government attitudes into a range of initiatives designed to peg the civil service and expand political influence on appointments and the policy process. More reform is expected in the early 2020s under Johnson.

Managerial reform has combined two forms of decentralisation: the penchant for agencification at an early stage of reform; and using third parties for delivering services. Years of austerity have reinforced the use of consultants and contractors for implementation to a much greater extent than elsewhere. The effect of Brexit has been to have consultants serving as clear capacity stopgaps for the public service. Other features have been the strong role of parliamentary committees, particularly and unusually in the lower house. Ministers have supplemented the use of more formal inquiries by ad hoc appointments of policy tsars. There are also formalised relationships between think tanks and politicos.

The United Kingdom has been an inveterate innovator, the results being apparent in several types of policy unit at the centre of government. There have been faltering agendas for improving policy over two decades, but a combination of skills and capacity weaknesses and the disruption provided by Brexit has increased reliance on the civil service and expanded the demand for policy staff in relevant departments. The United Kingdom has also been an early adopter of the policy profession focus. However, the civil service has been bedevilled by high turnover of senior officials (and ministers), which has had significant consequences for policy capacity and continuity (Freeguard et al., 2019; Riddell, 2019).

One important consequence has been the question of what direction PAS is moving. The rhetoric has been about open government and engagement, but questions exist about the impact. A persuasive argument has been mounted by Richardson (2018) that the policy style of Britain has traditionally been 'impositional' but that it became more consensual with greater engagement with interest groups in the 1970s, depicted as a move from government to governance. However, the effect of austerity was to produce a return to an impositional policy style, which may have to change post-Brexit as it will be necessary to engage with interest groups to a greater extent. More generally, the position of PAS at the end of the 2010s reflects the state of flux and confusion about the state of government in the United Kingdom.

Responses to Challenged Core PAS Capability

There have been five types of response to address capability and relationship issues. They differ in character, level and system impact, covering variously quality and relevance of advice, skills of public servants, policy networks, and either relationships with ministers or external engagement with recipients of government services (ranging from consultative processes to design and innovation).

The broader relationship between public servants and ministers has been a central theme of this book. The first type of response is to address the nature of advice both in conception and implementation. New Zealand has arguably given more attention to the issue than elsewhere, with consideration focusing both on the quality of the advice ministers receive and strengthening public servants' ability to provide fearless advice (Scott, 2010; Hipkins, 2019). Elsewhere the tendencies have been somewhat lopsided and more concerned with the ability of ministers to command public servants in the policy process.

The second response is external engagement, and while this mantra has echoed across the four and been pursued through co-design, the most sustained campaign has been conducted in the United Kingdom, particularly in the most recent phase of Open Policy Making.[1] Two other expanding endeavours have been the creation of policy labs and the emphasis on some variation of the policy profession (discussed next). The fifth is simply the employment of more policy staff to handle new government agendas and specific lacunae that have arisen, policy capability being more of a by-product.

Engagement, Design and Policy Innovation

Recent experiments have occurred with variations on policy labs. Public sector innovation (PSI) labs have proliferated across anglophone countries (McGann, Blomkamp and Lewis, 2018), although many are marginal to the focus here. For Australia and New Zealand, PSI units are divided between government and non-government units that are reliant on funding from the government. However, most are not in national government departments, and much of their work does not directly relate to policy development (although other specialisations, 'evaluation and system development' and 'user and customer-experience', can be relevant). The government does not receive direct credit for these initiatives because they derive from leadership in individual departments (McGann, Lewis and Blomkamp, 2018).[2] The United Kingdom's policy lab, based in the Cabinet Office, covers the public service by supporting policy teams in co-design approaches to policymaking.[3] Canadian labs are located in various departments, and the PCO has expanded the original Results and Delivery unit to also include an oversight and coordination function for Canadian innovation lab efforts.

Policy Professionalisation and Capacity Building

New Zealand and the United Kingdom have given serious attention to improvements to the policy function through mounting programs for developing the policy profession. In both countries, two related approaches – functional areas and heads of profession – have been adopted as a means of cross-government capability development (Jensen et al., 2014; McCrae, Harris and Andrews, 2015; McCrae and Gold, 2017). The heads of profession approach or the 'policy profession' is common to both. In contrast, Australia has not implemented such generic networks, but the public service has been galvanised into action and in a concrete form in 2019.

Previous attempts at enhancing policy advice across the New Zealand government, including central prescriptions and guidelines, failed at the implementation phase. The Department of the Prime Minister and Cabinet's 'policy project' was established because of complex policy problems (DPMC, 2014, 1–2). The 'policy project' has been based on collaboration and co-design involving a community of policy leaders with the overall purpose of embedding collective responsibility and improving the quality of advice across the state services. The objective of collective ownership was difficult to achieve early on (Davison, 2016).

Three policy improvement frameworks were designed to improve consistency in the quality of advice, practitioner skills and organisational capability with a long-term objective of improving system capability (Washington, 2016; Kibblewhite, 2018b). Two policy frameworks were at the level of the individual policy adviser (skills and quality), while capability applied at the organisational level. The head of the policy profession is the chief executive of the Department of the Prime Minister and Cabinet, who is responsible for improving the 'policy system' and is supported by a policy profession board consisting of eight chief executives and three deputy chief executives with policy responsibilities. A contrast with the other systems is the emphasis on and progress with 'frank and fearless advice' and to some extent policy stewardship (Kibblewhite, 2018b). There has been political support from two prime ministers.

One-third of policy agencies, including central agencies, were reported as having taken up the policy quality framework; another third had made use of the policy skills framework; and several agencies have applied the policy capability framework. There has been funding and institutional commitment and plans to measure improvements in the quality of policy advice and the usage of the frameworks (Washington and Mintrom, 2018, 40–1). The Board has since taken on the role of a policy career board with responsibility for cross-agency support for developing a cohort of about ninety policy leaders (Kibblewhite, 2018b). A significant new stage occurred in 2019 when the State Sector Leadership (consisting of all chief executives) agreed to the development of a revised policy quality framework, which has been accepted by the profession and was being used by all agencies as of 2019.

The policy role in the United Kingdom has been a core generic activity of civil servants (and over half the permanent secretaries have had backgrounds in policy and economics (McCrae and Gold, 2017, 45), but the push towards specialisms has led to the differentiation of functional areas (covering mainly corporate functions) and professions, of which policy is one.[4] There is a standard depiction for a profession, in this case 'an informal network for civil servants who work in, or are involved with, the formation of policy for government'. The functions are to raise standards, provide career development opportunities and promote collaboration, all within a governance structure. There is a cross-government head of the policy profession, a departmental permanent secretary who convenes the leadership group, and the policy profession board, which is responsible for improvement agendas such as professional standards. Policy professional standards covers areas of skills and knowledge and a policy professional development framework provides a model for policy advisers to assess skills and capabilities against three tiers of standards (the public policy masters at LSE being the pinnacle).

The policy profession is becoming more institutionalised, although funding has been dependent on amounts negotiated with departments on an annual basis. Although a large specialist area, the support unit is small, and the head of the policy profession is a part-time permanent secretary. However, the membership of the policy profession board covers the main policy departments and has expanded to become more inclusive of Whitehall agencies.

This systemic change in the way Whitehall is envisaged has broader implications. It addresses the long-term reign of the generalist, which in the past favoured policy roles, to be succeeded by specialists. Civil servants have been appointed to one of twenty-eight specialisms in a 'transformation' of the workforce in which the chief executive of the civil service has favoured commercial, technical and project execution skills (Manzoni, 2018).[5] Policy as one of twenty-eight professions has more than 18,000 members, the second largest. Given the level of professional specialisation there are cognate professions with implications for policy including legal, project delivery and operational delivery (the latter is for delivering and supporting frontline services and has 230,000 members, 70 per cent of the civil service; Thompson, 2018). An evaluation of the policy profession reviewed and assessed the original actions, reinforcing the directions being taken, such as collective ownership and the collaborative approach (rather than the centralised and interventionist roles of functional areas), and building links with other centres of expertise within the policy ecosystem (e.g. with Policy Lab) (Policy Profession Board, 2019).

The Canadian policy community was established in 2017 following exploratory work by a task force. It is funded by departments and has a small team of staff managing it and ADM-level champions and board. Activities have focused on hosting annual conferences, but the group is developing training materials and a competency framework, operating cross-functional policy mobility through rotational public service placements (Percival, 2018; Shepherd and Stoney, 2018).

Australia's policy capability agenda was formalised in 2019 under the leadership of a secretaries' group with a dedicated staff in a policy hub and an associated website and roadmap (DPMC, 2019). The objectives (or actions) for enhancing the policy ecosystem include policy career pathways, cross-agency support to policy improvement, developing system leadership for policy capability (supported by a leaders network), annual assessment of policy capability, increasing 'the demand for long-term policy thinking' and clarifying political advisers' role in policy development (DPMC, 2019, 5).

There is a question of what context these programs have been operating in and how efficacious they might be. New Zealand arguably has the most conducive environment, with questions about the condition of and values for the public service being more integral. The UK profession is concerned with actions that assist with meeting government priorities and ministers' objectives and improving policy-making by focusing on the use of evidence, understandings of the 'political and democratic context' and enhancing policy delivery.[6] The Australian environment appears to favour a narrow public service role as the prime minister elected in 2019 has reinforced the government's responsible for the policy agenda (although little policy was offered in the May election) and downplayed the public service role in policy development. Instead the APS is assigned the role of advising on the challenges of implementation and delivering services (Grattan, 2019; Halligan 2020; Podger, 2019). The main public service leader of a stronger public service role and evidenced-based policy, the head of PMC, resigned to allow the PM to choose his own adviser.

Post-austerity and New Policy Needs

The post-GFC austerity programs of governments had an impact on new policy and public service cuts directly affected departmental capability. In 2019, the UK government declared that austerity was over, and the Australian government finally claimed the budget was in surplus. What this means for how PAS operates remains unclear, although the UK prime minister has moved into spending mode in some areas, while the Australian prime minister has made declarations about attending to the needs of 'middle Australia' (Morrison, 2019). Government agendas in specific fields may nevertheless override and produce new demand for policy capability.

The most astounding example is the UK case because of the impact of Brexit, which has placed heavy and new demands on departments to expand their policy capability. In effect departments have had to reconstruct a range of policy-related frameworks, regulations and procedures for a post-Brexit United Kingdom. This affects some departments more than others. The Department of International Trade, as one of two departments created to facilitate leaving the EU, struggled with staff recruitment and development to handle functions that included reducing barriers to trade and investment, delivering a new trade policy framework for a post-EU era and promoting British trade. Existing departments and agencies were also given Brexit-related resources for needed staff recruitment and development. For some departments the job markets were difficult, with competition from the private sector for specialists. There was a shortage of suitable personnel in many areas both within and outside the civil service, which meant recruiting staff and training them as civil servants and policy workers. Consequently, there was an influx of large numbers of staff who were often poorly equipped to immediately undertake policy work (UK11, UK15).

Implications of Trends for the Quality of Policymaking

The Public Service and Westminster PAS

The trends indicate the greater demands on internal actors as they confront environmental change and challenges. Their attention is funnelled through portfolios for which they have responsibility and may change regularly where the politics are unstable. Context matters greatly because policy domains vary widely in terms of the complexity of the issues and the number, expertise and significance of interests jostling for consideration (Tiernan, 2011; Howlett, Wellstead & Craft, 2017). What this means for policy work is unpromising for supporters of stout departmental capacity and expertise. The extent to which policy content will be a core policy role, and the primary expertise concentrated within a department, has been receding, although departments still need to retain staff with basic expertise and general-ised skills.

In all four PAS there have been calls for public servants to renew efforts to develop and maintain 'craft skills' in policy advising (Rhodes, 2015; Tiernan, 2015c; Prince, 2018). This is a reflection of the chan-ging nature of advisory practices, where public servants' advisory roles have been evolving given shifts in demand, supply dynamics flowing from austerity measures, and in some PAS more competition from non-public service supplies. The policy worker's role, on advisory matters, is no longer defined only by their ability to marshal substantive knowl-edge and expertise but increasingly based on political nous and process skills: consultation with stakeholders, drawing on expertise from within and beyond government, persuading others, and servicing the expectations of ministers and their advisers in addition to active stake-holder communities outside of government. For the ministers, much depends on how effectively they handle appointments to their private office and relationships with their department. The senior public ser-vice is dependent on the resources provided by government for funding capability and the calibre and competence of the ministerial staff.

The limits of ministerial discretion remained unclear. Many minis-ters valued independent advice but were often intolerant of challenges. It has been commonplace for the minister to prefer a department that is compliant, which has extended to ministers instructing officials not to challenge proposals (Scott, 2001, 95). Weak officials too frequently acquiesced (Tingle, 2015; Eichbaum and Shaw, 2018), one option being to 'hedge their bets', while a common pattern was depicted as 'self-censoring in the face of political determination' (Podger, 2007; Taylor, 2015). An alternative but potentially haphazard strategy was 'picking the battles' by determining which policies to challenge and limiting the number of issues on which to take a strong stand. There was extensive feedback about cases of incomplete candidness and the need to maintain good working relationships (Podger, 2007, 144; Hallsworth et al., 2011, 12).

The clear message from dismissals, high turnover and contractuali-sation is illustrated as follows. The incentives were shaped by strong political control and the contract system where it existed. Despite reports of more public roles for the senior public service (Grube, 2015, 2019), overt policy leadership by public servants could be career limiting. There was a reluctance 'to speak truth to power' because objections were regarded as obstructive and had career consequences (as instanced for the United Kingdom by King and Crewe, 2014, 335). Standing up to ministers was regarded as damaging to the careers of civil servants or risking job termination (CAG, 2016b, 6; Burgess, 2017).

Relatively little research exists on the success and impact of recommendations for different types of policy units (but see Levitt and Solesbury's [2012] attempt for the United Kingdom; and Russell and Benton [2011] on the House of Commons). Best documented are the weaknesses and failures of policy advice (although see the Institute for Government work on successful policy processes historically, Rutter, Marshall and Sims, 2012; and Luetjens, Mintrom and 't Hart, 2019).

Australia can be credited with the lowest ebb of the anglophone countries, at least during the 2010s. The quality of public debate was castigated by national leaders, who argued it had reached a nadir (Tiernan, 2012), and this was before it descended further under transient governments and prime ministers. Most Australian departments lost not only the capacity to develop policy and provide frank advice but also the memory of how it was made (Tingle, 2015, 11, 17; Stark, 2018; Halligan, 2020).

Across the four PAS the churn of senior officials has long been flagged as problematic in these systems, receiving attention in both political and public service quarters for its corrosive effects on institutional memory and the time required to build effective working relations essential to a well-functioning PAS (Bourgault, 2014; Riddell, 2019; Sasse and Norris, 2019).

Growing attempts to implement a renewed public service understanding of a stewardship role may offer a means of rationalising, which is of particular relevance if it incorporates a long-term responsibility for the public service. However, only in New Zealand are these issues being taken seriously by academics, public servants and politicians collectively (Boston, 2017; Hipkins, 2019).

The Costs of Increased Responsiveness and Contestability

While PAS research has often emphasised the pluralised nature of these systems – including greater contestability, which is often argued to improve policymaking – there are potentially negative implications as well. From a content-based perspective the increased politicisation of PAS, in terms of direct political inputs via partisan advisers and more activist ministers, heightens tensions regarding the use of evidence and a predisposition for short-termism in advisory work.

The consequences of a politically driven public service have been a focus on the short-term, as well as the neglect of public policy issues (Boston, 2016, 2017). The weaknesses in UK policymaking were indicated by the lack of progress with acknowledged issues over a ten-year period. Policy making was not innovative, joined up, flexible and creative, nor was it the subject of evaluation, review and learning (as perceived by civil servants and ministers) (Hallsworth et al., 2011, 7). The Australian Treasury was 'dragged closer to government and in the process became a less effective policy adviser. The consequent lack of a consistent government economic reform narrative over the last decade is plain for all to see' (Tilley, 2019). There were systemic barriers that had not been addressed by reform. One civil servant's explanation was: '[I]f you've got to be evidence-based, and inclusive, and joined up and consulted, and outward-looking, you can't deliver a policy in the week – but ministers want policies tomorrow' (quoted in Hallsworth et al., 2011, 8).

The pace of policymaking has increased, leaving less time for considered advice. Ministerial hastiness in the short-term has been established to be a significant factor in policy failures. According to UK interviewees, ministers' 'desire to capture the news agenda, generate headlines, or be seen to be acting, could lead to over hasty announcements' (Hallsworth et al., 2011, 6). A substantial number of the 'blunders of government' investigated by King and Crewe (2014, 339) were the product of hasty processes. Speedy policymaking by activist ministers and the reticence of civil servants were responsible. Moreover, a perverse effect of the delivery culture that Thatcher and Blair instilled at the centre was that ministers and officials produced results but 'the wrong commodities' (King and Crewe, 2014, 343). Australia has also had cases of speedy and mishandled implementation: for instance, the Building Education Revolution policy (Althaus, 2011) and the Home Insulation Program fiasco (Hanger, 2014; Shergold, 2015). The Canadian handling of the Phoenix pay problem produced an 'incomprehensible failure' of implementation, according to the auditor general, which has been attributed to procedures and policy as well as culture (SSCNF, 2018).

In this environment the salience of evidence in policy fluctuates and varies across regimes. There are two strands to how evidence has been handled: whether it is accorded significance or ignored. The role of evidence in policymaking is widespread, especially in technical and scientific fields and specific public services. There are conscious attempts to elevate its importance, such as the United Kingdom's What Works Network of about ten centres that produces and evaluates evidence about public services in mainly sub-national fields with national support from the Cabinet Office for prioritising evidence (What Works Network, 2018).[7] There are also open hostilities to evidence-based policymaking such as those that characterised the Harper years in Canada, with attempts to alter the mandatory long-form census, contentious relationships with some expert and scientific communities on environmental matters, and privileging interest groups over departmental evidence-based analysis, such as the establishment of employment insurance tax credits for independent business (Curry, 2014).

The second strand arises from pre-emptory behaviour by ministers in policymaking. There are substantial anecdotal details of ministers making policy declarations without acquiring evidence first. Senior policy officials surveyed in Australia, New Zealand and the United Kingdom (2012–14) provided more concrete indications based on their experience. The majority agreed in those three countries that ministers were indifferent to facts; three-quarters (over 80 per cent in New Zealand) agreed that retrofitting of evidence occurred after decisions. More experienced public servants believed that there had been a dramatic decline in using evidence in policymaking (Stoker and Evans, 2016, 16–19).

The lack of evidence-based policy (EBP) has been regarded as a limitation of Australian policymaking, although talked up by prime ministers (Banks, 2018; and for the United Kingdom, see RSS, 2016). Policy-based evidence-making (or PBE: policy-based evidence) had entered the lexicon of and was widespread in Whitehall (Diamond, 2019, 43, 74; UK11, 2018). The policy active ministers of anglophone countries have regularly initiated their own policy (e.g. Michael Gove, a high-profile secretary of state in the United Kingdom's Cameron and May governments: Bennett, 2019); UK secretary of state Andrew Lansley single-handedly engineered the 'final solution' for the NHS (King and Crewe, 2014, 401–2). In Australia and Canada, ministers have ignored or privileged certain forms of evidence. For example, in 2014 Finance Minister Joe Oliver introduced a $550 million tax credit for small businesses based solely on analysis provided by the Federation of Independent Business (CFIB), an industry group. Department of Finance officials later revealed they had not completed analysis or provided advice on the initiative, and the independent Parliamentary Budget Office rebuked the quality of analysis and methodology used by the CFIB (Wherry, 2014). The Trudeau government also demonstrated selective use of evidence in returning the recently adjusted age of eligibility for retirement benefits back to 65 from 67. This ran counter to the advice from most Canadian economists, the OECD and the finance minister's own independent advisory panel on economic growth (Curry and Silcoff, 2017). The rational assumption that better evidence will improve the quality of policymaking conflicts with political realities and processes featuring bargaining and the need to reconcile different interests and expectations (Head, 2017). An alternative option is the 'good governance of evidence', which entails combining systematic and validated evidence within policy processes that reflect and are responsive to the citizens affected (Parkhurst, 2017).

Managing the Policy Advisory System?

At the strategic level there is not much evidence of government management of the policy advisory system with a view to enhancing policymaking and governance. All countries have had recent reviews of the public sector, which usually addressed advice but not the advisory system itself. Moreover, in the 'age of austerity', which has been more pronounced in some countries (e.g. the United Kingdom) than others, the dominant whole of government process has been the efficiency drive, with reviews (such as the Commissions of Audit in Australia) calling the shots with often-major impacts on PAS.

Desultory attention then has been given to managing the policy advice *system*, with attention focusing on components. An agenda has been most apparent in New Zealand and the United Kingdom. However, the consequences of politicisation and externalisation are rarely given sustained and systematic consideration (but note earlier reports by oversight agencies). This lack of attention to the policy advisory system means that the costs attendant on the use of specific instruments and approaches are ignored until there is a crisis. The

options chosen invariably have effects including unintended consequences. The costs of outsourcing delivery can be a lack of transparency, issues with the level of savings and risks of failure (as evidenced
by the outsourcing supremo, the United Kingdom), and an inability to
avoid the regular underperformance of private sector contractors. The
greater rigour and data entailed in obtaining high-quality evidence for
policymaking has financial costs but political irrelevance. Heightened
responsiveness to ministers can lead to multiple distortions: the short-
term over the long-term, political priorities over public interest, and the
disestablishment of the public service. There is a lack of clear evidence
that capability reviews and other initiatives have measurably lifted the
policy capability of the centre. Innovation units and policy labs seem to
be the initiative of public service leaders that are developed piecemeal
by specific departments. Too many ambiguities and tensions remain
with the relationship between ministers and department heads. The
oversight of political advisers remains questionable, and, with mounting issues about the capabilities and roles of ministers themselves, the
potential for optimising the system is affected by the poorly performing
parts.

The legislation for inquiries has been modernised but ad hoc ministerial reviews by policy tsars and task forces often seem to operate in
grey areas where transparency is lacking, the results unclear and
reports are withheld by governments. Prescriptions are bandied about
such as adaptability (OECD, 2017). But how open-ended can the
arrangements be? Some OECD countries have clearer rules about
expectations for ad hoc inquiries.

The clearest exception in this area has been the increased attention to
advisory matters surrounding government transitions. Led by the centre in all four PAS, transition planning and support have received
resources and attention given the importance for governments and
the public service to making a credible start. There are considerable
implications for PAS, as transition advice covers a range of issues
related to how cabinets and decision-making processes are structured,
staffing both the public service and ministers, and most importantly
providing government with advice on turning campaign policy priorities into concrete programs and policy, but also ensuring government
is made aware of considerations that may shape their thinking or
reprioritise their stated policy agendas ('t Hart and Uhr, 2011;
Zussman, 2013). Transitions are also arenas that feature significant

involvement of externals in all four cases with, to varying degrees, transition teams drawing from the ranks of former public service officials, private sector and partisan-political circles of advisers, and former ministers (Riddell and Haddon, 2009). Incoming governments often seek to ensure some 'friendlies' are on the team, to gain perspectives on organisational and process matters and to provide candid advice on how to make the most of the initial governing period. The New Zealand case is perhaps the outlier, given the realities of coalition governments necessitating longer and more intricate transitions supports. Minority parliaments and coalition governments in the other three PAS, along with instability in the United Kingdom and Australia in the 2010s, have underscored the continued relevance of the public service – and select externals and political advisers – to transitions and the initial governing period.

Relevance of the Experience of Westminster Systems for Other PAS

Policy advisory systems exist in some shape or form in all countries and within various administrative traditions. The language of PAS has been widely picked up in the 2010s, and studies have been emerging that are charting similarities and differences beyond the dominant Westminster system perspectives (OECD, 2017; van den Berg, 2017; Veit et al., 2017; Bressers et al., 2018).

The anglophone experience resonates particularly with OECD countries because of the commonalities arising from public management reform and some convergence in approaches. Politicisation has been an international phenomenon (Peters and Pierre, 2004; Roban, 2012), and, despite the strong traditional differences in the conduct of relationships between politicians and bureaucrats, this is now less the case. The OECD itself, in addition to its member countries, has begun to unpack the importance of advisory systems to the operation of the OECD as a whole, as well as the idiosyncratic features of some of the member countries. Analysis further supports the diversity of possible governance arrangements for PAS, as well as the operational distinctions owing to capacity differences, working arrangements, and policy and country-specific factors (OECD, 2017). Non-Westminster countries are not immune from many of the pressures facing Westminster PAS, including short-termism, a growing emphasis on 'results', and calls for more open and transparent government. Across the OECD and at the individual country level there is, however, clear agreement on the importance of PAS to good governance.

The coalition and minority government experiences of Westminster PAS in the 2000s are also of relevance for systems that operate on permanent modes of consensus and neo-corporatist and compromise-based policymaking styles (van den Berg et al., 2014; Hustedt, 2019). Countries such as Belgium, the Netherlands and Germany also offer different institutional structures and governance arrangements that raise questions about how notions of politicisation, externalisation, and control and autonomy operate and impact PAS (Fobe et al., 2013; Bressers et al., 2018). Non-democratic PAS raise a host of other important questions about where government control can be more intensive and pervasive, but also important issues related to how pressures for openness and transparency might affect authoritarian PAS (Uldanov, 2019).

There can be opportunities and lessons for developing countries too, particularly as they grapple with perennial questions of PAS organisation and capacity building, including both state and non-state advisory bodies.

Future of Westminster PAS

The future directions for PAS are unclear because of hyper-change and uncertainties arising with new community and political movements and importantly unstable and insecure governments. What was thought to be dramatic change in the 2000s has been seemingly magnified in the 2010s. PAS and its constituent elements detailed in this book will however continue to provide the framework for policy activity. The Westminster PAS remains imbedded but not inviolable, as the culture of contestability pushes at boundaries established by the administrative tradition. Current trends point to the continued shuffling of various advisory roles and fluctuation in their significance, with on-going tensions and pressures that will stretch Westminster PAS. There will be continued conflicts and messiness around who is providing what types of policy advice as well as blurred authorities and resources to do so effectively, particularly for the public service.

Much will depend on ad hoc arrangements and the stylistic preferences of the executive. Prime ministers and ministers remain the focus,
with particularly strong centres in PAS in Canada and Australia and the
public service attempting to sift and sort increasing advice from various
channels within and around the core executive. Ministers will continue
to push for more political control and responsiveness, with the public
service seeking to focus some attention on longer-term advisory considerations, against a backdrop of increasingly acute permanent campaigning. Intense competition will continue to be a hallmark of all four
PAS, with public servants and ministers (and their offices) struggling to
ensure policy coherence. The centre will continue to look to its levers to
drive coordination and ensure select policy priorities receive sufficient
oxygen within the system. In the United Kingdom and New Zealand
this will be even more pronounced, given the coalition politics now
entrenched in the latter and the greater constraints on prime ministerial
unilateralism in both.

The public service will remain under-resourced in all four PAS but
continue to execute professionally in an increasingly 'just in time'
manner. Successive efforts at capacity building will continue in all
four cases but in more targeted ways that benefit mid- to senior-level
policy officials. More experimentation will be required, with advisory
units within the public service being deployed as surge units directed to
advance key government priorities or to clean up problematic files. The
public service will continue to depend on other PAS actors to fill gaps,
particularly on technical substantive matters. The use of 'independent'
inquiries will remain popular because they are flexible and short-term,
satisfy expectations about cross-boundary collaboration, allow outsiders to be inserted and (depending on how they are constituted) are
politically controllable. Pressures for responsiveness will extend
beyond the ministerial suite too; where possible, open policymaking
and increased public consultation, participation and transparency will
continue where viable or practical for political purposes. The non-core
agencies endowed with some independence will continue to make
policy contributions in specialised areas.

Two more extreme potential scenarios can be envisaged given trends
identified in earlier chapters. A politicised model incorporates an even
greater role for political and partisan appointments at the centre in the
prime minister's department and office. Prime ministers and select
ministers will more emphatically claim leadership on matters of policy,

which will increasingly privilege short-term hyper-partisan objectives, relegating the public service to delivery modes focused on process management and implementation. A further possibility, which has been articulated by politicians, is a step change towards a variant of European approaches where 'ministerial cabinets' drive policy and public servants, or where heads of departments become the political appointments of ministers (and possibly party members) and extensions to other senior appointments.

An externalised scenario shifts the sourcing of advice even further outside, producing an on-demand PAS with a heavy reliance on externals and bringing in capacity as needed and then letting it go. There would be a continued role for the public service in select substantive areas but a focus on managing process. Insourcing has been entrenched in some areas (e.g. IT for decades; and Brexit is a recent policy example). The on-demand nature of policy advising produces a more ad-hoc style of advisory activity than the public service dominated PAS of old. There are signs of this taking root in Australia (notwithstanding counter efforts to re-energise the public service as a substantive policy adviser with a greater stewardship role). In an on-demand model the public service would, in concert with ministers' offices, assume a greater role in brokering advice: knowing what communities of practice or consulting firms to tap, how to optimise external advice within government and engagements outside of it, and who to avoid.

PAS will continue to be a product of the uncertain and often turbulent environments in which PAS now operate and how the core actors, the operating style chosen by the political executive and policy issues coalesce. Overall, trends point to a PAS that is unstable and unpredictable, subject to tensions and contradictions between components, and an administrative tradition that may become of questionable value when sorely challenged by political executives (Halligan, 2020).

Instability of PAS

It seems highly likely that PAS will remain unstable. The long-standing flexibilities of PAS in responding to new political executives and the policy issues du jour have been tested by minority or coalition governments in all four PAS, and by a relatively quick succession of prime ministers in Australia and the United Kingdom (three from the same party in as many years). Within governments, stark and irreconcilable differences on major issues have arisen: in Australia, between the moderate and hard conservatives in Turnbull's short-lived government (Evans, Grattan and McCaffrie, 2019); and in the United Kingdom, 'Cabinet's chasm-like fissure over the right sort of Brexit' under May, the latter producing 'decision-making paralysis across Whitehall' (Rutter, 2019, 61).

To date, PAS thinking has tended to assume that governments are capable of making informed decisions about the choice of advisory instruments and sources. The policy advisory system adapts accordingly. For many purposes it is appropriate for the political executive to be regarded as a given and relatively stable in Westminster PAS analysis. However, as the departures have mounted alarmingly, there are reasons for questioning these assumptions. Government control has been receding because of its own actions but also due to the environmental pressures arising from the tempo of change and issue outbursts. Further, there are general questions about how well governments are responding to the complexity of policy issues, where complicated policy sectors see interests multiply and overall volatility. Another issue is whether the political system can produce governments that have the competence for good governance, as evidenced by several cases of serial incompetence in recent times.

The unpredictability of PAS is signalled by abrupt shifts in direction that point to the dysfunctional nature of how the PAS system has been operating. Take the rise of royal commissions in Australia in recent years after they had become regarded as almost dormant. The use of this instrument is seen as a result of ineffective government policy-making, and the clamour for them reflects a lack of faith in government (Hayne, 2019).

PAS has always invited competitive advice, with courts of old and new featuring advisers jockeying for the ear of decision makers and with those sitting on the outside looking for access (Savoie, 1999; Rhodes, 2014). PAS has also purposefully been reformed with the aim of increasing competitiveness. In part this has occurred through the institutionalisation of new advisory bodies or reforms to existing ones (e.g. partisan advisers, parliamentary officers) and through managerial reforms that introduced competitive market principles inside government, as well as with purchase advisers outside of it (Boston, 1996; Richards, 2008; Rhodes, Wanna and Weller, 2009). In all four

PAS, the second-order changes noted in this chapter point to a more distributed PAS, although in the Canadian and New Zealand PAS there is considerably less capacity outside of the public service, specifically in the think tank landscape. This may present challenges for governments seeking to increase contestability of policy advice beyond government proper. It may see a continued rise in the policy-specific functions of partisan advisers or more status quo options where governments simply cannot look to domestic alternative supplies to the degree possible in the United Kingdom or Australia. Conversely, the concerns have amplified about the dependence on consultants in Australia and, to a degree, in the United Kingdom around Brexit-related issues. While there is certainly an ebb and flow of advisory supply in response to demand and pressing policy needs, there is also a requirement to actively seek to manage and balance advisory inputs. In the backdrop of this is a public service institution that has seen its role gradually evolve, with increasingly loud calls for attention to the basic foundational policy capacity it is able to muster.

Contradictions and Tensions

The nature of PAS is also increasingly marked by ongoing tensions around short- versus long-term policy advice considerations. While not new, the four classic Westminster PAS reviewed here point to growing 'issues management' and short-termism that sees public service fire-fighting capacity on the rise without the ability to make comparable investments in the longer-term capacity (Page and Jenkins, 2005; Howlett, Wellstead and Craft, 2017). This is manifested in many ways but can be exacerbated where there are shorter electoral cycles that exert pressure on PAS through the need for coalition building and ongoing PAS recalibration.

A key challenge then for PAS is: who is going to take the longer (or in some cases even a medium-term) view? In a traditional public-service-centred PAS there was an inherent understanding that the public service was the institution that provided context and considerations that would inform decision-making beyond the horizon of single governments. At least there was a notional idea that someone out there was thinking beyond the next ballot box. These issues have received attention in formal public service reviews with some concrete responses, including foresight agencies like Horizons Canada (a repurposed version of the policy research initiative unit), investments in longer-term planning, and various efforts to introduce professional standards and communities of practices as previously noted.

The coordination of PAS moving forward will also continue to be put to the test. The growing attention to the concentration of power and governing from the centre around prime ministers reflects the challenges of using control and power appropriately, but also securing coordination in a pluralised and porous PAS where policy files are brought to the centre to keep them moving or where the centre is 'holding on' by seeking some degree of coherence and planning amongst all the policy work of government (Dahlstrom et al., 2011). Central agencies in particular have been, to varying degrees, providing enterprise-wide perspectives and contestability within PAS, as well as trying to get everyone working in the same direction. Moving forward, the centre of government will face continued pressures to perform that function, and Westminster PAS will have to revisit how it secures coherence and coordination. The on-again, off-again use of senior official committees, centralised delivery, results and strategy units in all four Westminster PAS are manifestations of attempts to coordinate from the centre (Harris and Rutter, 2014; Craft and Wilson, 2018). The long-standing tensions around control and autonomy of advisory bodies are in many ways a coordination problem. Perennial attempts at securing improved policy coherence through coordination will undoubtedly continue, and Westminster PAS will continue to experiment with loose and tight forms of coordination and how best to manage advisory inputs inside and outside of its span of control. Growing pressures for externalisation, which produce additional advisory inputs but, as explored already, also feature calls to bring advisory activity outside and into the open, will add to the need for adept management at the centre. Generalising about the Westminster resilience can be problematic because of variations among the four countries.

A Tenuous Westminster Tradition?

Once the Westminster approach was a fail-safe, but this is no longer necessarily the case. At the end of the 2010s, many observers argued that there was a crisis in governance within the anglophone systems with far-reaching consequence for PAS. The question of the 'unstable state' in an 'unstable world' and approaches to policy capacity have been around for some time (Parsons, 2004) but in some respects have evolved and have been arguably amplified by populism (Boston, 2017; Young, 2018; Blick, 2019). The dimensions of the crisis centre on the loss of trust in government and its ability to engage in policymaking, self-serving behaviour of election-fixated politicians, discreditable policy discourse and ineffective policy, and the abuse of power by political executives. Constitutional issues have also come to the fore. In late 2019, the crisis was arguably the most acute in Australia and the United Kingdom. For Australia, the deterioration in governance is pronounced: 'Trust in all sorts of institutions, governmental and private, has been damaged or destroyed ... . We seem unable to conduct reasoned debates about policy matters. Policy ideas seem often to be framed only for partisan or sectional advantage with little articulation of how or why their implementation would contribute to the greater good' (Evans, Grattan and McCaffrie, 2019; Hayne, 2019, 7). For the United Kingdom, the multiple dimensions of the Brexit crisis have challenged the British political tradition (Hall and Marsh, 2019), which has direct implications for the administration tradition.

The adaptability of PAS in the Westminster tradition results in potential for large swings in how political-administrative relations are managed, stylistic preferences, and how PAS norms are respected or boundaries pushed. The experiences of Canada and New Zealand indicate some resilience: the excesses of Harper were replaced by Trudeau's more mainstream style; and legislation in NZ is expected to give expression to traditional Westminster principles. In contrast, Australia and the United Kingdom have experienced extended periods of third-order challenges to their arrangements, which are expected to continue under the prime ministers elected in 2019. Finally, NZ has also been the most effective at adapting Westminster PAS to recognise and respect Indigenous peoples and their cultural and political traditions, while Canada and Australia are experiencing greater pressures to be more inclusive (Gregory and Maynard 2019).

It is clear that the four PAS are shaped by both administrative and country traditions. The distinctive quality of the anglophone tradition is that it both facilitates and constrains change, a combination that distinguishes it from other traditions and has played an important role in the modernisation process in all four countries. However, the question of the constraining role of the tradition came under challenge because new modes of operation and relationships posed questions about the viability of the Westminster tradition. The internal tensions in the traditional framework have been repeatedly exposed in the twenty-first-century environment, such as the notion that the civil service can be 'both politically neutral and completely tied to "the government of the day"' (Talbot, 2019, 65). Were these pressure points matters that could be readily accommodated, or were they raising issues about the fundamentals of good governance? There have been costs in terms of public service capability and the reliance on ministers and political executives, whose policy competence does not match their authority.

In other words, the constraining influence of Westminster principles has been found wanting, and the administrative tradition continues to be vulnerable in respects that are relevant to policymaking. The reliance on interpretation and continued practice of Westminster principles has always made them susceptible to stretching and even abuse. There are, however, increasing warnings by those studying and working within Westminster systems that we may have already passed a tipping point. Many have voiced concerns about short-termism, excessive partisanship, constant campaigning, the growing use of partisan and external advisers, and a hollowed-out public service, which have challenged the viability of Westminster (Savoie, 2003, 2008, 2019; Aucoin, 2012; Diamond, 2019; Grube, 2019).

One response has been to formalise, and in some cases legally codify, aspects that were previously conventions or norms (e.g. cabinet manuals, ministerial guidance and codes of conduct for political advisers). Some are more comprehensive and effective than others, and several aspects of PAS will always remain outside of the control or authority of government, such as the capacity of externals or types of policy issues that require responses. Paradoxically, some of the biggest pathologies of PAS are owing to the path dependencies that have developed around how advisory systems operate, how various advisory units are stood up and used, and how investments and retrenchments have shaped how these systems operate. The future of PAS, then, will to a degree hinge on the extent to which these four PAS, and the broader Westminster principles that underpin them, are formalised or left flexible and how governments navigate path dependencies.

There are major issues to be confronted about reconciling good public policy and the complexities of policymaking in the volatile environment of the twenty-first century. Governments will continue to need advice, but it is already clear that the types and nature of that advice sought by ministers can no longer be assumed or predicted. Westminster PAS has evolved to such a degree that it is less clear who will provide advice, what the nature of the advice will be, and if and how governments in Canberra, London, Ottawa or Wellington will effectively use it.

Appendix A

Interview List

Country	Title	Dates
Australia		
A1	Secretary	March 2018
A2	Secretary	March 2018
A3	Deputy secretary	April 2018
A4	Deputy secretary	April 2018
A5	Deputy secretary	April 2018
A6	Secretary	May 2018
A7	Secretary	May 2018
A8	Secretary	July 2018
A9	Minister	3 August 2018
A10	Senior adviser	1 August 2018
A11	COS	1 August 2018
A12	COS	1 August 2018
A13	DPMC official	1 August 2019
Canada		
C1	Minister	May 2019
C2	Minister	May 2019
C3	Deputy minister	13 December 2017
C4	Deputy minister	1 May 2018
C5	PCO official	30 August 2018
C6	PCO official	8 September 2018
C7	PCO official	6 October 2017
C8	Director of policy, minister's office	18 October 2018
C9	Director of policy, minister's office	13 December 2017
C10	Director of policy, minister's office	14 December 2017
C11	Director of policy, minister's office	19 October 2018
C12	Senior PMO official	8 September 2017
C13	Senior PCO official	8 December 2016
C14	Senior PCO official	15 December 2016
C15	Deputy minister	14 December 2017

(*cont.*)

Country	Title	Dates
United Kingdom		
UK1	Senior No 10 adviser	17 April 2018
UK2	Senior No 10 adviser	20 April 2018
UK3	Senior No 10 adviser	17 April 2018
UK4	Senior No 10 adviser	20 April 2018
UK5	Ministerial special adviser	20 April 2018
UK6	Ministerial special adviser	19 April 2018
UK7	Permanent secretary	23 April 2019
UK8	Consultant	11 October 2018
UK9	Consultant	10 October 2018
UK10	Senior civil servant	9 August 2018
UK11	Senior civil servant	9 August 2018
UK12	Senior civil servant	13 August 2018
UK13	Senior civil servant	13 August 2018
UK14	Senior civil servant	20 August 2018
UK15	Senior civil servant	21 August 2018
UK16	Senior civil servant	22 August 2018
UK17	Senior civil servant	23 August 2018
UK18	Former permanent secretary	28 August 2018
UK19	Senior think tank official	20 April 2018
UK20	Think tank official	20 April 2018
UK21	Minister	30 January 2018
New Zealand		
NZ1	Former minister	30 July 2018
NZ2	Minister	10 August 2018
NZ3	Minister	7 August 2018
NZ4	Minister	8 August 2018
NZ5	Ministerial adviser	8 August 2018
NZ6	Ministerial adviser	8 August 2018
NZ7	Ministerial adviser	10 August 2018
NZ8	Ministerial adviser	9 August 2018
NZ9	Former PMO adviser	9 August 2018
NZ10	DPMC adviser	8 August 2018
NZ11	Former chief executive & think tank expert	31 July 2018
NZ12	Chief executive	31 July 2018
NZ13	Think tank expert	1 August 2018
NZ14	Deputy chief executive	1 August 2018

(*cont.*)

Country	Title	Dates
NZ15	Deputy chief executive	1 August 2018
NZ16	Former senior public servant & think tank expert	3 August 2018
NZ17	Policy specialist	3 August 2018
NZ18	Senior executive	16 August 2017
NZ19	Deputy chief executive	16 August 2017

Appendix B

Cases of Independent Reviews

Australia

Alexander, E., and D. Thodey (2018). *Independent Review into the Operation of the Public Governance, Performance and Accountability Act 2013 and Rule.* Canberra: Commonwealth of Australia.

Belcher, B. (2015). *Independent Review of Whole-of-Government Internal Regulation: Report to the Secretaries Committee on Transformation, Volume 1 Recommendations.* Canberra: Department of Finance.

Independent Review of the APS (2019, 19 March). *Independent Review of the APS: Priorities for Change.* Canberra: Commonwealth of Australia.

Shergold, P. (2015). *Learning from Failure: Why Large Government Policy Initiatives Have Gone so Badly Wrong in the Past and How the Chances of Success in the Future Can Be Improved. An Independent Review of Government Processes for Implementing Large Programs and Projects.* Canberra: Commonwealth of Australia.

Canada

TBS/Treasury Board of Canada Secretariat (2006) *From Red Tape to Clear Results: The Report of the Independent Blue-Ribbon Panel on Grant and Contribution Program.* Ottawa: TBS.

New Zealand

Scott, G. (2010). *Improving the Quality and Value of Policy Advice. Committee Appointed by the Review of Expenditure on Policy Advice.* Wellington: Government of New Zealand.

School of Government (2017). *Independent Review of the Performance Management Framework*. Wellington: Victoria University of Wellington.

United Kingdom

Department of Health and Social Care (2018). *Modernising the Mental Health Act: Increasing Choice, Reducing Compulsion: Final report of the Independent Review of the Mental Health Act 1983*, December.

Home Office (2019, in progress) *Independent Review of Prevent: Ways of Working. Led by Lord Alex Carlile, the review is analysing information to underpin evidence-based recommendations on the government's strategy for supporting people vulnerable to being drawn into terrorism.* www.gov.uk/government/publications/inde pendent-review-of-prevent/independent-review-of-prevent-ways-of-working.

Read, M. (2013). *Practical Steps to Improve Management Information in Government: An Independent Report* Commissioned by the Minister for the Cabinet Office and Chief Secretary to the Treasury. London.

Notes

2 Comparative Contexts

1. In Australia, for example, there is the 'long-standing reliance on government as the major agency of development'. The Australian instrumental view towards government is attributed to utilitarianism with government regarded 'as the instrument of the people' (Emy and Hughes, 1991, 117–18; see also Encel, 1960; Wettenhall, 2006).
2. The fluidity of relationships when confronted by a highly complex issue is apparent from the May government's handling of Brexit (Shipman, 2017).
3. The term 'ministry' may also be used instead of 'department'. Departmental lists in New Zealand and the United Kingdom also include several minor offices.
4. Note however that Canada has been operating with thirty-nine ministers, compared to Australia's twenty-nine, plus twelve parliamentary secretaries.

4 Public Services and Policy Advice

1. For example, New Zealand has Greater Christchurch recovery and Australia has Indigenous Affairs for program integration.
2. The disciplines included comparative institutional analysis, effectiveness analysis, program evaluation, micro-simulation modelling and quantitative/performance analysis (Scott, 2010).
3. Main sources are www.apsc.gov.au/priorities/capability-reviews and APSC (2014).

5 Ministerial Partisan Advisers and the Politicisation of PAS

1. See https://publications.parliament.uk/pa/cm200809/cmselect/cmpu badm/504/09050701.htm, Q18.
2. Labour changed the rules governing party spills to prevent precisely the types of rapid turnovers and conflict that characterised the Liberal coalition from 2007 to 2018.

3. These were typically restricted to PMO chief of staff or more rarely PMO director of policy interventions. In another signal of their established nature and influence in Canada, the PCO formally changed the guidelines to allow ministerial partisan advisers, not just PMO staff, to participate in cabinet activity on an as-needed basis as support staff for ministers (Craft, 2018).

4. Up until the 1960s there was of course a tradition of public servants staffing Canadian prime ministers' offices, but in modern practice the only exception to partisan-only appointments has been the Mulroney appointment of Derek Burney, a career diplomat, to PMO chief of staff from 1987 to 1989.

6 Alternative Advice from within Government

1. There are variations and exceptions. An agency may report to both the executive and parliament. A few commissions of inquiry may have an ongoing remit to report at intervals. These are not covered here.

2. For example, a commission of inquiry appointed in New Zealand in 2018 was described as having the powers of a royal commission.

3. It is unclear whether this latter total includes 'public inquiries' discussed subsequently.

4. See www.publicinquiries.com.au/defining.htm).

5. See www.gov.uk/government/news/sir-amyas-morse-to-lead-indepen dent-review-of-the-loan-charge; www.pmc.gov.au/news-centre/gov ernment/independent-review-australian-public-service.

6. The practice has been associated with the United States, where it has referred to high-level officials (termed 'czars') who have oversight of a particular policy or problem area, the usage of which increased under Presidents G. W. Bush and B. Obama.

7. Levitt and Solesbury (2012, p. 13) excluded about 110 national clinical directors who are expert practitioners appointed in the Department of Health, mostly for several years; business ambassadors; and non-executive directors appointed to boards of departments and public bodies.

8. The posts are first subject to allocation to parties in accordance with their representation.

9. The Commission had predecessors, but they were constituted on a different basis and with narrower foci and standing.

10. The UK commission is the Law Commission of England and Wales. The Australian commission was renamed the Australian Law Reform Commission in 1996 under new legislation.

11. E.g. the key government disagreed with most recommendations of a New Zealand Law Commission report (2012) on the Official Information Act (Palmer and Butler, 2016); and the Morrison government ignored the report of the Australian Law Reform Commission into family law in September 2019 by appointing a joint parliamentary committee chaired by two senators with strong positions on the operation of the courts.
12. The Australian Productivity Commission had predecessors, but they were constituted on a different basis and with narrower foci and standing.

7 External Advice

1. Externalization of policy advice can be understood as a process in which 'various advisory activities previously undertaken largely by internal government actors are shifted outside government bureaucracies' (Veselý, 2013, 200) and as 'the extent to which actors outside government exercise influence [in policy making]' (Craft and Howlett, 2013, 188).
2. We adopt the UK National Audit Office definition of consultancy as 'The provision to management of objective advice relating to strategy, structure, management or operations of an organisation, in pursuit of its purposes and objectives. Such advice is provided outside the "business-as-usual" environment when in-house skills are not available and will be time-limited. Consultancy may include the identification of options with recommendations, or assistance with (but not the delivery of) the implementation of solutions' (CAG/Comptroller and Auditor General (UK), 2016a, 14).
3. https://gov.uk/guidance/contestable-policy-fund (accessed 20 September 2018).
4. See https://assets.publishing.service.gov.uk/government/uploads/system/uploads/attachment_data/file/220506/review_fincrisis_response_290312.pdf.

9 Trends, Tensions and the State of Neo-policy Advisory Systems

1. https://openpolicy.blog.gov.uk/what-is-open-policy-making/.
2. At the centre of government, Australia's Department of the Prime Minister and Cabinet has a Policy Innovation and Projects division but no public identity of relevance here.

3. https://openpolicy.blog.gov.uk/about/.
4. The 'functional model' covers 'priority areas of common, cross-departmental activity for which central leadership is required' and includes many professions. The distinction is not entirely clear except professions cover a wider range of expertise that includes niche and broad areas (e.g. policy, operational delivery). See https://assets .publishing.service.gov.uk/government/%20uploads/system/%20uploa ds/attachment_data/file/418869/The_Functional_Model.pdf.
5. Manzoni's presentation to the Institute for Government, April 2018, available in video form, appeared to advocate a civil service composed of specialists (as opposed to the traditional generalists), who might at an advanced stage in their career become generalists. This was illustrated by the commercial function.
6. See www.gov.uk/government/organisations/civil-service-policy-profes sion/about.
7. See www.gov.uk/guidance/what-works-network.

References

Abelson, D. E. (2002). *Do Think Tanks Matter? Assessing the Impact of Public Policy Institutes.* Kingston and Montreal: McGill-Queen's University Press.

Abelson, D. E. (2009). *Do Think Tanks Matter? Assessing the Impact of Public Policy Institutes.* 2nd ed. (revised and expanded). Kingston and Montreal: McGill-Queen's University Press.

Abelson, D. E. (2016). *Northern Lights: Exploring Canada's Think Tank Landscape.* Kingston and Montreal: McGill-Queen's University Press.

Abelson, D. E. (2018). Any better ideas? Think tanks and policy analysis in Canada. In L. Dobuzinskis and M. Howlett (eds.), *Policy Analysis in Canada.* Bristol: Policy Press, pp. 275–96.

Abelson, D. E., and E. A. Lindquist (2000). Think tanks across North America. In R. K. Weaver and J. G. McGann (eds.), *Think Tanks and Civil Societies: Catalyst for Ideas and Action.* Piscataway, NJ: Transaction Publishers, pp. 37–66.

Aberbach, J. D., and B. A. Rockman (1989). On the rise, transformation, and decline of analysis in the US government. *Governance: An International Journal of Policy, Administration, and Institutions* 2(3): 293–314.

Aberbach, J. D., and B. A. Rockman (1994). Civil servants and policymakers: Neutral or responsive competence? *Governance: An International Journal of Policy, Administration, and Institutions* 7(4): 461–9.

AGRAGA/Advisory Group on the Reform of Australian Government Administration (2009). *Reform of Australian Government Administration: Building the World's Best Public Service.* Canberra: Commonwealth of Australia.

Althaus, C. (2011). Assessing the capacity to deliver – the BER experience. *Australian Journal of Public Administration* 70(4): 421–36.

ANAO (Australian National Audit Office) (2010). *Effective Cross-Agency Agreements.* Audit Report No. 41 2009–2010. Canberra: ANAO.

APSC (Australian Public Service Commission) (2014). *State of the Service Report 2013–14.* Canberra: APSC.

APSR (Australian Public Service Review) (2019). *Interim Report.* Department of the Prime Minister and Cabinet, Canberra. www .apsreview.gov.au/priorities.

Aucoin, P. (1995). *The New Public Management: Canada in Comparative Perspective.* Montreal: Institute for Research on Public Policy.

Aucoin, P. (2002). Beyond the 'new' in public management. In C. Dunn (ed.), *A Handbook of Canadian Public Administration.* Don Mills, ON: Oxford University Press, pp. 32–57.

Aucoin, P. (2010). Canada. In C. Eichbaum and R. Shaw (eds.), *Partisan Appointees and Public Servants: An International Analysis.* Boston, MA: Edward Elgar Publishing, pp. 64–93.

Aucoin, P. (2012). New political governance in Westminster systems: Impartial public administration and management performance at risk. *Governance: An International Journal of Policy, Administration, and Institutions* 25(2): 177–99.

Aucoin, P., M. Jarvis and L. Turnbull (2011). *Democratizing the Constitution: Reforming Responsible Government.* Toronto: Emond Publishing.

Aucoin, P., J. Smith and G. Dinsdale (2004). *Responsible Government: Clarifying Essentials, Dispelling Myths and Exploring Change.* Ottawa: Canadian Centre for Management Development.

Auditor-General (Australia) (2017). *Australian Government Procurement Contract Reporting 2017–2018.* ANAO Report No.19 2017–18. Canberra: ANAO. ISSN 2203–0352 (Online).

Baker, R. J. S. (1972). *Administrative Theory and Public Administration.* London: Hutchinson University Library.

Bakvis, H. (1997). Advising the executive: Think tanks, consultants, political staff and kitchen cabinets. In P. Weller, H. Bakvis and R. A. W. Rhodes (eds.), *The Hollow Crown: Countervailing Trends in Core Executives.* Basingstoke: Macmillan Press, pp. 84–125.

Bakvis, H. (2000). Rebuilding policy capacity in the era of the fiscal dividend. *Governance: An International Journal of Policy, Administration, and Institutions* 13(1): 71–103.

Bakvis, H. (2013). In the shadows of hierarchy: Intergovernmental governance in Canada and the European Union. *Canadian Public Administration* 56(2): 203–18.

Bakvis, H., and L. Juillet (2004). *The Horizontal Challenge: Line Department, Central Agencies and Leadership.* Ottawa: The Canada School of Public Service.

Balls, K. (2019, 17 August). How No. 10 Downing Street is taking back control. *The Spectator.*

Banks, G. (2011, 22 September). Independent Policy Advice and the Productivity Commission. Chancellor's Lecture, Swinburne University.

Banks, G. (2012, 1 November). Productivity Policies: The 'To Do' List. Economic and Social Outlook Conference, Securing the Future, Melbourne.

Banks, G. (2013). *The Governance of Public Policy: Lectures in Honour of Eminent Australians*. Melbourne: Australian and New Zealand School of Government.

Banks, G. (2014). Making public policy in the public interest. In S. Prasser and H. Tracey (eds.), *Royal Commissions and Public Inquiries: Practice and Potential*. Ballarat: Connorcourt Publishing, pp. 112–32.

Banks, G. (2015, 6–7 July). Institutions to Promote Pro-productivity Policies: Logic and Lessons. Global Dialogue on the Future of Productivity Growth: Towards an OECD Productivity Network. Mexico City.

Banks, G. (2018, 20 November). *Whatever Happened to 'Evidence Based Policy Making'?* Alf Rattigan Lecture. Melbourne: ANZSOG. www .anzsog.edu.au/preview-documents/research-output/5307-alf-rattigan-lec ture-2018.

Barberis, P. (1996). *The Elite of the Elite: Permanent Secretaries in the British Higher Civil Service*. Aldershot: Dartmouth.

Beeby, D. (2011, 20 September). Tories hire $90,000-a-day consultant to help cut spending. *The Globe and Mail*. www.theglobeandmail.com/news/ politics/tories-hire-90000-a-day-consultant-to-help-cut-federal-spending/ article4256641/.

Behm, A. (2015). *No, Minister: So You Want to Be Chief of Staff?* Melbourne: Melbourne University Press.

Bell, S., and A. Hindmoor (2009). *Rethinking Governance: The Centrality of the State in Modern Society*. Cambridge: Cambridge University Press

Bennett, O. (2019). *Michael Gove: A Man in a Hurry*. London: Biteback Publishing.

Bentham, J. (2006). The IPPR and Demos: Think tanks of the new social democracy. *Political Quarterly* 77(2): 166–74.

Benton, M., and M. Russell (2013). Assessing the impact of parliamentary oversight committees: The select committees in the British House of Commons. *Parliamentary Affairs* 66(4): 772–97

Berardo, R., and J. Scholz (2010). Self-organizing policy networks: Risk, partner selection, and cooperation in estuaries. *American Journal of Political Science* 54(3): 632–49.

Beveridge, R. (2012). Consultants, depoliticization and arena-shifting in the policy process: Privatizing water in Berlin. *Policy Sciences* 45(1): 47–68.

Bingham, L. B., T. Nabatchi and R. O'Leary (2005). The new governance: Practices and processes for stakeholder and citizen participation in the work of government. *Public Administration Review* 65(5): 547–58.

Blick, A. (2018). Special advisers in the United Kingdom: Tensions in Whitehall. In R. Shaw and C. Eichbaum (eds.), *Ministers, Minders and Mandarins: An International Study of Relationships at the Executive Summit of Parliamentary Democracies*. London: Edward Elgar, pp. 180–97.

Blick, A. (2019). *Populism and the UK Constitution*. London: Constitution Society. https://consoc.org.uk/publications/populism-and-the-uk-constitution/.

Blick, A., and G. Jones (2010). *Premiership: The Development, Nature and Power of the Office of the British Prime Minister*. Charlottesville, VA: Societas.

Blick, A., and G. Jones (2013). *At Power's Elbow: Aides to Prime Ministers from Robert Walpole to David Cameron*. London: Biteback Publishing.

Bogdanor, V. (ed.) (2005). *Joined-Up Government*. Oxford: Oxford University Press.

Boston, J. (1994). Purchasing policy advice: The limits to contracting out. *Governance: An International Journal of Policy, Administration, and Institutions* 7(1): 1–30.

Boston, J. (2012). Reflections on new political governance in Westminster systems. *Governance: An International Journal of Policy, Administration, and Institutions* 25(2): 201–205.

Boston, J. (2016). *Governing for the Future: Designing Democratic Institutions for a Better Tomorrow*. Bingley: Emerald.

Boston, J. (2017). *Safeguarding Your Future: Governing in an Uncertain World*. Wellington: BWB Texts.

Boston, J., D. Bagnall and A. Barry (2019). *Foresight, Insight and Oversight: Enhancing Long-Term Government through Better Parliamentary Scrutiny*. Wellington: Institute for Governance and Policy Studies.

Boston, J., and D. Gill (2011). Working across organizational boundaries: The challenge for accountability. In B. Ryan and D. Gill (eds.), *Future State: Directions for Public Management in New Zealand*. Wellington: Victoria University Press, pp. 212–46.

Boston, J., and Halligan, J. (2012). Political management and new political governance: Reconciling political responsiveness and neutral competence. In H. Bakvis and M. Jarvis (eds.), *From New Public Management to New Political Governance: Essays in Honour of Peter C. Aucoin*. Kingston and Montreal: McGill-Queen's University Press, pp. 204–41.

Boston, J., and D. Bullock (2010). Multi-party governance: Managing the unity-distinctiveness dilemma in executive coalitions. *Party Politics* 18(3): 349–68.

Boston, J., J. Martin, J. Pallot and P. Walsh (1996). *Public Management: The New Zealand Model*. Auckland: Oxford University Press.

Boucher, A. (2013). Bureaucratic control and policy change: A comparative venue shopping approach to skilled immigration policies in Australia and Canada. *Journal of Comparative Policy Analysis* 15(4): 349–67.

Boucher, M. (2018). Who you know in the PMO: Lobbying the Prime Minister's Office in Canada. *Canadian Public Administration* 61(3): 317–40.

Bourgault, J. (2014). Federal deputy ministers: Serial servers looking for influence. In J. Bourgault and C. Dunn (eds.), *Deputy Ministers in Canada: Comparative and Jurisdictional Perspectives*. Toronto: University of Toronto Press, pp. 364–400.

Bourgault, J. (2018). Governance Issues for Deputy Ministers in Canadian Government in 2015. Draft manuscript.

Bourgault, J., and C. Dunn (eds.) (2014a). Conclusion: Deputy ministers in Canada – evolution of deputy ministers as archetypal figures. In J. Bourgault and C. Dunn (eds.), *Deputy Ministers in Canada: Comparative and Jurisdictional Perspectives*. Toronto: University of Toronto Press, pp. 429–50.

Bourgault, J., and C. Dunn (eds.) (2014b). *Deputy Ministers in Canada: Comparative and Jurisdictional Perspectives*. Toronto: University of Toronto Press.

Bousted, M. (2017, 4 August). The consequences of Gove's ideological reforms are now being felt everywhere. *TES*.

Bowen, P. (2016). *The Parliamentary Budget Office: Supporting Australian Democracy*. Papers on Parliament no. 64. Canberra: Department of the Senate.

BPSAG/Better Public Services Advisory Group (2011). *Better Public Services Advisory Group Report*. Wellington: New Zealand Government.

Brans, M., I. Iris-Geneva and M. Howlet (eds.). (2017). *Routledge Handbook of Comparative Policy Analysis*. New York: Routledge.

Bressers D., M. J. W. van Twist, M. A. van der Steen and J. M. Schulz (2018). The contested autonomy of policy advisory bodies: The trade-off between autonomy and control of policy advisory bodies in the Netherlands, the United Kingdom, and Sweden. In E. Ongaro and S. Van Thiel (eds.), *The Palgrave Handbook of Public Administration and Management in Europe*. London: Palgrave Macmillan, pp. 1189–1211.

British Broadcasting Corporation (2020). PM's senior aide Dominic Cummings calls for civil service changes. www.bbc.com/news/uk-politics -50978329.

Bromell, D. (2017). *The Art and Craft of Policy Advising: A Practical Guide.* Gewerbestrasse: Springer.

Brown, G. (2017). *My Life, Our Times.* London: Penguin Random House.

Burgess, V. (2017, 12 July). APS leadership turnover set for another jolt – for better or for worse. Mandarin.

Bushell-Embling, D. (2017, 26 July). PM&C develops digital briefing system. *Govtech Review.* www.govtechreview.com.au/content/gov-digital/article/ pm-amp-c-develops-digital-briefing-system-790769450.

Cabinet Office (UK) (2010). Code of conduct for special advisers. http://do wnload.cabinetoffice.gov.uk/special-advisers/code-of-conduct.pdf.

Cabinet Office (UK) (2018). Annual report on special advisers. https://assets .publishing.service.gov.uk/government/uploads/system/uploads/attach ment_data/file/766413/AnnualReportOnSpecialAdvisers2018.pdf.

CAG/Comptroller and Auditor General (UK) (2006, December). *Central Government's Use of Consultants.* HC 128. London: National Audit Office.

CAG/Comptroller and Auditor General (UK) (2010, October). *Central Government's Use of Consultants and Interims.* HC 488. London: National Audit Office.

CAG/Comptroller and Auditor General (UK) (2016a, 13 January). *Cross Government Use of Consultants and Temporary Staff.* HC 603. London: National Audit Office.

CAG/Comptroller and Auditor General (UK) (2016b, 23 February). *Accountability to Parliament for Taxpayers' Money.* HC 849. Session 2015–16. London: National Audit Office.

CAG/Comptroller and Auditor General (UK) (2016c, 21 July). *Spending Review 2015.* HC 571. London: National Audit Office.

CAG/Comptroller and Auditor General (UK) (2018, 23 May). *Investigation into Government-Funded Inquiries.* HC 836. Session 2017–19. London: National Audit Office.

CAG/Comptroller and Auditor General (UK) (2019, 7 June). *Departments' Use of Consultants to Support Preparations for EU Exit.* HC 2105. London: National Audit Office.

Caird, J. S. (2016, 30 November). Public inquiries: Non-statutory commissions of inquiry. House of Commons Library, Briefing Paper Number 02599.

Campbell, C., and J. Halligan (1992). *Political Leadership in an Age of Constraint: The Experience of Australia.* Sydney: Allen and Unwin; Pittsburgh, PA: University of Pittsburgh Press.

Campbell, C., and G. K. Wilson (1995). *The End of Whitehall: Death of a Paradigm?* Oxford and Cambridge: Blackwell.

Campbell, C., and G. Szablowski (1979). *The Superbureaucrats: Structure and Behaviour in Central Agencies.* Toronto: Gage.

Carroll, B. W. (1990). Politics and administration: A trichotomy? *Governance: An International Journal of Policy, Administration, and Institutions* 3(4): 345–66.

Carson, D., and A. Wellstead (2015). Government with a cast of dozens: Policy capacity risks and policy work in the northern territory. *Australian Journal of Public Administration* 74(2): 162–75.

Cashore, B., and M. Howlett (2007). Punctuating which equilibrium? Understanding thermostatic policy dynamics in Pacific Northwest forestry. *American Journal of Political Science* 51(3): 532–51.

Castles, F. (1989). Big government in weak states: The paradox of state size in the English-speaking nations of advanced capitalism. *Journal of Commonwealth and Comparative Politics* 27(3): 267–93.

Chapman, R. (1996). The end of the civil service? In P. Barberis (ed.), *The Whitehall Reader: The UK's Administrative Machine in Action.* Buckingham: Open University Press, pp. 187–91.

Chowdhury, A. R. (2019). International–domestic linkages in a developing country context: The case of the Rohingyas in Bangladesh. *Policy Studies* 40(3–4): 303–19.

Christensen, T., and P. Lægreid (2007). The whole of government approach to public sector reform. *Public Administration Review* 67(6): 1057–64.

Clarke, A. (2019). *Opening the Government of Canada: The Federal Bureaucracy in the Digital Age.* Vancouver: University of British Columbia Press.

Clarke, A., and J. Craft (2017). The vestiges and vanguards of policy design in a digital context. *Canadian Public Administration* 60(4): 476–97.

Clift, B. (2018). *The IMF and the Politics of Austerity in the Wake of the Global Financial Crisis.* Oxford: Oxford University Press.

Cole, H. (2017, 27 March). WHATS-CAB: 18 Cabinet ministers used WhatsApp recently – including Amber Rudd who accused the messaging app of helping terrorists. *The Sun.* www.thesun.co.uk/news/3191673/eighteen-cabinet-ministers-used-whatsapp-recently-including-amber-rudd-who-accused-the-messaging-service-of-helping-terrorists/

Coleman, W. (2016). *Financial Services, Globalization, and Domestic Policy Change.* London: Macmillan.

Connaughton, B. (2010). 'Glorified gofers, policy experts or good generalists': A classification of the roles of the Irish ministerial adviser. *Irish Political Studies* 25(3): 347–69.

Corry, D. (2011). Power at the centre: Is the National Economic Council a new way of organizing things? *The Political Quarterly* 82(3): 459–68.

Cowie, G., and M. Sandford (2018, 24 September). *Statutory commissions of inquiry: The Inquiries Act 2005.* House of Commons Library, Briefing Paper No. SN06410.

Craft, J. (2015a). Conceptualizing partisan advisers as policy workers. *Policy Sciences Journal* 48(2): 135–58.

Craft, J. (2015b). Revisiting the Gospel: Appointed political staffs and core executive policy coordination. *International Journal of Public Administration* 38(1): 56–65.

Craft, J. (2016). *Backrooms and Beyond: Partisan Advisers and the Politics of Policy Work in Canada.* Toronto: University of Toronto Press.

Craft, J. (2017a). Partisan advisers and political policy failure avoidance. *Public Administration* 95(2): 327–41.

Craft, J. (2017b). Governing on the front foot: The permanent campaign and Canada's evolving 'Bargain(s)'. In A. Marland, T. Giasson and A. Esselment (eds.), *The Permanent Campaign in Canada.* Vancouver: UBC Press, pp. 28–46.

Craft, J. (2018). Canada: Flexing the political arm of government. In R. Shaw and C. Eichbaum (eds.), *Ministers, Minders and Mandarins: An International Study of Relationships at the Executive Summit of Parliamentary Democracies.* London: Edward Elgar, pp. 34–52.

Craft, J., and M. Daku (2017). A comparative assessment of elite policy recruits in Canada. *Journal of Comparative Policy Analysis* 19(3): 207–26.

Craft, J., and M. Howlett (2012). Policy formulation, governance shifts and policy influence: Location and content in policy advisory systems. *Journal of Public Policy* 32(2): 79–98.

Craft, J., and M. Howlett (2013). The dual dynamics of policy advisory systems: The impact of externalization and politicization on policy advice. *Policy and Society* 32(3): 187–97.

Craft, J., and J. Halligan (2017). Assessing 30 years of Westminster policy advisory system experience. *Policy Sciences* 50(1): 47–62.

Craft, J., and M. Wilder (2017). Catching a second wave: Context and compatibility in advisory system dynamics. *Policy Studies Journal* 45(1): 215–39.

Craft, J., and P. Wilson (2018). Policy analysis and the central executive. In L. Dobuzinskis and M. Howlett (eds.), *Policy Analysis in Canada.* Bristol: Policy Press, pp. 147–64.

Curry, B. (2014, 19 November). Finance Minister Joe Oliver says business tax credit did not require internal analysis. *Globe and Mail.*

Curry, B., and S. Silcoff (2017, 13 April). Encourage seniors to delay retirement, growth council tells Morneau. *Globe and Mail*.

Dahlstrom, C., B. G. Peters and J. Pierre (eds.). (2011). *Steering from the Centre: Strengthening Political Control in Western Democracies*. Toronto: University of Toronto Press.

Davies, J. S. (2011). *Challenging Governance Theory: From Networks to Hegemony*. Bristol: Polity Press.

Davison, N. (2016). *Whole of Government Reforms in New Zealand: The Case of the Policy Project*. London: Institute for Government.

Delacourt, S. (2019, 19 February). Here's the downside of concentrating power in the prime minister's office. *Toronto Star*.

Dent, H. (2002). Consultants and the public service. *Australian Journal of Public Administration* 61(1): 108–13.

DIA/Department of Internal Affairs (2018). *Different Types of Government Reviews*. Wellington: Department of Internal Affairs. www.dia.govt.nz/ Different-types-of-government-reviews.

Diamond, P. (2014). *Governing Britain: Power, Politics and the Prime Minister*. London: I. B. Tauris.

Diamond, P. (2017). The Westminster system under the Cameron coalition: 'Promiscuous partisanship' or institutional resilience? *Public Policy and Administration* 34(3): 1–21.

Diamond, P. (2019). *The End of Whitehall? Government by Permanent Campaign*. New York: Palgrave.

Di Francesco, M. (2001). Process not outcomes in new public management? Policy coherence in Australian government. *Australian Review of Public Affairs* 1(3): 103–16.

Di Francesco, M. (2012). Grand designs? The 'managerial' role of ministers within Westminster-based public management policy. *Australian Journal of Public Administration* 71(3): 257–68.

Dobuzinskis, L. and M. Howlett (eds.) (2018). *Policy Analysis in Canada*. Bristol: Policy Press.

Dobuzinskis, L., M. Howlett and D. Laycock (eds.) (2007). *Policy Analysis in Canada: The State of the Art*. Toronto: University of Toronto Press.

DPMC/Department of the Prime Minister and Cabinet (2014). *The Policy Project – Responsive Today, Shaping Tomorrow*. Wellington: DPMC.

DPMC/Department of the Prime Minister and Cabinet (2019). *APS Policy Capability Roadmap: A Practical Plan to Lift Policy Capability across the AP*. Canberra: Australian Government.

Drezner, D. (2014). The system worked: Global economic governance during the Great Recession. *World Politics* 66(1): 123–64.

Drezner, D. (2018). *The Idea Industry*. New York: Oxford University Press.

Dror, Y. (1984). Policy analysis for advising rulers. In R. Tomlinson and I. Kiss (eds.), *Rethinking the Process of Operational Research and Systems Analysis*. Oxford: Pergamon Press.

Dunleavy, P., et al. (2017). Audit 2017: How effective is the Westminster Parliament in scrutinising central government policy-making? www.democraticaudit.com/2017/08/31/audit-2017-how-effective-is-the-westminster-parliament-in-scrutinising-central-govern ment-policy-making/.

Dunleavy, P., A. Park and R. Taylor (eds.) (2018). *The UK's Changing Democracy: The 2018 Democratic Audit*. London: LSE Press.

Dunn, D. (1997). *Politics and Administration at the Top: Lessons from Down Under*. Pittsburgh: University of Pittsburgh Press.

Dunn, W. (1980). The two-communities metaphor and models of knowledge use. *Knowledge: Creation, Diffusion, Utilization* 1(4): 515–36.

Dwivedi, O. P., and J. I. Gow (1999). *From Bureaucracy to Public Management: The Administrative Culture of the Government of Canada*. Toronto: Broadview Press.

Easton, S. (2018, 4 July). Australian Public Service to start running citizen-satisfaction surveys. *The Mandarin*. www.themandarin.com.au/95214-australian-public-service-to-start-running-citizen-satisfaction-surveys/.

Edwards, L. (2009). Testing the discourse of declining policy capacity: Rail policy and the Department of Transport. *Australian Journal of Public Administration* 68(3): 288–302.

Edwards, M., J. Halligan, B. Horrigan and G. Nicoll (2012). *Public Sector Governance in Australia*. Canberra: ANU Press.

Eichbaum, C. (2017, 8 August). Free and frank advice fast disappearing. *The Dominion Post*.

Eichbaum, C. (2019, 29 July). The 2019 Public Service Reset – tweak or transformation? Presentation notes. Wellington: New Zealand Institute of Public Administration.

Eichbaum, C., and R. Shaw (2007). Ministerial advisers and the politics of policy-making: Bureaucratic permanence and popular control. *Australian Journal of Public Administration* 66(4): 453–67.

Eichbaum, C., and R. Shaw (2008). Revisiting politicization: Political advisers and public servants in Westminster systems. *Governance: An International Journal of Policy, Administration, and Institutions* 21(3): 337–63.

Eichbaum, C., and R. Shaw (2010a). New Zealand. In C. Eichbaum and R. Shaw (eds.), *Partisan Appointees and Public Servants: An International Analysis of the Role of the Political Adviser*. Cheltenham: Edward Elgar, pp. 114–50.

Eichbaum, C., and R. Shaw (2010b). *Partisan Appointees and Public Servants: An international Analysis*. Cheltenham: Edward Elgar.

Eichbaum, C., and R. Shaw (2011). Political staff in executive government: Conceptualising and mapping roles within the core executive. *Australia Journal of Political Science* 46(4): 583–600.

Eichbaum, C., and R. Shaw (2017). The future of public administration: Speaking truth to power or fluffing the lines? Paper to the 2017 Conference of the New Zealand Political Studies Association. University of Otago, 29 November–1 December 2017.

Eichbaum, C., and R. Shaw (2018). The future of public administration: Speaking truth to power or fluffing the lines? Paper for the 2018 IPSA Conference, Borders and Margins, Brisbane, 21–25 July.

Eichbaum, C., and R. Shaw (2019). Two faces of politicisation: Administrative and functional politicization within the New Zealand core executive. International Conference on Public Policy, Montreal, 26–8 June.

Elgie, R. (1997). Models of executive politics: A framework for the study of executive power relations in parliamentary and semi-presidential regimes. *Political Studies* 45(2): 217–31.

Elston, T. (2012). Developments in UK executive agencies: Re-examining the 'disaggregation-reaggregation' thesis. *Public Policy and Administration* 28(1): 66–89.

Elston, T. (2014). Not so 'arm's length': Reinterpreting agencies in UK central government. *Public Administration* 92(2): 458–76.

Emy, H., and O. Hughes (1991). *Australian Politics: Realities in Conflict*. 2nd ed. Melbourne: Macmillan.

Encel, S. (1960). The concept of the state in Australian politics. *Australian Journal of Politics and History* 61(1): 62–76.

Esselment, A., J. Lees-Marshment and A. Marland (2014). The nature of political advising to prime ministers in Australia, Canada, New Zealand and the UK. *Commonwealth and Comparative Politics* 52(3): 358–75.

Esselment, A., and P. Wilson (2015). Political staff and the permanent campaign. Paper presented to the Annual Meeting of the Canadian Political Science Association. Ottawa, June 4.

European Commission (2017). Quality of public administration: A toolbox for practitioners. European Union.

Evans, M., M. Grattan and B. McCaffrie (eds.) (2019). *From Turnbull to Morrison: Australian Commonwealth Administration 2016-2019 – Understanding the Trust Divide*. Melbourne: Melbourne University Press.

Evans, M., M. Halupka and G. Stoker (2019). Trust and democracy in Australia. In M. Evans, M. Grattan and B. McCaffrie (eds.), *From Turnbull to Morrison: Australian Commonwealth Administration*

2016–2019 – *Understanding the Trust Divide*. Melbourne: Melbourne University Press, pp. 17–35.

Fellegi, I. (1996). *Strengthening our Policy Capacity: Report of the Deputy Ministers Task Force*. Ottawa: Supply and Service Canada.

Fleischer, J. (2009). Power resources of parliamentary executives: Policy advice in the UK and Germany. *West European Politics* 32(1): 196–214.

Flinders, M. (2000). Governance in Whitehall. *Public Administration* 80(1): 51–75.

Flinders, M. (2002). Shifting the balance? *Political Studies* 50(1): 23–42.

Flinders, M. (2008). *Delegated Governance and the British State: Walking without Order*. Oxford: Oxford University Press.

Flinders, M., and J. Buller (2006). Depoliticization: Principles, tactics and tools. *British Politics* 1(3): 293–318.

Fobe, E., M. Brans, V. Diederik and J. Van Damme (2013). Institutionalized advisory systems: An analysis of member satisfaction of advice production and use across 9 strategic advisory councils in Flanders (Belgium). *Policy and Society* 32(3): 225–40.

Fonberg, R., and T. Fyfe (2013, 10 September). The critical role of policy advice. *Canadian Government Executive*.

Foster, C. D. (2001). The civil service under stress: The fall in civil service power and authority. *Public Administration* 79(3): 725–49.

Fraussen, B., and D. Halpin (2017). Think tanks and strategic policy-making: The contribution of think tanks to policy advisory systems. *Policy Sciences* 50(1): 105–24.

Freeguard, G., A. Cheung, A. Lilly, M. Shepheard, J. Lillis, L. Campbell, J. Haigh, J. Taylor and A. de Costa. (2019). *Whitehall Monitor 2019*. London: Institute for Government.

Gains, F., and G. Stoker (2011). Special advisors and the transmission of ideas from the policy primeval soup. *Policy and Politics* 39(4): 485–98.

Gleeson, D., D. Legge, D. O'Neill and M. Pfeffer (2011). Negotiating tensions in developing organizational policy capacity: Comparative lessons to be drawn. *Journal of Comparative Policy Analysis: Research and Practice* 13(3): 237–63.

Glenn, T. (2018). Canadian legislatures, public policy and policy analysis. In L. Dobuzinskis and M. Howlett (eds.), *Policy Analysis in Canada*. Bristol: Policy Press, pp. 211–32.

Gold, J. (2014). *International Delivery: Centres of Government And The Drive For Better Policy Implementation*. London: Institute for Government; Toronto: Mowat Centre.

Gold, J. (2017). *Tracking Delivery: Global Trends and Warning Signs in Delivery Units*. London: Institute for Government.

Goldenberg, E. (2006). *The Way It Works: Inside Ottawa*. Toronto: McClelland & Stewart.

Government of New Zealand. (2018a). Government to reduce reliance on consultants. Wellington. www.beehive.govt.nz/release/government-reduce-reliance-consultants.

Government of New Zealand (2018b). Cabinet Minute: GOV-18-MIN-0030 – Reducing state services agencies' reliance on purchasing external capability. http://www.ssc.govt.nz/sites/all/files/GOV-18-MIN-0030.pdf.

Gow, J. I. (1994). *Learning from Others: Administrative Innovation among Canadian Governments*. Toronto: Institute of Public Administration of Canada and the Canadian Centre for Management Development.

Gow, I. (2004). *A Canadian Model of Public Administration?* Ottawa: Canadian School of Public Service.

Grattan, M. (2019, 27 July). PM attempts to calm the circus. *The Canberra Times*: 36.

Greenway, A. (2019, 4 September). Officials who fear change should be wary, *Civil Service World*.

Gregory, R., and Z. Lonti (2008). Chasing shadows? Performance measurement of policy advice in New Zealand government departments. *Public Administration* 86(3): 837–56.

Grube, D. (2015). Responsibility to be enthusiastic? Public servants and the public face of 'promiscuous partisanship'. *Governance: An International Journal of Policy, Administration, and Institutions* 28(3): 305–20.

Grube, D. (2019). *Megaphone Bureaucracy: Speaking Truth to Power in the Age of the New Normal*. Princeton, NJ: Princeton University Press.

Grube, D., and C. Howard (2016). Is the Westminster system broken beyond repair? *Governance: An International Journal of Policy, Administration, and Institutions* 29(4): 467–81.

Gruhn, Z., and F. Slater (2012). *Special Advisers and Ministerial Effectiveness*. London: Institute for Government.

Gurr, B. (2019, 24 July). Boris Johnson's cabinet: Dominic Cummings, brains of Brexit campaign, is hired to make it happen. *The Times*. www.thetimes.co.uk/edition/news/boris-johnson-s-cabinet-dominic-cummings-brains-of-brexit-campaign-is-hired-to-make-it-happen-j2sgzgs0l.

Haddon, C. (2016). Developments in the civil service. In R. Heffernan, C. Hay, M. Russell and P. Cowley (eds.), *Developments in British Politics Ten*. 10th ed. London: Palgrave, pp. 161–82.

Haddon, C. (2019). *Becoming Prime Minister*. London: Institute for Government.

Hall, M., and D. Marsh (2019, September). Brexit shows both the importance of the British Political Tradition and the extent to which it is under threat. LSE Blogs.

Hall, Peter. (1993). Policy paradigms, social learning, and the state: The case of economic policymaking in Britain. *Comparative Politics* 25(3): 275–96.

Halligan, J. (1995). Policy advice and the public sector. In B. G. Peters and D. Savoie (eds.), *Governance in a Changing Environment*. Kingston and Montreal: McGill-Queen's University Press, pp. 138–72.

Halligan, J. (1996). The diffusion of civil service reform. In H. Bekke, J. L. Perry and T. A. J. Toonen (eds.), *Civil Services in Comparative Perspective*. Bloomington: Indiana University Press, pp. 288–317.

Halligan, J. (2001). Politicians, bureaucrats and public sector reform in Australia and New Zealand. In B. G. Peters and J. Pierre (eds.), *Politicians, Bureaucrats and Administrative Reform*. London: Routledge, pp. 157–68.

Halligan, J. (2003). Anglo-American civil service systems: Comparative perspectives. In J. Halligan (ed.), *Civil Service Systems in Anglo-American Countries*. Cheltenham: Edward Elgar, pp. 1–9.

Halligan, J. (2006). The reassertion of the centre in a first generation NPM system. In T. Christensen and P. Laegreid (eds.), *Autonomy and Regulation: Coping with Agencies in the Modern State*. Cheltenham: Edward Elgar, pp. 162–80.

Halligan, J. (2007). Reintegrating government in third generation reforms of Australia and New Zealand. *Public Policy and Administration* 22(2): 217–38.

Halligan, J. (2010). The fate of administrative ttradition in anglophone countries during the reform era. In M. Painter and B. G. Peters (eds.), *Tradition and Public Administration*. London: Palgrave, pp. 129–42.

Halligan, J. (2011). Central steering in Australia. In C. Dahlström, B. G. Peters and J. Pierre (eds.), *Steering from the Centre: Strengthening Political Control in Western Democracies*. Toronto: University of Toronto Press, pp. 99–122.

Halligan, J. (2013). The evolution of public service bargains of Australian senior public servants. *International Review of Administrative Sciences* 79 (1): 111–29.

Halligan, J. (2015). Anglophone systems: Diffusion and policy transfer within an administrative tradition. In F. van der Meer, J. Raadschelders and T. Toonen (eds.), *The Civil Service in the 21st century*. 2nd ed. Basingstoke: Palgrave, pp. 57–76.

Halligan, J. (2016). Mapping the Central State in Australia. Paper for Panel 13 Mapping the State: Old and New Explanatory Perspectives, Research Committee 27, IPSA 2016 World Congress, Poznan, 23–28 July.

Halligan, J. (2019). Nadir or renaissance for the Australian public service? In M. Evans, M. Grattan and B. McCaffrie (eds.), *From Turnbull to Morrison: Australian Commonwealth Administration 2016–2019* –

Understanding the Trust Divide. Melbourne: Melbourne University Press, pp. 144–159.

Halligan, J. (2020). *Reforming Public Management and Governance: Impact and Lessons from Anglophone Countries*. Cheltenham: Edward Elgar.

Halligan, J., R. Miller and J. Power (2007). *Parliament in the 21st Century: Institutional Reform and Emerging Roles*. Melbourne: Melbourne University Press.

Hallsworth, M., S. Parker and J. Rutter (2011). *Policymaking in the Real World: Evidence and Analysis*. London: Institute for Government.

Halligan, J., and J. Power (1992). *Political Management in the 1990s*. Melbourne: Oxford University Press.

Halligan, J., and R. Reid (2016). Conflict and Consensus in Committees of the Australian Parliament. *Parliamentary Affairs* 69(2): 230–48.

Halligan, J., and G. Smith (2019). Intensity of collaboration between Australian government agencies and the effect on program success. Paper for the annual conference of the International Research Society of Public Management, Wellington: Victoria University of Wellington, 16–18 April.

Hamburger, P., B. Stevens and P. Weller (2012). A capacity for central coordination: The case of Department of the Prime Minister and Cabinet. *Australian Journal of Public Administration* 70(4): 377–90.

Hamburger, P., and P. Weller (2012). Policy advice and a central agency: The Department of the Prime Minister and Cabinet. *Australian Journal of Political Science* 47(3): 363–76.

Hanger, I. (2014). *Report of the Royal Commission into the Home Insulation Program*. Canberra: Commonwealth of Australia.

Harris, J., and J. Rutter (2014). *Center Forward: Effective Support for the Prime Minister at the Center of Government*. London: Institute for Government.

Hayne, K. M. (2019, 26 July). On Royal Commissions. Address to CCCS Conference, Melbourne Law School.

Hazell, R. (2012). How the coalition works at the centre. In R. Hazell and B. Yong (eds.), *The Politics of Coalition: How the Conservative-Liberal Democrat Government Works*. Oxford: Hart Publishing, pp. 57–76.

Hazell, R., and B. Yong (eds.) (2012). *The Politics of Coalition: How the Conservative-Liberal Democrat Coalition Works*. Oxford: Hart Publishing.

Head, B. (2015). Policy analysis and public sector capacity. In B. Head and K. Crowley (eds.), *Policy Analysis in Australia*. Bristol: Policy Press, pp. 53–67.

Head, B. (2017). Reconsidering evidence-based policy: Key issues and challenges. *Policy and Society* 29(2): 77–94.

Head, B., and K. Crowley (eds.) (2015). *Policy Analysis in Australia*. Bristol: Policy Press.

Heady, B. (1974). *British Cabinet Ministers*. London: Allen and Unwin.

Hernando, M., P. Hartwig and D. Stone. (2018). Think tanks in 'hard times' – the Global Financial Crisis and economic advice. *Policy and Society* 37(2): 125–39.

HC CPA/House of Commons Committee of Public Accounts (2016a). *Accountability to Parliament for Taxpayers' Money*. HC 732. Thirty-ninth Report of Session 2015–16. London: House of Commons.

HC CPA/House of Commons Committee of Public Accounts (2016b). *Oral Evidence: Accountability to Parliament for Taxpayers' Money*. HC 732. London: House of Commons.

HC CPA/House of Commons Committee of Public Accounts (2016c, 23 November). *Managing Government Spending and Expenditure*. HC 710. Twenty-seventh Report of Session 2016–17. London: London: House of Commons.

HC PAC/House of Commons Public Administration Select Committee (2005). *Government by Inquiry*. HC 51-I. First Report of Session 2004–05. London: House of Commons.

Heintzman, R. (1997). Canada and public administration. In J. Bourgault, M. Demers and C. Williams (eds.), *Public Administration and Public Management Experiences in Canada*. Sainte-Foy: Les Publications du Quebec, pp. 1–12.

Henry, K. (2007, 14 March). Treasury's effectiveness in the current environment. Address to Treasury staff.

Hindmoor, A., P. Larkin and A. Kennon (2009). Assessing the influence of select committees in the UK: The Education and Skills Committee, 1997–2005, *Journal of Legislative Studies* 15: 71–89.

Hipkins, C. (Minister of State Services) (2019). Cabinet Paper: Public Service Legislation: Paper 2 – A Unified Public Service. Wellington. https://ssc.govt.nz/assets/Legacy/resources/Paper-2-A-Unified-Public-Service.pdf.

Hird, J. A. (ed.) (2018). *Policy analysis in the United States*. Bristol: Policy Press.

HM Government (2011). *Open Public Services White Paper*. CM 8145. London: HM Government.

HM Government (2012, June). *The Civil Service Reform Plan*. London: HM Government.

HM Government (2013). Civil service reform plan: One year on report. http://my.civilservice.gov.uk/reform/civil-service-reform-one-year-on/.

HM Government (2014). *The Civil Service Reform Plan: Progress Report*. London: HM Government.

Höchtl, J., P. Parycek and R. Schöllhammer (2016). Big data in the policy cycle: Policy decision making in the digital era. *Journal of Organizational Computing and Electronic Commerce* 26: 1–2, 147–69.

Hodgetts, J. E. (1983). Implicit values in the administration of public affairs. In K. Kernaghan (ed.), *Canadian Public Administration: Discipline and Profession*. Toronto: Butterworths pp. 29–41.

Holland, I. (2009). *Senate Committees and Legislative Process*. Parliamentary Studies Paper 7. Canberra: Parliamentary Studies Centre, Australian National University.

Hood, C. (2010). *The Blame Game: Spin, Bureaucracy, and Self-Preservation in Government*. Princeton, NJ: Princeton University Press.

Hoole, G. (2014). Commissions of inquiry in Canada. In S. Prasser and H. Tracey (eds.), *Royal Commissions and Public Inquiries: Practice and Potential*. Ballarat: Connorcourt Publishing, pp. 331–55.

Howard, M. (2017). *Submission #54 to Joint Committee of Public Accounts and Audit Inquiry Based on ANAO Report No 19, 2017–18*. Canberra: Australian Government Procurement Contract Reporting.

Howlett, M. (2009). Governance modes, policy regimes and operational plans: A multi-level nested model of policy instrument choice and policy design. *Policy Sciences* 42(1): 73–89.

Howlett, M., and E. Lindquist (2004). Policy analysis and governance: Analytical and policy styles in Canada. *Journal of Comparative Policy Analysis* 6(3): 225–49.

Howlett, M., and A. Migone (2013a). Policy advice through the market: The role of external consultants in contemporary policy advisory systems. *Policy and Society* 32(3): 241–54.

Howlett, M., and A. Migone (2013b). The permanence of temporary services: The reliance of Canadian federal departments on policy and management consultants. *Canadian Public Administration* 56(3): 369–90.

Howlett, M., and A. Migone (2014a). Making the invisible public service visible? Exploring data on the supply of policy and management consultancies in Canada. *Canadian Public Administration* 57(2): 183–216.

Howlett, M., A. Migone and S. L. Tan. (2014b). Duplicative or complementary? The relationship between policy consulting and internal policy analysis in Canadian government. *Canadian Journal of Political Science* 47(1): 113–34.

Howlett, M., and A. M. Wellstead (2011). Policy analysts in the bureaucracy revisited: The nature of professional policy work in contemporary government. *Politics & Policy* 39(4): 613–33.

Howlett, M., A. Wellstead and J. Craft (eds.) (2017). *Policy Work in Canada: Professional Practices and Analytical Capacities*. Toronto: University of Toronto Press.

Hunn, D., and H. G. Lang (1989). *Review of the Prime Minister's Office and Cabinet Office*. Wellington: State Services Commission.

Hustedt, T. (2019). Studying policy advisory systems: Beyond the Westminster-bias? *Policy Studies*. DOI:10.1080/01442872.2018.1557627.

Hustedt, T., and S. Veit (2017). Policy advisory systems: Change dynamics and sources of variation. *Policy Sciences* 50(1): 41–6.

Independent Review of the APS (2019). *Independent Review of the APS: Priorities for Change*. Canberra: Commonwealth of Australia.

Institute for Government (2016). Ministers reflect: Ian Duncan Smith. www .instituteforgovernment.org.uk/ministers-reflect/wp-content/uploads/201 6/09/Iain-Duncan-Smith.pdf.

Inwood, G. J. (2005). *Continentalizing Canada: The Politics and Legacy of the Macdonald Royal Commission*. Toronto: University of Toronto Press.

Inwood, G., and C. Johns (eds.) (2014). *Commissions of Inquiry and Policy Change: A Comparative Analysis*. Toronto: University of Toronto Press.

Inwood, G., and C. Johns (2016). Commissions of inquiry and policy change: Comparative analysis and future research frontiers. *Canadian Public Administration* 50(3): 382–404.

Inwood, G., and C. Johns (2018). Commissions of Inquiry and Policy Analysis. In L. Dobuzinskis and M. Howlett (eds.), *Policy Analysis in Canada*. 2nd ed. Bristol: Policy Press, pp. 233–54.

Inwood, G. J., C. M. Johns and P. L. O'Reilly (2012). *Intergovernmental Policy Capacity in Canada: Inside the Worlds of Finance, Environment, Trade, and Health*. Kingston and Montreal: McGill-Queen's University Press.

IPAA/Institute of Public Administration Australia (2012, April). Public policy drift: An IPAA policy paper.

IRPP (2018, 27 February). Government of Canada announces major contribution to the IRPP to create a centre of excellence on the Canadian federation. News release. http://irpp.org/news-release/government-canada -announces-major-contribution-irpp-create-centre-excellence-canadian-f ederation/.

James, O., and A. Nakamura (2014). Coordination in UK central government. In P. Lægreid, K. Sarapuu, L. Rykkja and T. Randma-Liiv (eds.), *Organizing for Coordination in the Public Sector: Practices and Lessons from 12 European Countries*. Basingstoke: Palgrave Macmillan, pp. 91–102.

Jeffrey, B. (2010). *Divided Loyalties: The Liberal Party of Canada, 1984–2008*. Toronto: University of Toronto Press.

Jensen, K., R. Scott, L. Slocombe, R. Body and L. Cowey (2014). *The management and organisational challenges of more joined-up government: New Zealand's better public services reforms. State Sector Performance Hub, Working Paper, 2014–1*. Wellington: New Zealand Government.

Jervis, R. (1997). *System Effects: Complexity in Political and Social Life*. Princeton, NJ: Princeton University Press.

Johnstone, R. (2019, 25 July). Permanent civil service 'an idea for the history books': New No.10 adviser Dominic Cummings' views on Whitehall. *Civil Service World*. www.civilserviceworld.com/articles/news/permanent-civil -service-%E2%80%98-idea-history-books%E2%80%99-new-no10-adv iser-dominic-cummings-views.

Jones, C. M., and G. J. Inwood (2018). Commission of inquiry and policy analysis. In L. Dobuzinskis and M. Howlett (eds.), *Policy Analysis in Canada*. Bristol: Policy Press, pp. 233–54.

Jones, G. (2016). *The Power of the Prime Minister: 50 Years On*. Research Paper. London: The Constitution Society.

Kavanagh, D., and D. Richards (2001). Departmentalism and joined-up government. *Parliamentary Affairs* 54(1): 1–18.

Kay, A., and C. Daugbjerg (2015). De-institutionalising governance? Instrument diversity and feedback dynamics. *Asia Pacific Journal of Public Administration* 37(4): 236–46.

Keep, M. (2018, 13 July). Office for Budget Responsibility, Briefing Paper, Number CBP 5657, House of Commons Library.

Kellner, P., and N. Crowther-Hunt (1980). *The Civil Servants: An Inquiry into Britain's Ruling Class*. London: Macdonald.

Kemp, D. (1986). The recent evolution of central policy control mechanisms in parliamentary systems. *International Political Science Review* 7(1): 56–66.

Kibblewhite, A. (2015, 26 May). Great policy: Responsive today, shaping tomorrow. Address to IPANZ.

Kibblewhite, A. (2018a). The New Zealand Policy Project: Reflections on the first three years. *Civil Service Quarterly* 16. https://dpmc.govt.nz/sites/de fault/files/2018-04/UK%20Civil%20Service%20Quarterly_1.pdf.

Kibblewhite, A. (2018b, 18 December). The future of the policy profession. Speech at Policy Managers Forum, Wellington.

Kibblewhite, A., and P. Boshier (2018). Free and frank advice and the Official Information Act: Balancing competing principles of good government. *Policy Quarterly* 14(2): 3–9.

King, A., and I. Crewe (2014). *The Blunders of our Governments*. London: Oneworld.

Kingston, A. (2017, 12 October). Inside the 'progressive' think tank that really runs Canada. *Maclean's*. www.macleans.ca/politics/ottawa/inside-the-progressive-think-tank-that-really-runs-canada/.

Kinne, Brandon. (2013). Network Dynamics and the Evolution of International Cooperation. *American Political Science Review* 107(4): 766–85.

Kirby, M., and H. Segal (2016). *A House Undivided: Making Senate Independence Work*. A Public Policy Forum report. Ottawa: Public Policy Forum.

Knill, C. (1999). Explaining cross-national variance in administrative reform: Autonomous versus instrumental bureaucracies. *Journal of Public Policy* 19(2): 113–39.

Lægreid, P., and L. H. Rykkja. (2016). Administrative reform in the Nordic countries – processes, trends and content. In C. Creve, P. Lægreid and L. H. Rykkja (eds.), *Nordic Administrative Reforms: Lessons for Public Management*. London: Palgrave Macmillan, pp. 105–28.

Lægreid, P., T. Randma-Liiv, L. H. Rykkja and K. Sarapuu (2016). Coordination challenges and administrative reforms. In G. Hammerschmid, S. Van de Walle, R. Andrews and P. Bezes, *Public Administration in Europe: The View from the Top*. Cheltenham: Edward Elgar, pp. 244–58.

Lawlor, A., and E. Crandall (2013). Committee performance in the Senate of Canada: Some sobering analysis for the chamber of 'sober second thought'. *Commonwealth and Comparative Politics* 51(4): 549–68.

Lee, J. M., G. W. Jones and J. Burnham (1998). *At the Centre of Whitehall: Advising the Prime Minister and Cabinet*. Basingstoke: Palgrave Macmillan.

Leifeld, P., and V. Schneider (2012). Information exchange in policy networks. *American Journal of Political Science* 56(3): 731–44.

Levitt, R., and W. Solesbury (2012). *Policy Tsars: Here to Stay but More Transparency Needed: Final Report*. London: Kings College.

Levitt, R., and W. Solesbury (2013a). New development: Policy tsars – Whitehall's expert advisers revealed. *Public Money and Management* 33 (1): 77–80.

Levitt, R., and B. Solesbury (2013b). Open policy making: don't tsars count? Manchester Policy Blogs: Whitehall Watch. http://blog.policy.manchester.ac .uk/whitehallwatch/2013/10/open-policy-making-dont-tsars-count/ (accessed 6 November 2018).

Lijphart, A. (1984). *Democracies: Patterns of Majoritarian and Consensus Government in Twenty-One Countries*. New Haven, CT: Yale University Press.

Lindquist, E. (1998). A quarter century of Canadian think tanks: Evolving institutions, conditions and strategies. In D. Stone, A. Denham and M. Garnett (eds.), *Think Tanks across Nations: A Comparative Approach*. Manchester: Manchester University Press, pp. 127–44.

Lindquist, E. (2006a). Organizing for policy implementation: The emergence and role of implementation units in policy design and oversight. *Journal of Comparative Policy Analysis* 8(4): 311–24.

Lindquist, E. (2006b). Organizing for policy implementation: Comparisons, lessons and prospects for cabinet implementation units. *Journal of Comparative Policy Analysis* 8(4): 421–35.

Lindquist, E. (2006c). *A Critical Moment: Capturing and Conveying the Evolution of the Canadian Public Service*. Ottawa: Canadian School of Public Service.

Lindquist, E. A. (2014). The responsiveness solution? Embedding horizontal governance in Canada. In J. O'Flynn, D. Blackman and J. Halligan (eds.), *Crossing Boundaries in Public Management and Policy: The International Experience*. London and New York: Routledge, pp. 190–210.

Lindquist, E., and C. Eichbaum (2016). Remaking Government in Canada: Dares, Resilience, and Civility in Westminster Systems. *Governance: An International Journal of Policy, Administration, and Institutions* 29(4): 553–71.

Lindquist, E., and A. Tiernan. (2011). The Australian public service and policy advising: Meeting the challenges of 21st century governance. *Australian Journal of Public Administration* 70(4): 437–50.

Lindvall, J. (2009). The real but limited influence of expert ideas. *World Politics* 61(4): 703–30.

Littoz-Monnet, A. (2017). *The Politics of Expertise in International Organizations: How International Bureaucracies Produce and Mobilize Knowledge*. London: Routledge.

Lloyd, L. (2019). *The Brexit Effect: How Government Has Changed since the EU Referendum*. London: Institute for Government.

Lodge, G., and B. Rogers (2006). *Whitehall's Black Box: Accountability and Performance in the Senior Civil Service*. London: Institute for Public Policy Research.

Lodge, M. (2010). Public service bargains in British central government: Multiplication, diversification and reassertion? In M. Painter and B. G. Peters (eds.), *Tradition and Public Administration*. London: Palgrave, pp. 99–113.

Lodge, M., and D. Gill (2011). Toward a new era of administrative reform? The myth of post-NPM in New Zealand. *Governance: An International Journal of Policy, Administration, and Institutions* 24(1): 141–66.

Lodge, M., and K. Wegrich (2014). *The Problem-Solving Capacity of the Modern State: Governance Challenges and Administrative Capacities.* Oxford: Oxford University Press.

LSE GV314 Group (2012). New life at the top: Special advisers in British government. *Parliamentary Affairs* 65(4): 715–32.

Luetjens, J., M. Mintrom, and P. `t Hart. (2019). *Successful Public Policy: Lessons from Australia and New Zealand.* Australian National University/ Australia New Zealand School of Public Service.

MAC/Management Advisory Committee (2004). *Connecting Government: Whole of Government Responses to Australia's Priority Challenges.* Canberra: Commonwealth of Australia.

May, Peter J. (1991). Reconsidering Policy Design: Policies and Publics. *Journal of Public Policy* 11(2): 187–206.

McBride, S., and J. Merolli (2013). Alternatives to austerity? Post-crisis policy advice from global institutions. *Global Social Policy* 13(3): 299–320.

McConnell, A. (2010). *Understanding Policy Success: Rethinking Public Policy.* Basingstoke: Palgrave Macmillan.

McCrae, J., and J. Gold (2017). *Professionalising Whitehall.* London: Institute for Government.

McCrae, J., J. Harris and E. Andrews (2015). All in it together: Cross-departmental responsibilities for improving Whitehall. Institute for Government after the Election. www.instituteforgovernment.org.uk/site s/default/files/publications/All%20in%20it%20together.pdf.

MacDermott, K. (2008). *Whatever Happened to 'Frank' and 'Fearless'? The Impact of New Public Management on the Public Service.* Canberra: ANU E Press.

Macdonald, D. (2011). *The Shadow Public Service: The Swelling Ranks of Federal Government Outsourced Workers.* Ottawa: Canadian Centre for Policy Alternatives.

McGann, M., E. Blomkamp and J. M. Lewis (2018) The rise of public sector innovation labs: Experiments in design thinking for policy. *Policy Sciences* 51: 249–67.

McGann, M., J. M. Lewis and E. Blomkamp (2018). *Mapping Public Sector Innovation Units in Australia and New Zealand: 2018 Survey Report.* Melbourne: The Policy Lab, University of Melbourne.

McIlroy, T. (2017, 25 August). Infrastructure boss Mike Mrdak lashes prime minister and cabinet and prime ministers' office. *The Canberra Times.*

McLeay, E. (1995). *The Cabinet and Political Power in New Zealand.* Auckland: Oxford University Press.

McLevey, J. (2014). Think tanks, funding, and the politics of policy knowledge in Canada. *Canadian Review of Sociology* 51(1): 54–75.

Maer, L., and R. McCaffrey (2018). Special advisers. Briefing Paper, No 3018. House of Commons Library.

Maley, M. (2000). Conceptualising advisers' policy work: The distinctive policy roles of ministerial advisers in the Keating government, 1991–96. *Australian Journal of Political Science* 35(3): 449–70.

Maley, M. (2010). Australia. In C. Eichbaum and R. Shaw (eds.), *Partisan Appointees and Public Servants: An International Analysis of the Role of the Political Adviser*. Cheltenham: Edward Elgar, pp. 94–113.

Maley, M. (2011). Strategic links in a cut-throat world: Rethinking the role and relationships of Australian ministerial staff. *Public Administration* 89 (4): 1469–88.

Maley, M. (2015). The policy work of Australian political staff. *International Journal of Public Administration* 38(1): 46–55.

Maley, M. (2018a). Understanding the divergent development of the ministerial office in Australia and the UK. *Australian Journal of Political Science* 53(3): 320–35. DOI:10.1080/10361146.2018.1450356.

Maley, M. (2018b). Australia: Applying an institutional lens to political staff. In R. Shaw and C. Eichbaum (eds.), *Ministers, Minders and Mandarins: An International Study of Relationships at the Executive Summit of Parliamentary Democracies*, London: Edward Elgar, pp. 15–33.

Maley, M. (2019). Border crossings: The employment of public servants in ministers' offices in Australia. International Conference on Public Policy, Montreal, 26–28 June.

Manson, A., and D. Mullan (eds.) (2003a). *Commission of Inquiry: Praise or Reappraise?* Toronto: Irwin Law.

Manson, A., and D. Mullan (2003b). Introduction. In A. Manson and D. Mullan (eds.), *Commission of Inquiry: Praise or Reappraise?* Toronto: Irwin Law, pp. 1–10.

Manzoni, J. (2018, 1 May). A civil service fit for the future. Presentation to the Institute for Government, London, video. www.instituteforgovern ment.org.uk/events/civil-service-fit-future.

Marando, D., and J. Craft (2017). Digital era policy advising: Clouding ministerial perspectives? *Canadian Journal of Public Administration* 60 (4): 498–516.

March, D., D. Toke, C. Befrage, D. Tepe and S. McGough (2009). Policy networks and the distinction between insider and outsider groups: The case of the countryside alliance. *Public Administration* 87(3): 621–38.

Marland, A., T. Giasson and A. Esselment (eds.) (2018). *Permanent Campaigning in Canada*. Vancouver: University of British Columbia Press.

Marsh, D., D. Richards and M. J. Smith (2001). *Changing Patterns of Governance in the United Kingdom: Reinventing Whitehall?* Basingstoke: Palgrave.

Marsh, I., and D. Stone (2004). Australian think tanks. In D. Stone and A. Denham (eds.), *Think Tank Traditions: Policy Research and the Politics of Ideas*. Manchester: Manchester University Press, pp. 247–63.

Massola, J. (2016, 12 October). Malcolm Turnbull and senior cabinet ministers using WhatsApp could pose security risk: experts. *Sydney Morning Herald*. www.smh.com.au/politics/federal/malcolm-turnbull-and-senior-cabinet-ministers-using-whatsapp-could-pose-security-risk-experts-20161012-gs0cuj.html.

Matthews, F. (2013). *Complexity, Fragmentation, and Uncertainty: Government Capacity in an Evolving State*. Oxford: Oxford University Press.

May, K. (2016a, 7 March). Perception of politicization of the public service is a problem for Liberals. *Ottawa Citizen*. https://ottawacitizen.com/news/national/perception-of-policitization-of-the-public-service-is-a-problem-for-liberals.

May, K. (2016b, 25 March). PS needs to pick up pace of reforms: Privy council clerk. *Ottawa Citizen*. https://ottawacitizen.com/news/local-news/ps-needs-to-pick-up-pace-of-reforms-privy-council-clerk.

May, P., C. Koski and C. Stramp (2016). Issue expertise in policymaking. *Journal of Public Policy* 36(2): 195–218.

Meltsner, A. (1975). Bureaucratic policy analysts. *Policy Analysis* 1(1): 115–31.

Mendes, P. (2003). Australian neoliberal think tanks and the backlash against the welfare state. *Journal of Australian Political Economy* 51: 29–56.

Mintrom, M., and J. Luetjens (2016). Design thinking in policymaking processes: Opportunities and challenges. *Australian Journal of Public Administration* 75(3): 391–402.

Monk, D. (2012). Committee inquiries in the Australian parliament and their influence on government: Government acceptance of recommendations as a measure of parliamentary performance. *Journal of Legislative Studies* 18: 137–60.

Montpetit, É. (2011). Between detachment and responsiveness: Civil servants in Europe and North America. *West European Politics* 34(6): 1250–71.

Morrison, A. (2014). Picking up the pace in public services. *Policy Quarterly* 10(2): 43–8.

Morrison, S. (2019). Speech. Institute of Public Administration, Canberra: Parliament House.

Moynihan, D. P., and J. Soss (2014). Policy feedback and the politics of administration. *Public Administration Review* 74(3): 320–32.

Mulgan, G. (2014). *Making Open Government Work*. London: Palgrave Macmillan.

Mulgan, R. (1997). *Politics in New Zealand*. 2nd ed. Auckland: Auckland University Press.

Mulgan, R. (2007). Truth in government and the politicization of public service advice. *Public Administration* 85(3): 569–86.

NAO/National Audit Office (2015). *The Centre of Government: An Update*. HC 1031. Session 2014–15. London: National Audit Office.

Ng, Y. (2018). *The Rise of Political Advisors in the Westminster System*. New York: Routledge.

Norman, R. (2008). At the centre or in control? Central agencies in search of new identities. *Policy Quarterly* 4(2): 33–8.

Norris, E., and M. Shepheard (2017). *How Public Inquiries Can Lead to Change*. London: Institute for Government.

Norton, P. (2005). *Parliament in British Politics*. Basingstoke: Palgrave Macmillan.

OECD/Organisation for Economic Cooperation and Development (2007). *Political Advisers and Civil Servants in European Countries*. Sigma papers, No. 38. Paris: OECD Publishing.

OECD/Organisation for Economic Cooperation and Development (2011). *Ministerial Advisors: Role, Influence and Management*. Paris: OECD Publishing.

OECD/Organisation for Economic Cooperation and Development (2015). Country notes: United Kingdom. *Journal on Budgeting* 15(2): 241–6.

OECD/Organisation for Economic Cooperation and Development (2017). *Policy Advisory System Supporting Good Governance and Sound Public Decision Making*. OECD Public Governance Reviews. Paris: OECD Publishing. https://doi.org/10.1787/9789264283664-en.

O'Flynn, J., D. Blackman and J. Halligan (eds.) (2014). *Crossing Boundaries in Public Management and Policy: The International Experience*. London and New York: Routledge.

Osborne, S. (2010). The (new) public governance: A suitable case for treatment? In S. Osbourne (ed.), *The New Public Governance*. Abingdon: Routledge, pp. 1–16.

Owen, J., and L. Lloyd. (2018). *Costing Brexit: What Is Whitehall Spending on Exiting the EU?* London: Institute for Government.

Page, E., and B. Jenkins (2005). *Policy Bureaucracy: Government with a Cast of Thousands*. Oxford: Oxford University Press.

Page, E., and V. Wright (eds.) (2007). *From the Active to the Enabling State: The Changing Role of Top Officials in European Nations*. Basingstoke: Palgrave Macmillan.

Page, K. (2015). *Unaccountable: Truth and Lies on Parliament Hill*. Toronto: Penguin.

Painter, M., and J. Pierre (eds.) (2005). *Challenges to State Policy Capacity Global Trends and Comparative Perspectives*. Basingstoke: Palgrave Macmillan.

Painter, M., and B. G. Peters (2010a). The analysis of administrative tradition. In M. Painter and B. G. Peters (eds.), *Tradition and Public Administration*. Basingstoke: Palgrave Macmillan, pp. 3–16.

Pal, L. (2012). *Frontiers of Governance: The OECD and Global Public Management Reform*. London: Palgrave.

Palmer, G., and A. Butler (2016). *A Constitution for Aotearoa New Zealand*. Wellington: Victoria University Press.

Palmer, G., and M. Palmer (2004). *Bridled Power: New Zealand's Constitution and Government*. 4th ed. South Melbourne: Oxford University Press.

Parliament of Australia (2018). Royal Commissions and Commissions of Inquiry. https://www.aph.gov.au/About_Parliament/Parliamentary_Depar tments/Parliamentary_Library/Browse_by_Topic/law/royalcommissions.

Parker, G. (2008, 21 May). Policy Exchange powers party's 'liberal revolution'. *Financial Times*, 4.

Parker, S., A. Paun, J. McClory and K. Blatchford (2010). *Shaping Up: A Whitehall for the Future*. London: Institute for Government.

Parkhurst, J. (2017). *The Politics of Evidence: From Evidence-Based Policy to the Good Governance of Evidence*. Routledge Studies in Governance and Public Policy. Abingdon: Routledge.

Parkinson, M. (2018, 19 October). Brexit, multilateralism and how the media impacts policy work. *Mandarin*. www.themandarin.com.au/100211-dr-mar tin-parkinson-brexit-multilateralism-and-how-the-media-impacts-policy-wo rk/?utm_campaign=TheJuice&utm_medium=email&utm?newsletterwork/ utm_campaign=TheJuice&utm_medium=email&utm_source=newsletter.

Parsons, W. (2003). Modernising policy-making for the twenty-first century: The professional model. In T. Butcher and A. Massey (eds.), *Modernizing Civil Services*. Cheltenham: Edward Elgar, pp. 147–84.

Parsons, W. (2004). Not just steering but weaving: Relevant knowledge and the craft of building policy capacity and coherence. *Australian Journal of Public Administration* 63(1): 43–57.

Patapan, H., J. Wanna and P. Weller (2005). *Westminster Legacies: Democracy and Responsible Government in Asia and the Pacific.* Sydney: UNSW Press.

Patrick, A. (2016). *Credlin & Co: How the Abbott Government Destroyed Itself.* Carlton: Black Inc.

Paun, A. (2010). *United We Stand: Coalition Government in the UK.* London: Institute for Government.

Paun, A. (2013). *Supporting Ministers to Lead.* London: Institute for Government.

Paun, A., and K. Blatchford (2014). The performance target solution? Cross-cutting public service agreements in the United Kingdom. In J. O'Flynn, D. Blackman and J. Halligan (eds.), *Crossing Boundaries in Public Management and Policy: The International Experience.* London and New York: Routledge.

Pautz, H. (2012). The think tanks behind 'Cameronism'. *The British Journal of Politics and International Relations* 15(3): 362–77.

Payne, S., and G. Parker (2020, February 13). Sajid Javid resigns as UK chancellor of the exchequer. *Financial Times.* www.ft.com/content/a15 c78ec-4e3f-11ea-95a0-43d18ec715f5 (subscription required).

Peck, J., and N. Theodore (2015). *Fast Policy: Experimental Statecraft and the Thresholds of Neoliberalism.* Minneapolis: University of Minnesota Press.

Percival, S. (2018, 29 March). A policy community for the federal public service and beyond. *Policy Options.*

Perl, A., M. Howlett and M. Ramesh (2018). Policymaking and truthiness: Can existing policy models cope with politicized evidence and wilful ignorance in a 'postfact' world? *Policy Sciences* 51: 581–600.

Perl, A., and D. J. White (2002). The changing role of consultants in Canadian policy analysis. *Policy & Society* 21(1): 49–73.

Peters, B. G. (1996). *The Policy Capacity of Government.* Research Paper No. 18. Ottawa: Canadian Centre for Management Development.

Peters, B. G. (2003). Administrative traditions and the Anglo-American democracies. In J. Halligan (ed.), *Civil Service Systems in Anglo-American Countries.* Cheltenham: Edward Elgar.

Peters, B. G. (2011). Governance responses to the fiscal crisis—comparative perspectives. *Public Money & Management* 31(1): 75–80. DOI:10.1080/09540962.2011.545551.

Peters, B. G. (2015). *Pursuing Horizontal Coordination: The Politics of Public Sector Coordination.* Lawrence: University of Kansas Press.

Peters, B. G., and A. Barker. (1993). *Advising West European Governments: Inquiries, Expertise and Public Policy.* Edinburgh: Edinburgh University Press.

Peters, B. G., and J. Pierre. (2004). *Politicization of the Civil Service in Comparative Perspective: The Quest for Control.* New York: Routledge.

Peters, B. G., and D. Savoie (2000). *Governance in the Twenty-First Century: Revitalizing the Public Service.* Kingston and Montreal: McGill-Queen's University Press.

Phipps, D., and S. Morton (2013). Qualities of Knowledge Brokers: Reflections from Practice. *Evidence and Policy* 9(2): 255–65.

Pierre, J. (1995). Conclusions: A framework of comparative public administration. In J. Pierre (ed.), *Bureaucracy in the Modern State: An Introduction to Comparative Public Administration.* Aldershot: Edward Elgar, pp. 205–18.

Pierre, J. (1998). Public consultation and citizen participation: Dilemmas of policy advice. In B. Guy Peters and Donald J. Savoie (eds.), *Taking Stock: Assessing Public Sector Reforms.* Kingston and Montreal: McGill-Queen's University Press, pp. 137–63.

Platt, B. (2019, 18 March). Privy Council Clerk Michael Wernick resigns after controversy over SNC-Lavalin testimony. National Post.

Plowden, W. (ed.) (1987). *Advising the Rulers.* Oxford: Basil Blackwell.

Podger, A. (2007). What really happens: Departmental secretary appointments, contracts and performance pay in the Australian Public Service. *Australian Journal of Public Administration* 66(2): 131–47.

Podger, A. (2019, 10 September). Protecting and nurturing the role and capability of the Australian Public Service. Parliamentary Library Lecture.

Policy Horizons Canada (2016). Canada 2030: Scan of Emerging Issues – Governance. www.horizons.gc.ca/en/content/canada-2030-scan-emer ging-issues-government-2030.

Policy Profession Board (2019). *Looking Back to Look Forward: From 'Twelve Actions' to 'Policy Profession 2025'.* London: Policy Profession, UK Government.

Pollitt, C. (1990). *Managerialism and the Public Services: The Anglo-American Experience.* Oxford: Basil Blackwell.

Pollitt, C. (2007). New Labour's re-disorganisation: Hyper-modernism and the costs of reform – a cautionary tale. *Public Management Review* 9(4): 529–43.

Pollitt, C. (ed.) (2013). *Context in Public Policy and Management.* Cheltenham: Edward Elgar.

Pollitt, C. (2016). Managerialism redux? *Financial Accountability and Management* 32(4): 429–47.

Pollitt, C., and G. Bouckaert (2011). *Public Management Reform: A Comparative Analysis: New Public Management, Governance and the Neo-Weberian State.* 3rd ed. Oxford: Oxford University Press.

Pollitt, C., and C. Talbot (eds.) (2004). *Unbundled Government: A Critical Analysis of the Global Trend to Agencies, Quangos and Contractualisation*. London: Taylor and Francis.

Power, M. (2005). The theory of the audit explosion. In E. Ferlie, L. Lynn and C. Pollitt (eds.), *The Oxford Handbook of Public Management*. Oxford: Oxford University Press, pp. 326–44.

Pralle, S. (2006). The 'mouse that roared': Agenda setting in Canadian pesticides politics. *Policy Studies* 34(2): 171–94.

Prasser, S. (2006). *Royal Commissions and Public Inquiries in Australia*. Chatswood: LexisNexis Butterworths.

Prasser, S., and H. Tracey (2014a). Introduction. In S. Prasser and H. Tracey (eds.), *Royal Commissions and Public Inquiries: Practice and Potential*. Ballarat: Connorcourt, pp. 1–7.

Prasser, S., and H. Tracey (eds.) (2014b). *Royal Commissions and Public Inquiries: Practice and Potential*. Ballarat: Connorcourt.

Priddy, S. (2018). Commons select committee chairs in the 2017 parliament. Number CBP04400, House of Commons Library.

Prince, M. J. (1983). *Policy Advice and Organizational Survival*. Aldershot: Gower.

Prince, M. J. (2007). Soft craft, hard choices, altered context: Reflections on twenty-five years of policy advice in Canada. In L. Dobuzinskis, M. Howlett and D. Laycock (eds.), *Policy Analysis in Canada*. Toronto: University of Toronto Press, pp. 163–85.

Prince, M. J. (2018). Trends and directions in Canadian policy analysis and advice. In L. Dobuzinskis and M. Howlett (eds.), *Policy Analysis in Canada*. Bristol: The Policy Press, pp. 449–65.

Privy Council Office (2015). Open and Accountable Government. https://pm .gc.ca/sites/pm/files/inline-files/oag_2015_english.pdf.

Privy Council Office (2018). About commission of inquiry. www .canada.ca/en/privy-council/services/commissions-inquiry/about.html (accessed 20 November 2018).

Productivity Commission (2017). *Shifting the Dial: 5 Year Productivity Review*.Inquiry Report No. 84. Canberra: Commonwealth of Australia.

Public Service Commission (2010) *Use of Temporary Help Services in Public Service Organizations*. Ottawa: Public Service Commission.

Radin, B. A. (2000). *Beyond Machiavelli: Policy Analysis Comes of Age*. Washington, DC: Georgetown University Press.

Radwanski, A. (2016, 9 January). All Pearson, no Pierre: Inside Trudeau's inner circle. *Globe and Mail*.

Results and Delivery Unit, Privy Council Office (2016). Results and delivery in Canada: Building the culture and the systems. Presentation, Government of Canada.

Rhodes, R. A. W. (1997). *Understanding Governance: Policy Networks, Governance, Reflexivity and Accountability.* Buckingham: Open University Press.

Rhodes, R. A. W. (2011). *Everyday Life in British Government.* Oxford: Oxford University Press.

Rhodes, R. A. W. (2014). Core executives, prime ministers, statecraft and court politics: Towards convergence. In G. Davis and R. A. W. Rhodes (eds.), *The Craft of Governing: Essays in Honour of Professor Patrick Weller.* Crows Nest, NSW: Allen & Unwin pp. 53–72.

Rhodes, R. A. W. (2015). Recovering the Craft of Public Administration. *Public Administration Review* 76(4): 638–47.

Rhodes, R. A. W., and P. Weller (2001). *Changing World of Top Officials: Mandarins or Valets?* Buckingham: Open University.

Rhodes, R. A. W., and A. Tiernan (2014a). *The Gate Keepers: Lessons from Prime Ministers' Chiefs of Staff.* Carlton: Melbourne University Press.

Rhodes, R. A. W., and A. Tiernan (2014b). *Lessons in Governing: A Profile of Prime Ministers' Chiefs of Staff.* Carlton: Melbourne University Press.

Rhodes, R. A. W., and J. Wanna (2007). The limits to public value, or rescuing responsible government from the platonic guardians. *Australian Journal of Public Administration* 66(4): 406–21.

Rhodes R. A. W., J. Wanna and P. Weller (2009). *Comparing Westminster.* Oxford: Oxford University Press.

Rhodes, R. A. W., and P. Weller (2001). *The Changing World of Top Officials: Mandarins or Valets?* London: Open University Press.

Richards, D. (1997). *The Civil Service under the Conservatives 1979–1997: Whitehall's Political Poodles.* Brighton: Sussex Academic Press.

Richards, D. (2008). *New Labour and the Civil Service: Reconstituting the Westminster Model.* Basingstoke: Palgrave Macmillan.

Richards, D., and M. Smith (2002). *Governance and Public Policy in the United Kingdom.* Oxford: Oxford University Press.

Richards, D., and M. Smith (2006). Central control and policy implementation in the UK: A case study of the Prime Minister's Delivery Unit. *Journal of Comparative Policy Analysis* 8(4): 325–45.

Richards, D., and M. Smith (2016). The Westminster model and the 'indivisibility of the political and administrative elite': A convenient myth whose time is up? *Governance: An International Journal of Policy, Administration, and Institutions* 29(4): 499–516.

Richardson, J. (2018). *British Policy-Making and the Need for a Post-Brexit Policy Style.* London: Palgrave Macmillan.

Riddell, P. (2019). *15 Minutes of Power: The Uncertain Life of British Ministers.* London: Profile Books.

Riddell, P., and P. Barlow (2013). *The Lost World of Royal Commissions.* London: Institute for Government.

Riddell, P., and C. Haddon (2009). *Transitions: Preparing for Government Changes.* London: Institute for Government.

Roberts, J. (1987). *Politicians, Public Servants and Public Enterprise.* Wellington: Victoria University Press for the Institute of Policy Studies.

Robertson, G. (2018, 15 February). Minister of Finance speech to the Institute of Public Administration, New Zealand.

Robson, J., and R. P. Wilson (2018). Political staff and public servants: Still getting along. In A. Marland, T. Giasson and A. Lawlor (eds.), *Political Elites in Canada: Power and Influence in Instantaneous Times.* Vancouver: University of British Columbia Press, pp. 71–88.

Rouban, L. (2012). Politicization of the civil service. In B. G. Peters and J. Pierre, *Handbook of Public Administration.* London: Sage, pp. 380–91.

Rouban, L. (2014). Political–administrative relations: Evolving models of politicization. In F. M. Van der Meer, J. C. N. Raadschelders and T. A. J. Toonen (eds.), *Comparative Civil Service Systems in the 21st Century: Comparative Perspectives.* Basingstoke: Palgrave Macmillan, pp. 317–33.

RSS/Royal Statistical Society (2016). *Putting Evidence at the Heart of the Policy Debate.* London: RSS.

Rudd, K. (2008, 30 April). Address to heads of agencies and members of the senior executive service. Great Hall, Parliament House, Canberra.

Russell, M. (2015, December 4). The policy power of the Westminster Parliament: The empirical evidence. UK Constitutional Law Blog. https://constitution-unit.com/2015/11/26/the-policy-power-of-the-westminster-parliament-the-empirical-evidence/.

Russell, M., and M. Benton (2011). *Selective Influence: The Policy Impact of House of Commons Select Committees.* London: The Constitution Unit, UCL.

Russell, M., and P. Crowley (2016). The policy power of the Westminster Parliament: The 'parliamentary state' and the empirical evidence. *Governance: An International Journal of Policy, Administration, and Institutions* 29(1): 121–37.

Rutter, J. (2013). A better formula: Will civil service reform improve Whitehall's use of expert advice. In R. Doubleday and J. Wilsdon (eds.), *Future Directions for Scientific Advice in Whitehall.* Cambridge: Centre for Science and Policy, University of Cambridge and four other partners, pp. 39–48.

Rutter, J. (2019). Will civil service impartiality be a casualty of Brexit? In S. Barwick (ed.), *Impartiality Matters: Perspectives on the Importance of Impartiality in the Civil Service in a 'Post Truth' World.* London: Smith Institute, pp. 57–62.

Rutter, J., E. Marshall and S. Sims (2012). *The 'S' Factors: Lessons from IfG's Policy Success Sessions*. London: Institute for Government.

Rutter, T. (2018, 10 January). Unions: Ministerial code 'tinkering' not enough to protect civil servants from harassment. *Civil Service World*.

Saint-Martin, D. (1998). The new managerialism and the policy influence of consultants in government: An historical-institutionalist analysis of Britain, Canada and France. *Governance: An International Journal of Policy, Administration, and Institutions* 11(3): 319–56.

Saint-Martin, D. (2004). *Building the New Managerialist State: Consultants and the Politics of Public Sector Reform*. Oxford: Oxford University Press.

Salacuse, J. (2018). Advice in government and policy making. In E. MacGeorge and L. M. Van Swol (eds.), *The Oxford Handbook of Advice*. Oxford: Oxford University Press, pp. 321–42.

Salter, L. (2007). The public of public enquiries. In L. Dobuzinskis, M. Howlett and D. Laycock (eds.), *Policy Analysis in Canada: The State of the Art*. Toronto: University of Toronto Press, pp. 291–313.

Samojlenko, D., and S. Boots (2018). Getting prototypes out the door: The e-briefing app. Canadian Digital Service/Service numérique Canadian. https://digital.canada.ca/2018/01/29/getting-prototypes-out-the-door/.

Sasse, T., and E. Norris (2019). *Moving On: The Costs of High Staff Turnover in the Civil Service*. London: Institute for Government.

Savoie, D. J. (1994). *Reagan, Thatcher, Mulroney: In Search of a New Bureaucracy*. Pittsburgh, PA: University of Pittsburgh Press.

Savoie, D. J. (1999). *Governing from the Centre: The Concentration of Power in Canadian Politics*. Toronto: University of Toronto Press.

Savoie, D. J. (2003). *Breaking the Bargain: Public Servants, Ministers, and Parliament*. Toronto: IPAC/University of Toronto Press.

Savoie, D. J. (2008). Court Government and the Collapse of Accountability in Canada and the United Kingdom. Toronto: IPAC/University of Toronto Press.

Savoie, D. J. (2011). Steering from the centre: The Canadian way. In C. Dahlström, B. G. Peters and J. Pierre, *Steering from the Centre: Strengthening Political Control in Western Democracies*. Toronto: University of Toronto Press, pp. 147–65.

Savoie, D. J. (2015). The Canadian public service: In search of a new equilibrium. In A. Massey and K. Johnson (eds.), *The International Handbook of Public Administration and Governance*. Cheltenham: Edward Elgar, pp. 182–98.

Savoie, D. J. (2019). *Democracy in Canada: The Disintegration of Our Institutions*. Kingston and Montreal: McGill-Queen's University Press.

Schlaufer, C. (2019). How does policy advice of the international monetary fund differ along the income of advised countries? *Policy Studies* 40(3–4): 287–302. DOI:10.1080/01442872.2018.1557620.

SCJHR (2019a, 27 February). Evidence. Standing Committee on Justice and Human Rights. House of Commons (Canada).

SCJHR (2019b, 6 March). Evidence. Standing Committee on Justice and Human Rights. House of Commons (Canada).

Schofield, J., and J. Fershau (2007). Committees inside Canadian legislatures. In L. Dobuzinskis, M. Howlett and D. Laycock (eds.), *Policy Analysis in Canada: The State of the Art.* Toronto: University of Toronto Press, pp. 351–74.

Scott, C., and K. Baehler (2010). *Adding Value to Policy Analysis and Advice.* Kensington: University of New South Wales Press.

Scott, G. (2001). *Public Management in New Zealand: Lessons and Challenges.* Wellington: New Zealand Business Roundtable.

Scott, G. (2010). *Improving the Quality and Value of Policy Advice: Committee Appointed by the Review of Expenditure on Policy Advice.* Wellington: Government of New Zealand.

Scott, R., and R. Boyd (2016). Results, targets and measures to drive collaboration: Lessons from the New Zealand Better Public Services reforms. In D. J. Gilchrist and J. R. Butcher (eds.), *Three Sector Solution: Delivering Public Policy in Collaboration with Not-for-Profits and Business.* Canberra: ANU Press, pp. 235–260.

Scott, R., and R. Boyd (2017). Joined-up for what? Response to Carey and Harris on adaptive collaboration. *Australian Journal of Public Administration* 76(1): 138–44.

Seldon, A., and G. Lodge (2013). *Brown at 10.* London: Biteback.

Senate (2019). Personal employee positions as at 1 April 2019. Senate Finance and Public Administration Committee, 2019–2020 Budget estimates, Parliament of Australia, tabled 4 April 2019.

Seymour-Ure, C. (1987). Institutionalization and informality in advisory systems. In W. Plowden (ed.), *Advising the Rulers.* Oxford: Blackwell, pp. 175–84.

Shaw, R., and C. Eichbaum (2011). *Public Policy in New Zealand: Institutions, Processes, and Outcomes.* 3rd ed. Auckland: Pearson.

Shaw, R., and C. Eichbaum (eds.) (2018a). *Ministers, Minders and Mandarins: An International Study of Relationships at the Executive Summit of Parliamentary Democracies.* London: Edward Elgar.

Shaw, R., and C. Eichbaum (2018b). New Zealand: Bargains, compacts and covenants in the core executive. In R. Shaw and C. Eichbaum (eds.), *Ministers, Minders and Mandarins: An International Study of*

Relationships at the Executive Summit of Parliamentary Democracies. London: Edward Elgar, pp. 145–62.

Shaw, R., and C. Eichbaum (2018c). Still allies? Revisiting New Zealand public servants' perceptions of ministerial advisors. Paper for the 2018 NZPSA Conference: Representation and Responsibility VUW, Wellington, 26–28 November 2018.

Shaw, R., and C. Eichbaum (2020). Bubbling up or cascading down? Public servants, political advisers and politicization. *Public Administration,* https://doi.org/10.1111/padm.12659.

Shepherd, R. P., and C. Stoney (2018). Policy analysis in the federal government: Conditions and renewal initiatives in the Trudeau era. In L. Dobuzinskis and M. Howlett (eds.), *Policy Analysis in Canada.* Bristol: Policy Press, pp. 71–97.

Shergold, P. (2015). *Learning from Failure: What Large Government Policy Initiatives Have Gone so Badly Wrong in the Past and How the Chances of Success in the Future Can Be Improved. An Independent Review of Government Processes for Implementing Large Programs and Projects.* Canberra: Commonwealth of Australia.

Shipman, T. (2017). *Fall Out: A Year of Political Mayhem.* London: William Collins.

Simpson, A. (2014). Commissions of inquiry – the New Zealand Way. In S. Prasser and H. Tracey (eds.), *Royal Commissions and Public Inquiries: Practice and Potential.* Ballarat: Connorcourt Publishing, pp. 316–30.

Simpson, A. (2018). Commissions of inquiry – Functions, power and legal status. *Te Ara – the Encyclopedia of New Zealand.* www.TeAra.govt.nz /en/commissions-of-inquiry/1–5 (accessed 16 November 2018).

Smith, H. (2018). *Doing Policy Differently: Challenges and Insights.* In *IPAA Speeches 2018.* Canberra: Institute of Public Administration, pp. 35–43.

Smith, M. J. (1999). *The Core Executive in Britain.* London: Macmillan.

Smith, M. (2011a). The paradoxes of Britain's strong centre: Delegating decisions and reclaiming control. In C. Dahlstrom, B. G. Peters and J. Pierre (eds.), *Steering from the Centre: Strengthening Political Control in Western Democracies.* Toronto: University of Toronto Press, pp. 166–90.

Smith, M. J. (2011b). Tsars, leadership and innovation in the public sector. *Policy and Politics* 39(3): 343–59.

Snyder, J. (1993). Introduction. In J. Snyder and R. Jervis (eds.), *Coping with Complexity in the International System.* Boulder, CO: Westview Press, pp. 6–13.

Spann, R. N. (1979). *Government Administration in Australia.* Sydney: George Allen & Unwin Australia.

Speers, K. (2007). The invisible public service: Consultants and public policy in Canada. In L. Dobuzinskis, M. Howlett and D. Laycock (eds.), *Policy Analysis in Canada: The State of the Art*. Toronto: University of Toronto Press, pp. 220–31.

Speers, K. (2018). The diminished invisible private service: Consultants and public. In L. Dobuzinskis and M. Howlett (eds.), *Policy Analysis in Canada*. Bristol: Policy Press, pp. 187–210.

SSCNF/Standing Senate Committee on National Finance (2018, 12 June). Issue No. 70, Evidence.

Stark, A. 2018). Explaining institutional amnesia in government. *Governance: An International Journal of Policy, Administration, and Institutions* 32(1): 143–58.

Starr, G. (2014). Public inquiries in the United Kingdom. In S. Prasser and H. Tracey (eds.), *Royal Commissions and Public Inquiries: Practice and Potential*. Ballarat: Connorcourt Publishing, pp. 301–15.

Stewart, J., and S. Prasser (2015). Expert advisory policy bodies. In B. Head and K. Crowley (eds.), *Policy Analysis in Australia*. Bristol: Policy Press, pp. 151–66.

Stone, D. (2015). The Group of 20 transnational policy community: Governance networks, policy analysis and think tanks. *International Review of Administrative Sciences* 81(4): 793–811.

Stone, D., and K. Moloney (eds.) (2019). *The Oxford Handbook of Global Policy and Transnational Administration*. Oxford: Oxford University Press.

St. Clair, A. L. (2006). The World Bank as a transnational expertised institution. *Global Governance: An International Journal of Policy, Administration, and Institutions* 12(1): 77–95.

Stoker, G., and M. Evans (2016). Evidence-based policy making and social science. In G. Stoker and M. Evans (eds.), *Evidence-Based Policy Making in the Social Sciences: Methods That Matter*. Bristol: Policy Press pp. 15–28.

Sundquist J. L. (1978). Research brokerage: The weak link. In National Research Council, *Knowledge and Policy: The Uncertain Connection*. Washington, DC: National Academies Press, pp. 126–45.

Sutherland, S. (1993). The public service and policy development. In M.M. Atkinson (ed.), *Governing Canada: Institutions and Public Policy*, Toronto: Harcourt Brace and Jovanovich Canada pp. 80–113.

Talbot, C. (2019). An impartial civil service – myth and reality. In S. Barwick (ed.), *Impartiality Matters: Perspectives on the Importance of Impartiality in the Civil Service in a 'Post Truth' World*. London: Smith Institute, pp. 63–71.

Talbot, C., and C. Johnson (2007). Seasonal cycles in public management: Disaggregation and re-aggregation. *Public Money and Management* 27(1): 53–60.

Taylor, M. (2015, 4 November). The critical fault line damaging departmental effectiveness? The relationship between politicians and senior officials. *Civil Service World*.

Thain, C. (2010). Budget reform in the United Kingdom: The rocky road to 'controlled discretion'. In J. Wanna, L. Jensen and J. de Vires (eds.), *The Reality of Budgetary Reform in OECD Countries: Trajectories and Consequences*. Cheltenham: Edward Elgar, pp. 35–64.

't Hart, P., and J. Uhr (eds.) (2011). *How Power Changes Hands: Transition and Succession in Government*. New York: Palgrave McMillan.

Thomas, P. G. (2003). The past, present and future of officers of parliament. *Canadian Public Administration* 46(3): 287–314.

Thompson, J. (2018, 5 July). Top things to know about the Operational Delivery Profession, Blog, *Civil Service Quarterly*. https://quarterly .blog.gov.uk/2018/07/05/top-things-to-know-about-the-operational-deli very-profession/.

Tiernan, A. (2006). Advising Howard: Interpreting changes in advisory and support structures for the prime minister of Australia. *Australian Journal of Political Science* 41(3): 309–24.

Tiernan, A. (2007). *Power without Responsibility: Ministerial Staffers in Australian Governments from Whitlam to Howard*. Sydney: University of New South Wales Press.

Tiernan, A. (2008). The Rudd transition: Continuity and change in the structures of advice and support to Australian prime ministers. *Papers on Parliament*, No. 49, August, pp. 59–77.

Tiernan, A. (2011). Advising Australian federal governments: Assessing the evolving capacity and role of the Australian public service. *Australian Journal of Public Administration* 70(4): 335–46.

Tiernan, A. (2012), 21 September). Improving public policy advice is a debate we have to have. *The Conversation*. https://theconversation .com/improving-public-policy-advice-is-a-debate-we-have-to-have -9729.

Tiernan, A. (2015a). The dilemmas of organizational capacity. *Policy and Society* 34(3–4): 209–17.

Tiernan, A. (2015b). Weathering the global financial crisis: Reflections on the capacity of the institutions of Australian governance. https://ssrn.com /abstract=1665974.

Tiernan, A. (2015c). Craft and capacity in the public service. *Australian Journal of Public Administration* 74(1): 53–62.

Tiernan, A., I. Holland and J. Deem. (2019). *Being a trusted and respected partner: The APS' relationship with ministers and their offices.* An ANZSOG research paper for the Australian Public Service Review Panel.

Tiernan, A., and P. Weller (2010). *Learning to Be a Minister: Heroic Expectations: Practical Realities.* Melbourne: Melbourne University Press.

Tilley, P. (2019). *Changing Fortunes: A History of the Australian Treasury.* Melbourne: Melbourne University Press.

Tingle, L. (2015). Political amnesia: How we forgot how to govern. *Quarterly Essay* 60: 1–86.

Truswell, E., and Atkinson, D. (2011). *Supporting Heads of Government: A Comparison across Six Countries.* Working paper. London: Institute for Government.

Uhrig, J. (2003). *Review of the Corporate Governance of Statutory Authorities and Office Holders Report.* Canberra: Commonwealth of Australia.

Uldanov, A. (2019). Policy advice in an authoritarian environment: Urban transport policies in Moscow and Beijing (2010–2017). *Policy Studies* 40 (3–4): 320–36.

van den Berg, C. F., C. Braun and T. Steen (2014). Consensus politics as administrative practice: The Europeanization of external advice-seeking? In Hans Vollaard, Jan Beyers and Patrick Dumont (eds.), *European Integration and Consensus Politics in the Low Countries.* London: Routledge, pp. 114–33.

van den Berg, C. F. (2017). Dynamics in the Dutch policy advisory system: Externalization, politicization and the legacy of pillarization. *Policy Sciences* 50(1): 63–84.

van den Berg, C. F., M. Howlett, A. Migone, M. Howard and F. Pemer (2020). *Policy Consultancy in Comparative Perspective.* London: Cambridge University Press.

van der Els, K. (2018). The future of evidence, expertise and think tanks – a foresight perspective on 'evidence-based' decision making. Blog post, Government of Canada.

Van Dorpe, K., and S. Horton (2011). The public service bargain in the United Kingdom: The Whitehall model in decline. *Public Policy and Administration* 26: 233–52.

Van Onselen, P., and W. Errington (2007). The democratic state as a marketing tool: The permanent campaign in Australia. *Commonwealth & Comparative Politics* 45(1): 78–94.

Varghese, P. (2016, 9 June). Parting reflections: Secretary's speech to IPAA.

Verschuere B. (2009). The role of public agencies in the policy making process. *Public Policy and Administration* 24(1): 23–46.

Veselý, A. (2013). Externalization of policy advice: Theory, methodology and evidence. *Policy and Society* 32(3): 199–209.

Veselý, A. (2017). Policy advice as policy work: A conceptual framework for multi-level analysis. *Policy Sciences* 50(1): 139–54.

Veit, S., T. Hustedt and T. Bach (2017). Dynamics of change in internal policy advisory systems: The hybridization of advisory capacities in Germany. *Policy Sciences* 50(1): 85–103.

von Trappe, L., and S. Nicol (2017). *Designing Effective Independent Fiscal Institutions*. Paris: OECD.

Vromen, A., and P. Hurley (2015). Consultants, think tanks, and public policy. In B. Head and K. Crowley (eds.), *Policy Analysis in Australia*. Bristol: Policy Press, pp. 167–82.

Wakamatsu, K. (1998). The role of civil servants in the formulation of policy: An analysis of the policy process on Commonwealth immigration from 1948 to 1964. Ph.D. thesis, Centre for Research in Ethnic Relations, University of Warwick.

Walker, R., S. Jung and G. Boyne (2013). Marching to different drummers? The performance effects of alignment between political and managerial perceptions of performance management. *Public Administration Review* 73(6): 833–44.

Waller, P. (2014). Special advisers and the policy-making process. In B. Yong and R. Hazell (eds.), *Special Advisers: Who They Are, What They Do and Why They Matter*. Oxford: Hart, pp. 87–109.

Walter, J. (1986). *The Ministers Minders: Personal Advisers in National Government*. Melbourne: Oxford University Press.

Walter, J. (2006). Ministers, minders and public servants: Changing parameters of responsibility in Australia. *Australian Journal of Public Administration* 65(3): 22–7.

Wanna, J. (2005). New Zealand's Westminster trajectory: Archetypal transplant to maverick outlier. In H. Patapan, J. Wanna and P. Weller (eds.), *Westminster Legacies: Democracy and Responsible Government in Asia and the Pacific*. Sydney: UNSW Press, pp. 153–85.

Wanna, J. (2014). Australia's future as a 'Westminster democracy': Threats to combat, stark choices to make. *Australian Journal of Public Administration* 73(1): 19–28.

Wanna, J., and P. Weller (2003). Traditions of Australian governance. *Public Administration* 81(1): 63–94.

Washington, S. (2016). *New Zealand's Reforms to Improve Policy*. London: Institute for Government.

Washington, S., and M. Mintrom (2018). Strengthening policy capability: New Zealand's policy project. *Policy Design and Practice* 1(1): 30–46. DOI:10.1080/25741292.2018.1425086.

Waterford, J. (2009, 16 May). On a west wing and a prayer. *The Canberra Times*, 8.

Watt, I., and B. Anderson (2017). *Parliamentary Budget Office Review 2016–17: Report of the Independent Review Panel*. Canberra: Joint Committee of Public Accounts and Audit, Parliament.

What Work Network (2018). *The What Work Network: Five Years On*. https://assets.publishing.service.gov.uk/government/uploads/system/upload s/attachment_data/file/677478/6.4154_What_works_report_Final.pdf.

Weaver, K., and P. B. Stares (2001). Guidance for governance: An overview. In K. Weaver (ed.), *Guidance for Governance: Comparing Alternative Sources of Public Policy Advice*. Tokyo: Nihon Kokusai Koryu Center, pp. 1–30.

Weible, C. (2008). Expert-based information and policy subsystems: A review and synthesis. *The Policy Studies Journal* 36(4): 615–35.

Weller P. (1987). Types of advice. In W. Plowden (ed.), *Advising the Rulers*. Oxford: Basil Blackwell, pp. 149–57.

Weller, P. (2015). Policy professionals in context: Advisors and ministers. In B. Head and K. Crowley (eds.), *Policy Analysis in Australia*. Bristol: Policy Press, pp. 23–36.

Weller, P. (2018). *The Prime Ministers' Craft: Why Some Succeed and Others Fail in Westminster Systems*. Oxford: Oxford University Press.

Weller, P., and M. Grattan, (1981). *Can Ministers Cope? Australian Ministers at Work*. London: Hutchinson of Australia.

Weller, P., and C. Haddon (2016). Westminster traditions: Continuity and change. *Governance: An International Journal of Policy, Administration, and Institutions* 29(4): 483–98.

Weller, P., J. Scott and B. Stevens (2011). *From Postbox to Powerhouse*. Sydney: Allen and Unwin.

Wells, P. (2018). The PM as dictator: The ultimate Harper insider on a theory of concentrated power. *Literary Review of Canada*. https://reviewcanada .ca/magazine/2018/05/the-pm-as-dictator/.

Wettenhall, R. (2006). The 'state tradition' in Australia: Reassessing an earlier view. *Journal of Contemporary Issues in Business and Government* 12(2): 15–46.

Wheatley, M., B. Maddox and T. K. Bishop (2018). *The 2019 Spending Review: How to Run It Well*. London: Institute for London.

Wherry, A. (2014). The EI hiring credit: Joe Oliver will take the CFIB's word for it. *Maclean's*. www.macleans.ca/politics/the-ei-hiring-credit-joe-oliver -will-take-the-cfibs-word-for-it/.

White, H. (2015). *Select Committees under Scrutiny: The Impact of Parliamentary Committee Inquiries on Government*. London: Institute for Government.

Wilby, P. (2017, 1 August). David Laws: 'The quality of education policymaking is poor'. *The Guardian*.

Wildavsky, A. B. (1979). *Speaking Truth to Power: The Art and Craft of Policy Analysis*. Boston: Little-Brown.

Wilks, S. (2013). *The Political Power of the Business Corporation*. Cheltenham: Edward Elgar.

Wilson R. (2006). Policy analysis as policy advice. In M. Moran, M. Rein and R. E. Goodin (eds.), *The Oxford Handbook of Public Policy*. New York: Oxford University Press, pp. 152–68.

Wilson, R. P. (2015). A profile of ministerial policy staff in the government of Canada. *Canadian Journal of Political Science* 48(2): 455–71.

Wilson, R. P. (2016a). Trust but verify: Ministerial policy advisors and public servants in the government of Canada. *Canadian Public Administration* 59(3): 337–56.

Wilson, R. P. (2016b). The inter-executive activity of ministerial policy advisors in the government of Canada. In C. Stoney and B. Doern (eds.), *How Ottawa Spends 2016–2017: The Trudeau Liberals in Power*. Kingston and Montreal: McGill–Queen's University Press, pp. 191–216.

Woolcott, R. (2018, 10 October). Where to for the Australia Public Service. Keynote address delivered by the Public Service Commissioner, APSwide conference, Canberra.

Workman S., B. D. Jones and A. Jochim (2009). Information Processing and Policy Dynamics. *The Policy Studies Journal* 37(1): 75–92.

Worthy, B. (2017). *The Politics of Freedom of Information: How and Why Governments Pass Laws That Threaten Their Power*. Manchester: Manchester University Press.

Wright, O. (2012). David Cameron aides at war with Civil Service in battle of Downing Street. *The Independent*. www.independent.co.uk/news/uk/poli tics/david-cameron-aides-at-war-with-civil-service-in-battle-of-downing-street-7763943.html.

Yong, B., and R. Hazell (2014). *Special Advisers: Who They Are, What They Do and Why They Matter*. London: Bloomsbury.

Young, A. (2018). Populism and the UK Constitution. *Current Legal Problems* 71(1): 17–52.

Zussman, D. (1986). Walking the tightrope: The Mulroney government and the public service. In M. J. Prince (ed.), *How Ottawa Spends: 1986–87: Tracking the Tories*. Toronto: Methuen, pp. 250–82.

Zussman, D. (2013). *Off and Running: The Prospects and Pitfalls of Government Transitions in Canada*. Toronto: University of Toronto Press.

Zussman, D. (2015). Public policy analysis in Canada: A 40-year overview. In E. Parson (ed.), *A Subtle Balance: Expertise, Evidence, and Democracy in Public Policy and Governance, 1970–2010*. Kingston and Montreal: McGill-Queen's University Press, pp. 11–36.

Zussman, D. (2016). Stephen Harper and the federal public service: An uneasy and unresolved relationship. In J. Ditchburn and G. Fox (eds.), *The Harper Factor: Assessing a Prime Minister's Policy Legacy*. Kingston and Montreal: McGill-Queen's University Press, pp. 44–61.

Index

For EU product safety concerns, contact us at Calle de José Abascal, 56–1°, 28003 Madrid, Spain or eugpsr@cambridge.org.

www.ingramcontent.com/pod-product-compliance
Ingram Content Group UK Ltd.
Pitfield, Milton Keynes, MK11 3LW, UK
UKHW020356140625
459647UK00020B/2506